GLOBAL
REGGAE

GLOBAL REGGAE

Edited by Carolyn Cooper

Canoe Press

Jamaica • Barbados • Trinidad and Tobago

C Fonds

Prince Claus Fund for
Culture and Development

Canoe Press
7A Gibraltar Hall Road, Mona
Kingston 7, Jamaica
www.uwipress.com

C
Fonds

Prince Claus Fund *for*
Culture and Development

Cover design and illustrations by Michael Thompson
(e-mail: mikethompson5@mac.com)
Book design by Maria Papaefstathiou
(e-mail: maria.pap@graphicart-news.com)
Photograph editing by Nikos Glykeas
(e-mail: nikglyk@icloud.com)

Printed in the United States of America.

Contents

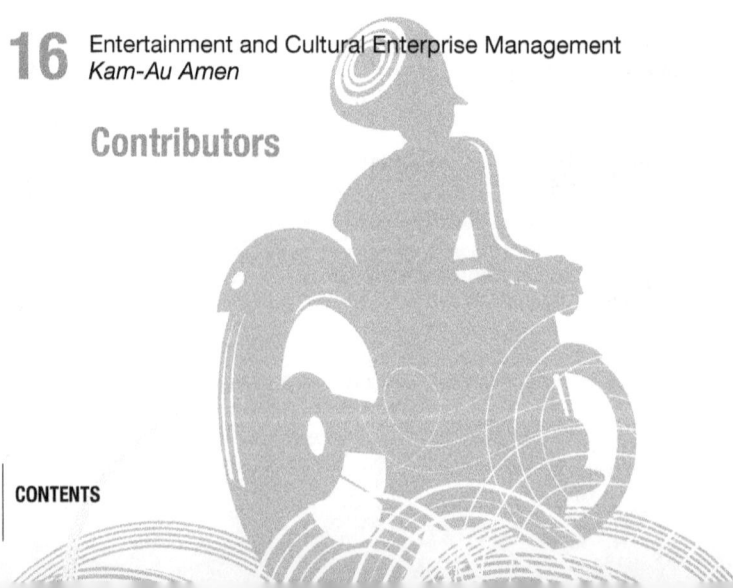

Acknowledgements

I am indebted to Professor Gordon Shirley, campus principal, University of the West Indies, Mona, Jamaica, for honouring the commitment of his predecessor, Sir Kenneth Hall, to provide substantial funding for hosting the Global Reggae Conference. Without this high-level institutional support, the vision could not have been realized. Dr Swithin Wilmot, dean of the Faculty of Humanities and Education, and Professor Mark Figueroa, dean of the Faculty of Social Sciences, provided welcome financial assistance, as did the UWI Development and Endowment Fund. Beyond the Mona campus, the Culture, Health, Arts, Sports and Education Fund (CHASE) also invested in the "Global Reggae" enterprise. The Bob Marley Foundation and Digicel also provided welcome support.

For almost a year, the members of the organizing committee spent many hours working to ensure that the conference was a success:

Carolyn Cooper, conference chair
Kam-Au Amen, conference coordinator
Donna Hope, programme coordinator
Cecil Gutzmore
Clinton Hutton
Cecile Johnson-Semaj
Dennis Howard
Herbie Miller
Lenford Salmon
Carlton Samuels
Hector Slack
Kingsley Stewart
Patricia Valentine

In addition, the staff of the Institute of Caribbean Studies as well as student assistants gave unstinting support: staff assistants were Andrea Todd, Elizabeth Douglas, Lorna Smith, Nicole Edwards-Bailey and Rohan Shaw; student assistants were Amina Blugh, Bertland Hope, Cassie-Ann James, Janielle Todd, Kerry-Ann Christie, Latoya Tulloch, Leon Burrell, Loeri Robinson, Maxandra Manning, Oral Taylor, Sanjae Blair Shane Redwood, Simeon Lorenzo

and Tyann Williams; and student group support was given by the Marcus Garvey Movement and the UWI Tourism Society.

Finally, the Prince Claus Fund for Culture and Development, based in the Netherlands, gave substantial support to this project, which enabled the publication of this book. For this I am most grateful. The fund's motto, "Culture is a basic need", motivates their commitment to the advancement of far-reaching initiatives such as the Global Reggae Conference and the production of this commemorative book.

I am most grateful to Michael "Freestylee" Thompson for so generously giving permission to reproduce his magnificent graphic art designs for the cover and chapter headings of this book. I also thank Maria Papaefstathiou for her brilliant design of this visually exciting cultural text.

INTRODUCTION

JAMAICAN
POPULAR MUSIC
A YARD
& ABROAD

CAROLYN COOPER

T his distinctive collection on reggae music in trans/
national perspective comprises the fourteen plenary
lectures that were delivered at the historic conference "Global Reggae" convened at the University of
the West Indies, Mona, Jamaica in February 2008. Keynote
speakers, representing all continents – except Antarctica
– and many islands, large and small, in the Caribbean and
the Pacific, were invited to share their analysis of the ways in
which Jamaican reggae has been appropriated and adapted
in a variety of cultural contexts across the globe.[1] The conference also focused on the impact of reggae music production
within Jamaica and assessed how the local economy could
benefit more directly from the investments of intellectual
property in this vibrant, multinational industry.

World-renowned Brazilian musician, cultural activist
and former minister of culture Gilberto Passos Gil Moreira

was selected to open the conference with a plenary lecture on reggae in Brazil. Regretfully, because of logistical difficulties, he was unable to attend. Gilberto Gil embodies the eclectic spirit of the "Global Reggae" conference. For almost half a century, this extraordinary musician has cut and mixed "local" beats like samba and bossa nova with rock, funk and reggae rhythms to produce a quintessentially Brazilian sound that resonates across the globe. His politically engaged lyrics, like the "word, sound and power" of so many foundational reggae songwriters and their dancehall offspring, resolutely chant down oppressive social and political systems.

Erna Brodber, distinguished historical sociologist and novelist, graciously agreed to amplify her conference paper "Reggae as Black Space" and present it as the opening plenary lecture. Artfully talking in the third person about herself and her peers, Brodber summarizes the predicament in which middle-class black Jamaicans found themselves in the early 1960s: "In short, the teenager, graduating from sixth form the year before independence, and so about to join the middle class, existed in an environment in which race and colour in their native land, Jamaica, were issues. But, were they openly discussed and did they feel that they had anything to do with their lives?"

It was in popular music that the oblique discourse of identity was belatedly confronted. Brodber lucidly argues that "reggae of the 1970s created a black space; it was an incubator for a kind of knowledge that needed to work its way out of the ground and into the minds of the young descendants of Africans enslaved in Jamaica. Not just chatter among the platters, the early reggae allowed meditation while you danced and even if you did not want to be black, you could at least understand why others would want to be." Brodber establishes the complex ideological "grounation" in which reggae music is rooted: Black Power, Garveyism, Rastafari and postcolonial/nationalist politics.

Peter Ashbourne's incisive chapter, "From Mento to Ska and Reggae to Dancehall", traverses the shifting terrain of the rural and urban soundscapes. Focusing on instrumentation, Ashbourne highlights experimentation, hybridization and innovation as recurring features of Jamaican music. Ideally, a compact disc should have accompanied this book, particularly for this chapter in which Ashbourne analyses with such precision the texture of reggae and dancehall compositions and for Michael Veal's penetrating chapter on dub, but this proved impractical.

The aesthetics of the cover version exemplifies a deep-rooted practice and philosophy of "mix up an' blenda" (Jamaican slang for heterogeneity) that produces ska and, much later, dancehall. As Ashbourne puts it, "The Jamaicanization of these covers started to occur. The musicians and singers making these recordings were, consciously or not, adding, replacing, changing or augmenting elements in the music with elements from their own experiences. Mento, Cuban rhythms, other elements from mainstream US and British pop culture were fair game for the fusion. The end result of this experimentation was the ska beat. 'Boogie in My Bones' by Laurel Aitken illustrates the fusion."

Radiating from the Jamaican centre, the chapters that follow illuminate the "glocalization" of reggae – its global dispersal and adaptation in diverse local contexts of consumption and transformation. A transcendent preoccupation is the politics and pragmatics of "authenticity". The languages of Jamaican popular music, both literal and metaphorical, are first imitated in pursuit of an undeniable "originality". Over time, as the music is indigenized, the Jamaican model loses its authority to varying degrees. The seductive embrace of exoticized Jamaican culture appears to yield inevitably to a much more profound refamiliarization with home. The revolutionary ethos of reggae music is translated into local languages that articulate the particular politics of new cultural contexts. The echoes of the Jamaican source gradually fade. It is a polyphonic, culture-specific authenticity that now resounds.

Amon Saba Saakana's chapter, "The Impact of Jamaican Music in Britain", vividly documents the complexities of cultural accommodation as reggae music travels with migrant Jamaicans to the "mother country". Saakana argues that "the conceptual base of British mythographers was a mental separation between the so-called West Indian and themselves. This mythogram was constructed around ideas of primitivism and a continuously refined British modernity."

Over time, the primitive seduces the refined and lines of separation become blurred. What was once disdained is now imitated. Saakana gives an amusing example: "Another curious sight was the *David Frost Show* on London Television in which each commercial break was introduced by Frost pointing his finger and saying, 'Soon come' [I'll soon be back]. For those who are not aware, Frost was a Cambridge man and quite upper crust in his speech and demeanour, but obviously very socialized, as he was once engaged to a Jamaican lady." Seduction takes many forms.

Saakana documents the role of entrepreneurship in the spread of reggae music in the United Kingdom, a fundamental element of the industry that still needs to be much more fully analysed and documented across the globe. Key players include Emile Shalet, founder of the Melodisc label; Siggy Jackson, who collaborated with Shalet to establish the Blue Beat label; Sonny Roberts and Lloyd Harvey, founders of Planitone Records; Richard Branson, who set up Virgin Records; and the don of them all, Chris Blackwell, who launched the Island Records empire.

In addition, Saakana examines the impact of radio – both "legitimate" and "pirate" – in the mainstreaming of Jamaican music. He also acknowledges the baseline role of the "sound man" and the sound system in colonizing the British sonic landscape. Finally, focusing on the politics of appropriation, Saakana underscores the ways in which "conscious cross-cultural insurgents" created new rhythms of rebellion against institutionalized racism: "Anti-racism activities produced the climate for the synthesizing of sounds: the punk rock movement, centred in London, was revived by the utilization of reggae as the basis for exploration."

In a sweeping summary, Saakana highlights the history of resistance against racism in the United Kingdom that enabled the rise of reggae as "hard core" rebel music:

> It would not be until the late 1970s, after years of African/Caribbean organizational structures to combat racism, several modern "slave" uprisings in the modern British urban centres throughout the country, the growing exposure of this experience in small magazines and journals, the rise of Bob Marley and the Wailers, the increasing visibility of reggae, its new-found model of relaunching recumbent careers as with Eric Clapton's Bob Marley–penned song, "I Shot the Sherrif", that British youth, already rebelling against the staid social *mores* of British life, now moved, visibly, to form structures such as Rock Against Racism and the Anti-Nazi League.

Ellen Koehlings and Pete Lilly, co-editors of *Riddim*, Germany's upscale reggae and dancehall magazine, with a bi-monthly circulation of forty-five thousand copies, examine the movement of reggae music beyond Britain to the continent. In "The Evolution of Reggae in Europe with a Focus on Germany", they ask (and answer) a penetrating question: "How did it come about that youths from European countries without significant Caribbean communities are able and motivated to recreate something that is genuinely Jamaican in origin but can, to a certain extent, even compete with what is happening in Jamaica today?"

Koehlings and Lilly give a nuanced account of the local cultural politics that precipitated the importation of popular music into Germany. They argue that indigenous folk music traditions had been appropriated by the Nazis and thus contaminated. This discredited body of music could not, therefore, be embraced as the source of contemporary idioms. German youth, distancing themselves from the genocidal discourse of xenophobia, tuned into the music of Britain and the United States to find a language that could articulate their "post-Holocaust" identity. Then they discovered Bob Marley, who embodied the spirit of rebellion against "ism and schism".

The early reception of reggae in Germany is conceived by Lilly and Koehlings as "a story of misunderstandings": "When Marley entered the German market with the album *Rastaman Vibration* in the mid-1970s, his audience mainly consisted of rock listeners. White middle-class kids with long hair and torn clothes were looking for a new Jimi Hendrix. Since there was no Jamaican community in Germany, Marley fans did not have much knowledge about Jamaica, the Jamaican language, Rastafari or the living conditions in a post-/neocolonial country."

At an academic conference at the University of Frankfurt in the 1990s, I discovered, much to my amusement, that uninitiated German reggae fans thought that the line "No[,] woman, no cry" meant that if you did not have a woman then you would not cry, woman becoming synonymous with grief.[2] This interpretation was certainly not what the songwriter intended. The empathetic song evokes domestic intimacy and the everyday pleasures of home, despite material poverty: "I remember when we used to sit inna government yard in Trench Town." Misunderstood, this comfortingly nostalgic song is transposed into another key. It becomes a seemingly misogynist, homosocial chanting down of demonized woman.

All the words of the line – "no", "woman", "cry" – appear to be transparently English. The largely English-derived vocabulary of Jamaican Creole can disguise meaning if the grammar and syntax of the sentence are not also taken into account. In the case of the phrase "no[,] woman, no cry", grammar, syntax and, in particular, context confirm that the language is not English, but Jamaican. Indeed, the grammatical function of the two "negatives" is not at all identical. The first "no" is an interjection; the second is a command. In English this would be translated as the following: "no, woman, don't cry!" The problem of mistranslation is compounded by faulty transcription of the lyrics. On the record jacket of the original Island Records release, the comma is omitted after the first "no", creating a simplistic parallelism of structure that seemed to support the assumption that "woman" equalled "cry[ing]". This collision of meanings confirms the importance of accurate transcription of lyrics and, more broadly, the value of liner notes as cultural cues that can facilitate comprehension of unfamiliar languages, both literal and metaphorical.

Koehlings and Lilly conclude their subtle analysis of the indigenization of reggae in Europe with a summary of the stages of evolution: "The development process of other continental European countries mirrors the one seen in Germany in that they began by first copying the Jamaican blueprint before turning initial misunderstanding into something productive, something that is Jamaican in form, but European in content. All this goes hand-in-hand with the gradual building of local infrastructures that include prosperous sound system scenes, a healthy live circuit, a recording industry, the existence of artists and producers and, most importantly, a strong *massive*."

Massive support for live reggae and dancehall music is most palpable at the summer festivals in Europe, the mother of them all being Rototom Reggae Sunsplash, first held in Italy for over a decade and a half, and now transplanted to the south of Spain. A vibrant feature of the festival is the daily "Reggae University" forum at which performing artists, journalists and academics meet with a now-knowledgeable, vocal audience to analyse reggae music in all its global diversity. Misunderstanding is being transformed into mutual understanding.

Returning from Europe to the Caribbean and South America, the chapters by Samuel Furé Davis, Teddy Isimat-Mirin and Leo Vidigal consider the regional dispersal of reggae and dancehall across language barriers – Spanish, French (Creole) and Portuguese, respectively. In "Reggae in Cuba and the Hispanic Caribbean", Furé Davis confirms that "in Cuba, the prevailing nationalist discourse has led to a very cautious official recognition of cultural diversity and foreign cultural influences, to the extent that the Rastafari culture is still disapproved of, and reggae music is marginalized and regarded with contempt".

Analysing the impact of Cuba's economic crisis in the "special period" of the 1990s, Furé Davis proposes that, "this period shook the grounds of Cubanness (*cubanía* or *cubanidad*)". Indeed, he argues that "with its complex dynamics of economic, political, and cultural changes, some social minority groups, such as the Rastas . . . increased in number, became more visible and acquired new meanings and roles; consequently, this foreign cultural expression was adopted and transformed within the new context". With reference to the wider Hispanic Caribbean, Furé Davis distinguishes between "reggae in Spanish" and "reggae Latino", arguing that not all "Hispanic reggae" was produced in Spanish. English was sometimes used, as in the case of the early music of the Costa Rican group Bamaselo. Furé Davis thus advocates adoption of the more representative term "reggae Latino", which "makes reference not only to the language but also to the musical fusion with the distinctive sounds of the region". Though he does deploy the generic label "Hispanic reggae" for its socio-historical resonance, Furé Davis convincingly argues in favour of the more precise designation: "This reggae Latino is not merely nurtured by the social contradictions of minorities in the metropolitan, hegemonic environment in the United States (the "American Dream") or in Europe (Spain); it stems from the social conditions of the (neo)colonized, marginalized and materially impoverished people in the South, in Latin America and the Caribbean."

Furé Davis also draws attention to what he calls "the historically determined circumstances that led to the absence of a Patwa or Creole language in the Hispanic Caribbean". This results in the loss of an "oppositional tool against the dominant language/culture of the metropolis". The language of Rastafari and reggae becomes a "high-grade" medium for communicating rhythms of resistance to imperial discourses, even in circumstances where the meaning of words is not understood. This is a recurring theme in the story of globalizing reggae.

In his chapter, "Reggae in the French Caribbean", Teddy Isimat-Mirin highlights the universal themes of roots reggae that resonated with the local audience: "the Third World order, equality and justice, black consciousness and repatriation to Africa". Beyond these global preoccupations, reggae and Rastafari inspired a localized "pride in Creole culture and recognition of a French Afro-Caribbean identity". But this was not without resistance from those conservative elements within the society that equated the culture of Rastafari and reggae with criminality, largely because of the primacy of the "holy herb".

Tracing the migration of popular reggae dancehall acts to France, Isimat-Mirin notes a major constraint in the widespread acceptance of French West Indian artistes in the metropole: "To go mainstream artistes from the Caribbean have to sing in French and avoid Creole expressions, but in doing so they were in danger of losing their initial fan base, support from the French

Caribbean fans and from our diaspora in France." This raises the problematic politics of "authenticity" as artistes try to strike a balance between mass-market, crossover success and long-term relevance to their core audience, however small.

In addition, Isimat-Mirin contests the efficacy of the criterion of collaboration with Jamaican artists as the absolute determinant of "authentic" reggae dancehall production in the French West Indies. Lamenting "the difficulty sometimes experienced in getting Jamaican artists to open up to other Caribbean and international acts", Isimat-Mirin argues that "even though Jamaica will forever be credited with giving birth to reggae music, they need to understand how some selected collaborations can open new avenues for the music". Furthermore, because of the particularity of the distinctive Creole identity in the French West Indies, Isimat-Mirin persuasively proposes that "the time has come, also, to move away from the Jamaican model." Affirming the "authenticity and viability of a specific 'Creole reggae'", Isimat-Mirin documents the accomplishments of the *Mozaik Creole* project that he initiated. He identifies the hybrid elements that constitute Creole reggae: "A shared goal of Guadeloupe and Martinique has been the search for an authentic reggae and dancehall sound, somewhere between traditional sounds (such as *gwo ka*, *bèlè*, *beguine*) and the authentic reggae groove and culture." "Authenticity" now becomes synonymous with "hybridity" as Creole reggae artists are liberated from a purist model of Jamaican originality.

Leo Vidigal's chapter, "Reggae Music Documentaries in Brazil", focuses in sharp detail on stereotypical representations of Jamaican culture, particularly popular music, in the Brazilian imaginary. Vidigal highlights the neocolonial politics that frame the documentaries *Maranhão em Ritmo de Reggae* (*Maranhão in Reggae's Rhythm* [1990]) and *Jamaica: O Paraíso do Reggae* (*Jamaica: Reggae's Paradise* [1992]). Of the latter, Vidigal notes: "The title *Jamaica: O Paraíso do Reggae* refers to the colonial discourse that has always associated the New World with the lost paradise, always ready to be discovered and rescued for the joy of a privileged élite (an approach that is still often used by tourist companies)."

In November 2010, as an academic tourist at the University of Sao Luis, Maranhão, I discovered many "street signs" that confirmed a Jamaican presence in the city, however much disfigured by tropes of paradise.[3] Known as "Brazilian Jamaica", the state of Maranhão can indeed lay claim to being a major centre of dispersed Jamaican culture, in particular reggae and Rasta-fari. But, as Vidigal argues, the cartography of *Maranhão em Ritmo de Reg-gae* maps both Jamaican and Maranhense culture in problematic ways: "[The narrator] presents the theme of reggae in Brazil regretting that, in Maranhão, 'the most popular songs were always imported from Jamaica.' The narrator qualifies this situation as a 'cultural distortion,' because Brazil is 'one of the richest countries in musical genres.' The terms and expressions used let slip a concept of culture as merchandise, unattached to its creators and admirers."

Turning from the Brazilian texts, Vidigal examines films shot in Jamaica that sensationalize the culture, such as *The Devil's Daughter*, a US production from the 1930s that exploited the local religion of Pocomania. But even documenta-ries made by Jamaicans in the post-independence period reproduce devilish stereotypes. Vidigal notes the similarity between the foreign film, *The Devil's Daughter*, and the local, two-part documentary, *This Is Ska*, both amplifying cultural "noise": "In the introduction to the movie, the disc jockey Tony Ver-ity describes ska as a 'hypnotic sound' which would cause the listeners to become 'caught up in a frenzy and [they] couldn't help moving to this pulsat-ing, almost religious beat'. The connection between the musical and spiritual spheres, translated in the rituals shot in *Pocomania,* seems to echo in the text, also characterizing dance as a bodily appropriation of a musical expression of a transcultural process." But what Vidigal accurately designates as "the hege-monic imaginary" is decidedly subverted by alternative narratives and visual texts that portray Jamaican culture in far more sophisticated ways. In his read-ing of *The Harder They Come*, Vidigal characterizes the iconic film in this way: "a full length music and movie hybrid that directed musically the space and time of a territory, catalysing the operation that would, way beyond mere asso-ciation, *fuse* 'Jamaica' and 'reggae'". It is this episteme, or "overstanding" – in the original Greek sense of the word and also in Rastafari discourse – that is both celebrated and contested over and over again in these chapters on the transposition of Jamaican reggae from local beat to global reverberation.[4]

The chapters by Roger Steffens and Klive Walker focus on reggae in the United States and Canada, respectively. In his autobiographical account of "Reggae Music in the Bloodstream", Steffens deploys a borrowed trope to emblematize his infectious encounter with reggae music: "I was living in Berke-ley, California, making my living by reading poetry, and I read an article by an Australian journalist named Michael Thomas in *Rolling Stone* in July of 1973. He said, 'Reggae music crawls into your bloodstream like some vampire amoeba from the psychic rapids of Upper Niger consciousness.' It led me to rush to the store and buy *Catch a Fire*." Having been invaded by the "vampire amoeba", Steffens tells a gripping tale of succumbing to the voracious predator. Retaining the informality of oral discourse, his transcribed talk conveys the drama of his Damascus Road conversion from poet to self-taught music journalist. Steffens also recounts his decades-long quest to put his hands on all those reggae documents he so presciently valued – documents that others might have considered ephemeral and unworthy of critical attention. His obsessive collection of reggae memorabilia, consolidated as the Roger Steffens Reggae Archives, constitutes incontestable evidence of the fanatic's precipitous fall over the "psychic rapids of Upper Niger consciousness".

Steffens's passionate tale is also the story of uneven exchange in the reggae music business, as evidenced, for example, in the case of the enterprising Hank Holmes:

> Hank worked in a one-stop – a wholesale/retail record store. The store specialized in cut-outs, over-pressings of soul albums for twenty-five cents an album. But Hank was reading the British magazines in the 1970s and took note of the little advertisements on the back that said "10 Reggae singles for £1". It turned out that these soul albums were known in England – in London, Manchester and Birmingham – as Northern Soul and they paid ten pounds or more a piece for those records. So Hank contacted some of these stores in England and said, "I'll sell these albums to you for ten pounds but I don't want money. I noticed your ad said ten singles for one pound. So why not just send me one hundred reggae singles for each of the albums I send you.

In a classic understatement, Steffens ingenuously observes: "The day I met him he had just received a new supply, four huge crates of reggae singles, with four hundred records in each crate. He had a little mail order company out of his house called Reggae Beat. So he was getting one hundred records for twenty-five cents – not a bad deal."

It certainly was not a "bad deal" for Holmes. But unsettling questions do arise, contesting the "goodness" of the deal. What of the depreciated reggae singles in comparison to the much appreciated soul albums? Who or what determined that ten reggae singles were worth only one pound in the UK retail trade? How could this pricing structure prove profitable in the long term? And for whom? Beyond the particularity of this 1970s West Coast moment, these questions, in long perspective, provoke interrogation of the economics, politics and ethics of the global distribution of reggae music and all the related material and intellectual property that now endlessly circulates.

Steffens also highlights the role of non-commercial radio stations in spreading the gospel of reggae. The fervour of the pop music fan is not unlike religious zeal. But mainstream US radio in the 1970s did not readily convert to reggae. As Peter Tosh put it in an interview soon after his final concert, "Me go to America and certain places out there man, fe months you wait fe hear all one reggae, and when them play is like them sorry fe you" ("I go to America and in certain places there you wait for months to hear even a single reggae song on the radio. And when they do play it, it's as if they're sorry for you") (Cooper 1984).

Steffens's own reggae radio show, the first in Los Angeles, spawned the *L.A. Reggae* television show and the widely influential black music magazine the *Beat*. With ready access to the media, entrepreneurial Steffens was also instrumental in mobilizing cultural tourists to attend Reggae Sunsplash: "It was like an annual convention of reggae lovers from around the world that helped spread the music even more." Steffens's career as music journalist, archivist, author, international lecturer and, above all, reggae fan, illustrates a recurring theme across the globe: the amateur often goes professional, all for the love of reggae.

In "The Journey of Reggae in Canada", Klive Walker discloses the "hidden potential" of Toronto, which has been "overlooked or seen as a minor contender with regard to reggae culture". Walker acknowledges the pioneering role of Jamaican-Canadian bands of the 1960s, such as the Sheiks, the Cougars, the Sounds of Joy and the Hitch-Hikers, who "treated Toronto audiences to quality doses of ska, rocksteady, soul, rhythm and blues, and funk at venues such as the West Indian Federation at College and Brunswick streets and two establishments in the heart of downtown Toronto on Yonge Street – Fitz Riley's Club Jamaica and the Blue Note". Walker coins the term "reggae in the Caribbean diaspora" to signify the fact that "reggae culture became the youth culture of successive generations of teenagers and twenty-somethings in the diaspora regardless of where in the English-speaking Caribbean they drew their heritage". As the Canadian reggae hip-hop artist Kardinal Offishall puts it rhythmically in "BaKardi Slang": "You think we all Jamaican, when nuff man a Trinis, Bajans, Grenadians and a whole heap of Haitians, / Guyanese and all of the West Indies combined / To make the T-dot O-dot one of a kind."[5]

Even for those Canadian youth who had no Caribbean roots, reggae music became a language they could understand and improvise on. Like Amon Saba Saakana, Walker underscores the primacy of Bob Marley in mainstreaming reggae: "He cemented an imprint of influence for rock and folk musicians who may have already been hip to reggae-flavoured rock through Eric Clapton or by punk bands like the Clash." For example, Canadian rock star Bruce Cockburn recorded a very popular reggae track on his 1979 album *Dancing in the Dragon's Jaws*, and another on the 1980 album *Humans*.

Caribbean diaspora artistes in Canada cover the full spectrum of reggae and related musical styles: For example, Ishan People and the Truths and Rights bands (roots reggae); Messenjah (rock and rhythm and blues); Lillian Allen, Clifton Joseph and Michael St George (dub poetry); Devon Martin, Kardinal Offishall, MC Collizhun and Motion (reggae hip-hop); Kid Fareigna and Carla Marshall (dancehall); Michie Mee and Maestro (Canadian hip-hop); Dream Warriors (hip-hop–jazz fusion); Jah Beng, Len Hammond, Humble, Sonia Collymore and Belinda Brady (singers); and Jeff Holdip and Jesse King (dub artistes). Klive Walker's comprehensive account of the journey of reggae in Canada confirms that there may have been many hard times; but the riddim does, indeed, continue to beat insistently.

Returning to the continent of Africa, the source of the resonating reggae beat, the contributions by Cheikh Ahmadou Dieng and Louis Chude-Sokei affirm the potency of both the sonic and ideological reverberations. Assuming the vestments of the traditional teller of tales, Dieng recounts the story of "Reggae Griots in Francophone Africa". His narrative voice evokes the riddling indirection of fable: "Once upon a time – that's how many stories begin – and it is often relevant because life is a story, in a way." Dieng celebrates orality; the word becomes flesh, however much disfigured by the trauma of colonization.

Defining the cultural context within which he recognizes resemblances between the mystic Baye Fall and Rastafari, Dieng observes that "in Senegal, the marginalized Baye Fall – not all – has always been tolerated as a smoker and a user of alcoholic beverages by many (even though the trend is changing). In the cultural psyche, the parallel perception or psycho-mental identification process is here: a negative perception of the Baye Fall leads inevitably to a negative perception of the Rasta. Here resemblance is identification; a positive perception of the Baye Fall leads to a positive perception of the Rasta." Speaking parabolically, Dieng navigates between the literal and the metaphorical: "If we travel in the imagination, we will certainly find the little dot where wisdom and madness intersect, where the self-declared fool jerks and spits out the truth from his guts. That is the stand of reggae and the realm of 'foolosophy' with its undeniable impact on the collective psyche." Dieng here cites Alpha Blondy, the self-styled "rastafoolosopher", who exemplifies the reggae artist as cunning griot; both praise-singer and wily critic of authority, the reggae griot chants down systems of oppression, whatever their disguises.

Louis Chude-Sokei's erudite chapter, "Roots, Diaspora and Possible Africas", theorizes the reclamation of reggae by Africans within the much broader context of an overarching narrative of exclusion in which "modern and contemporary Africa is often left out of or marginalized by the 'black Atlantic' framework, celebrated for its anteriority yet seconded to the echoes of its cultural influence". Chude-Sokei, himself born in Nigeria, raised in Jamaica and long-resident in the United States, tells an archetypal tale of the complex ways in which embodied echoes return and turn again: "Africans so often have to find their way into the conversations and assumptions of the 'black Atlantic' or the black diaspora by ironically mimicking and performing the questions and assertions of African authenticity or racial utopia produced by those very conversations and assumptions."

Chude-Sokei presents an excoriating meditation on the paradoxical rhetorics of reggae: "In keeping with its roots in colonialism, poverty and a fundamentalist sense of manhood, this millenarian and nakedly Utopian music also sublimated its fantasies of power and vengeance in its language of justice and liberation (there is always, after all, an echo of revenge in revolution and of murder in freedom)." In this polemical piece, murder is both a recurring trope and a literal sign of the seemingly inescapable conflation of justice and vengeance. Delineating the problematic ways in which the engagement of Jamaican reggae artists with "Africa" often alienates continental Africans from diasporic fantasies of power and authenticity, Chude-Sokei sardonically observes, with reference to the murdered Lucky Dube, that, "lacking the geographical distance that gives gravity to longing and authority to metaphor, perhaps murder will ultimately guarantee Lucky Dube authenticity in a diaspora that often renders Africa secondary to its imaginings of it, its soundings of it and its representations of itself in relation to it".

Signifying on the "alternative Africas produced in black diasporic sound", Chude-Sokei compellingly argues that "for Lucky Dube and the myriad musicians and fans on the continent, despite its fundamentalism and deep essentialism, reggae offered not an authentic or a true Africa but a series of possible Africas that could stand above and beyond the ethnic particularities of the continent and which could enable the intrusion of merely literal Africans into the black diaspora's conversations and into its creation of foundational assumptions". Indeed, the fundamental issue Chude-Sokei addresses so brilliantly in this provocative chapter is this: "how a music that begins as a statement of Jamaica becomes globalized and translated as the sound of the very world itself, and then is appropriated due to its relentless symbols of Africa by Africans themselves".

The chapters by Marvin Sterling, Brent Clough and Michael Veal demonstrate the startling ways in which reggae, dancehall and dub have become "the sound[s] of the very world itself". In "Gender, Class and Race in Japanese Dancehall Culture", Marvin Sterling examines the modes in which the embrace of Jamaican reggae and dancehall dislocates assumptions about social power in contemporary Japanese society. Conceptions of Japan as a homogenous ethnonation have been destabilized as a consequence of recessionary times that have created a class of underemployed youth engaged in a search for self. Disclaiming the fiction of a uniformly middle-class Japanese modernity, these youth constitute the core audience for transgressive Jamaican popular culture.

Sterling observes that "the Jamaican reggae call for a return to Afrocentred tradition is articulated in Japanese reggae as a return to the Japanese premodern". The samurai becomes the symbol of updated ancestral values. Sterling cites the following example:

> In his song, "Born Japanese", Nanjaman – if there can be a Jamaican "Ninjaman", why not a Japanese "Nanjaman"? – describes samurai as bearing "*yamato damashii*". This is a nationalistic term in which Japan's national soul is seen to reside with the dominant Yamato ethnic group. Nanjaman muses in his song about how those Japanese today bearing this spirit leap into the world in search of something truly important ("*hontōni daiji mono o sagashi ni*"), something beyond Japan's dishonest politicians and narrow pursuit of yen.

Daring Japanese women who have been seduced by dancehall culture literally leap into a world of "exotic" stereotypes. In their search for self, these women subject their bodies to contradictory readings that both contest and reinscribe patriarchal discourses. As I myself also propose with respect to the representation of female sexuality in Jamaican dancehall culture *a yard*, Sterling argues that, "seen in deep subcultural context, there is subversive potential to this dance in which large groups of women forgo gendered propriety to engage in a highly erotic dance that celebrates a woman's performance and control of her sexuality".[6] Sterling does acknowledge that the subversive potential of the celebratory dance can itself be subverted in the body politics and economics of capitalist reproduction: "However, as subcultural performance reaches broader and broader audiences, this potential often comes to submit to and reinforce the hegemonies of the mainstream. Reggae dance in this environment is stripped of its subcultural complexity, becoming just another opportunity for Japan's corporate patriarchy to commoditize and profit from the bodies of Japanese women."

In his subtly shaded reading of race in Japanese dancehall culture, Sterling argues that, "given the relative absence of black people in Japan, blackness is more readily seen as, and is more uncontestedly, reduced to manipulable symbolization". CD and DVD covers are prime examples of the manipulation of symbols of blackness. Analysing the CD cover image painted by the artist Ryoono, which features an ambiguous Japanese and Jamaican woman depicted simultaneously as geisha and donnette, Sterling concludes that "any reckoning of what she singularly is, given how emphatically the evidence points both one way *and* the next, would be pointless. But, perhaps, in the end, the woman is Japanese, to the extent that she is a product of Japanese creative agency, of a Japanese pleasuring in the Afro-Jamaican global in a way that is (il)legibly local". This alluring inscription of the illegibility of the local in the translocal discourse of Jamaican popular music beautifully illustrates the recurring theme of this collection.

Brent Clough's expansive chapter, "Oceanic Reggae", provides a fortuitous instance of the convergence of mutually intelligible meanings of local and global politics as reggae music, with its resounding message of resistance to neocolonialism, reverberates in New Zealand: "The anniversary of Marley's birthday, on 6 February, now has considerable significance as a day of celebration in New Zealand (or Aotearoa – its Māori name) because it falls on the modern state's contentious birthday, Waitangi Day. It has become a day when deeper questions attend notions of One People and One Love (*Aroha Tahi*) for those citizens of the Marley nation, indigenous or non-indigenous, who flock to reggae concerts around the country." In Clough's comprehensive account of the "naturalization" of reggae music across the Pacific, exported Jamaican culture becomes the transformative agency through which multiple host societies articulate indigeneity. The intimate act of laying claim to the culture of reggae and Rastafari engenders reclamation of native discourses that are now translated into a new language of global creolity. "Home" is the literal landscape of belonging; it is also a distant, mythicized territory of unfulfilled longing. In summary, Clough posits that

> if these glimpses of reggae's indigenization in Aotearoa, Australia, Hawai'i and parts of Melanesia have a common thread it is in the value musicians and audiences place on "roots" as a metaphor for the vital expression of local cultural identity. Paradoxically perhaps, this means for many Rastafari in Melanesia, Hawai'i, Aotearoa and Australia, that reggae calls them "home" to Ethiopia. This creates a desire which exists, not without tensions, alongside indigenous cultural nationalism and ongoing struggles to retain land and prepare for the worst of the omni-colonial future.

In "Dub: Electronic Music and Sound Experimentation", musicologist Michael Veal theorizes the dub aesthetic in lyrical language that simulates the deconstructive poetry of his subject: "fragments of the lyrics, delay units creating streams of liquefied sound, synthetic reverberation implying cavernous spaces, instruments sliding in and out of the mix, filter units manipulating the sonic frequencies". Veal graphically evokes the surreal inscape that is dub, foregrounding the destabilizing topography of the disjunctive music.

What Veal provides is a celebration of the dis/integrative ingenuity of pre-eminent Jamaican "enginicians" such as Lee "Scratch" Perry, Sylvan Morris, Errol Thompson, Overton "Scientist" Brown, Lloyd "King Jammy" James and Osbourne "King Tubby" Ruddock, whose collective genius irrevocably transformed global popular music: "Dub's 'aesthetic of fragmentation' has become one of the stylistic cornerstones of popular dance music in the digital age, and its fluid reinterpretation of song form laid one important foundation for the amorphous remix culture that is so central to contemporary pop music." Veal also asks a profound question that continues to perplex analysts of dub music: "How did such a technologically dependent style develop to such an advanced extent under these circumstances, in a nation of extremely limited economic resources, within a region marked by a diversity of traditional performing ensembles?"

Veal's penetrating question can be applied much more broadly to other arenas of competition, such as athletics, in which Jamaicans excel globally in

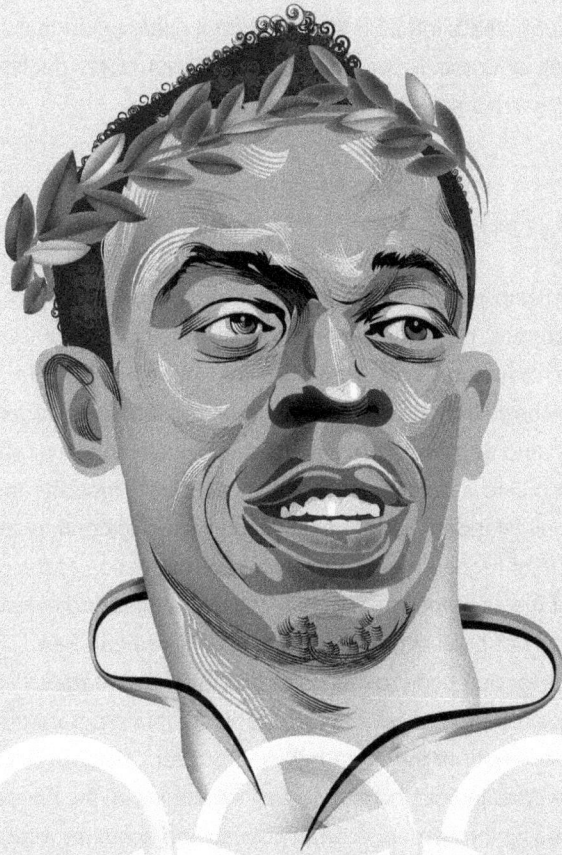

ΟΛΥΜΠΙΑΚΟΙ ΑΓΩΝΕΣ
OLYMPIC GAMES
USAINBOLTLONDON2012
THE HONOURABLE USAIN ST. LEO BOLT, OJ, C.D. JAMAICAN SPRINTER AND THREE-TIME OLYMPIC GOLD MEDALIST.

Usain Bolt, Olympic champion, by Michael Thompson. Courtesy of Michael Thompson.

complete disproportion to our geo-political size. Having identified several factors that could account for the emergence of dub, Veal does concede that "the elusive and unquantifiable 'character' of the Jamaican people" must also be taken into account. Veal's intuition is an insightful observation that Jamaicans would completely endorse. Proverbial wisdom unequivocally declares, "wi likl bot wi talawa" ("we're small but we're powerful").

Conclusion

From the inter/disciplinary perspectives of historical sociology, musicology, history, media studies, literature, anthropology, sociology, cultural studies, the creative/cultural industries and, above all, the metaphorical "life sciences", these plenary lectures from the "Global Reggae" conference eloquently exemplify the breadth and depth of current scholarship on Jamaican popular music. They lucidly articulate a cultural politics that acknowledges the far-reaching creativity of small-islanders with ancestral memories of continents of origin. The globalization of reggae music is, indeed, an affirmation of the unquantifiable potential of the Jamaican people to reclaim identities and establish ties of affiliation that are not at all circumscribed by the Caribbean Sea.

As a much-extended coda to this collection on global reggae, I include two *braata* chapters on the establishment of the academic programme in reggae studies at the University of the West Indies.[7] The first, "Reggae Studies at the University of the West Indies", constitutes my reflections on the dangerous politics of criss-crossing the border between popular and academic discourse. The second chapter, "Entertainment and Cultural Enterprise Management", is written by Kam-Au Amen, an entertainment business specialist, who designed the curriculum for the innovative undergraduate degree programme.

These appended chapters complement the primary texts on the globalization of reggae, illustrating the subtextual trials and tribulations of academic innovation in a "postcolonial" university. The institutionalizing of reggae studies deconstructs colonialist narratives of authoritative, Eurocentric scholarship. Indeed, reggae studies, like dub poetics, is an ec/centric enterprise that is literally located out-of-centre. Contesting conventional notions of what constitutes scholarship, reggae studies affirms the authority of orally transmitted knowledge, thus reclaiming for the academy the wisdom of the streets.

Notes

"A yard", Jamaican street talk for "at home". By extension, "yardies" are Jamaicans born in Jamaica or, especially, those born in the diaspora who assertively claim Jamaican heritage.

1. Teddy Isimat-Mirin was unable to attend the conference because of a family emergency. His piece is included in these proceedings.
2. Though performed and popularized by Bob Marley, "No[,] Woman, No Cry" is attributed to Vincent Ford. The song is found on the album *Natty Dread* (1974).
3. I was invited to give one of the keynote lectures at the Sixth International Symposium of the Center for Caribbean Studies in Brazil, "Afro-Caribbean Influences in the Americas". My paper was entitled " 'The Unity Is Submarine': Circuits of Culture in the 'Transterritorial' Caribbean".
4. According to the *Online Etymology Dictionary*, the origin of episteme is "Ionic Greek, *epistasthai* 'know how to do, understand,' literally 'overstand,' from *epi* 'over, near' (see *epi-*) + *histasthai* 'to stand'". http://www.etymonline.com/index.php?term=epistemology&allowed_in_frame=0. Accessed 28 January 2012.
5. "T-dot O-dot", street talk for Toronto, or T.O.
6. See, for example, the chapter "Lady Saw Cuts Loose: Female Fertility Rituals in the Dancehall", in Cooper 2004, 99–123.
7. The Jamaican Creole word *braata*, like the Spanish American *pilon*, signifies "a little amount of the same, as of some foodstuff that one is buying, added on for good measure" (Cassidy and Le Page 2002, 64).

References

Bob Marley and the Wailers. 1974. *Natty Dread*. Island, ILPS 9281.

Cassidy, F.G., and R.B. Le Page. 2002. *Dictionary of Jamaican English*. Kingston: University of the West Indies Press.

Cooper, Carolyn. 2004. *Sound Clash: Jamaican Dancehall Culture at Large*. New York: Palgrave Macmillan.

——. 1984. "Peter Tosh Interview". *Pulse*, June, 15.

CHAPTER 1

REGGAE AS BLACK SPACE

ERNA BRODBER

n 1961, sixth-form students, who were to become Jamaica's middle class in the post-independence period, would have known of the great difficulty black students in Little Rock, Arkansas, United States, were experiencing in trying to get into high school. They would have read about this in the popular evening daily news-paper the *Star*.

They would also have seen the advertisement in the issue of 10 November 1961 inviting young Jamaican women to choose to which of ten types of beauty they belonged and to apply, accordingly, to be judged and to get the winning prize in the national Miss Jamaica Beauty Contest. The year 1961 was the year for the "satinwood" type of beauty. The years of "ebony" and "mahogany" had either gone or were yet to come, for the next year's beauty type was going to be "golden apple". They would also have seen the following cartoon on page thirteen and wondered whether with their type of beauty – ebony or mahogany – they could get a job in the hotel industry on the "naught coast".

They could have read, too, about Millard Johnson's party, the People's Political Party, and its attempts to organize black people. Or, they might even have seen some of his publications in which he showed the faces of African leaders, so different phenotypically from Jamaica's Alexander Bustamante and Norman Manley – thick lips, broad nose, black skin, the first Africans they would have seen outside of Tarzan's half-naked friends giving them the chance to test the saying "Hugly no African".

They might have heard that Rastafarian dreadlocks were being forcibly trimmed by the police, seen Rastas made a joke of in the annual pantomime, shared jokes about them and their purchase of tickets to take them to Africa, or

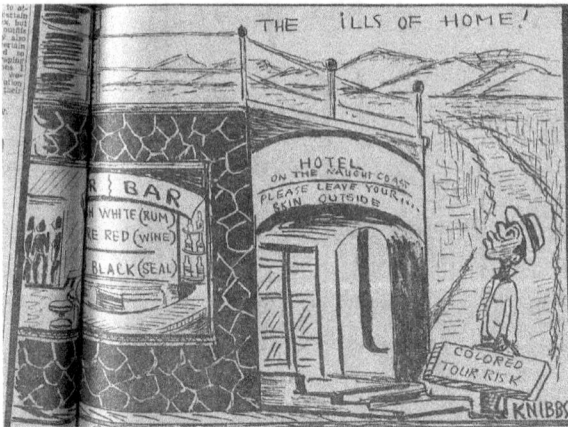

1.1 African Jamaicans suffered the indignities associated with colour prejudice in 1960s Jamaica as portrayed in the *Star* advertisement on 10 November 1961. Courtesy of the Gleaner Company.

1.2 Beauty contests of the 1960s favoured the lighter-skinned Jamaican woman, reflecting the colour and class prejudices of the era. *Star*, 10 November 1961. Courtesy of the Gleaner Company.

been frightened by the armed insurrection led by Claudius Henry, the Repairer of the Breach, and his son. They might even have been part of *Teenage Dance Party* on JBC (the Jamaica Broadcasting Commission, a government-owned radio and television station) and there danced to Beardman Shuffle, an imitation of the way dreadlocks (Rastafarians) danced. In short, the teenager, graduating from sixth form the year before independence, and so about to join the middle class, existed in an environment in which race and colour were issues in their native Jamaica. But were these issues openly discussed and did these teenagers feel that race and colour had anything to do with their lives? Their parents would never have encouraged them to seek jobs in the tourist industry on the "naught coast": there was the civil service, there was the library service and there was teaching. For the very bright who got scholarships, or those whose parents could afford the fees, there was university and courses such as law or medicine.

The *Star* had a section called "Sing a Song". The songs published on 13 November 1961, the day on which the previously mentioned cartoon and the advertisement announcing the beauty contest appeared, were "Wooden Heart" and "Amor, Amor", both popular American love songs. The teenager would have cut these out, learned the tunes by listening to the radio and been able to sing along, word for word. From her parents or nightclub-going elder sibling, she might have heard of Mapletoft Poulle, Baba Motta, Carlos Malcolm or Sonny Bradshaw and their attempts to promote Jamaican music, the same old "Linstead Market", "Sammy Dead" and "Come back Liza" but in jazz format. There were, however, Jamaican artists, Wilfred Edwards and Keith and Enid on the new radio station, JBC, and their ballads "Tell Me Darling" and "Worried over You" were as lovely and engaging as "Wooden Heart" or "Amor, Amor". This station is said to have been designed to promote the development of Jamaican culture, and it did lay down some tracks. Sonny Bradshaw, director of musical programmes at JBC, attracted the services of Aggrey Brown, the popular DaCosta Cup footballer and recently graduated head boy of Cornwall College, to host his *Teenage Dance Party*. The Top Ten was one of the features of this station. It was a list of the ten most popular tunes determined from the analysis of the purchases of the major record shops – Universal Mart, Gordon's Record Service, Clock Tower, K-G Radio Sales, Stanley Motta and Wonard's Radio Engineering. Up to 1964, no more than three locally created tunes had made the Top Ten in any week. Desmond Dekker's "Honour Thy

1.3 Rastafarians were stigmatized, ridiculed and feared in the 1960s because of their appearance. The growth of reggae was integral to the acceptance of Rastafari. Courtesy of the Gleaner Company.

Mother and Thy Father" was there, though, from 8 February to 26 April and the great "rent-a-tile" (meaning "slow dance"), Jimmy James's "Come to Me Softly", on the Gaydisc label, *ruled* from May to July of that year. Dekker's sociological eye was one to watch. Prince Buster was another one: his "Tongue Will Tell" spent several weeks on the Top

Ten in 1964. Dekker and Prince Buster came with a new slant in content. They were not crooning love songs to anybody or talking of unrequited love; they were talking of and to the people in their community, and the buying public was interested.

This conversation, to which the buying middle class was able to listen through the lyrics of art-

1.4 Prince Buster was one of the singers that revolutionized the approach to popular music in the 1960s. He addressed issues of violence and oppression instead of romantic love. Courtesy of the Gleaner Company.

1.5 Desmond Dekker and the Aces, Wilson James and Easton Howard, were like Prince Buster, in that they came with a new slant in content that highlighted the issues of the time. Courtesy of the Gleaner Company.

ists such as Dekker and Prince Buster, continued throughout the 1960s. Eavesdropping thus, the sixth-form graduate learned about "rude boys" in 1966 and 1967 from the Clarendonians and the Wailers, facilitated by Studio One. It was Peter Black, who later revealed himself to me as Fred Nunes, who brought this discourse officially to the attention of the middle class. He did so in an extended letter to the editor, published in the *Sunday Gleaner* of 11 June 1967. Black thought this conversation within the rude-boy culture was of great socio-political import, writing that "our local boys are men of true importance and ought not to be taken lightly." He wished, he said, to draw the editor's attention to this. Black looked at five songs – "Train", "Gun Man", "Tougher Than Tough", "Judge Dread" and "Court Dismissed" – in his article "Community Violence and Jamaican Pop Music". The article draws attention to an incident in "Tougher Than Tough" in which the judge, passing sentence on a rude boy, is from Ethiopia. Black interprets this thus: "The first point of note is the association of authority with a personality not of Jamaican origin."

He missed the point. The point was that within this musical culture, Ethiopia was highly rated: it was the source of power; it was, according to Psalm 68:31, where the people would stretch forth their hands unto God; moreover, according to Psalm 87:4, "this man was born there". This man was selected by God to rule his people. Indeed, the year before Black wrote his article, His Imperial Majesty Haile Selassie, Emperor of Ethiopia, clearly the man referred to in the Psalms mentioned above (according to Rastafari theology), had visited Jamaica and had left the establishment amazed at the passion with which ordinary Jamaicans had welcomed him. It should be noted, too, that this judge was accusing and charging the rude boy for "shooting black people". Clearly this judge cared, particularly, for a kind of people called "black people". He also missed the colour reference in the Ethiopian judge's statement: "I am black, sulphuric acid / I melt all iron." This was the opportunity for the sixth-form graduate to note that Ethiopia and black were invested with great power in parts of the society. This great power had a colour. It was black and could do impossible things. The righteous black man could melt the guns of rude boys. Black also missed the reference to trains in the song "Trains". He confesses, "I can make little of the trains, boats and planes which are 'coming now'." The reference here was to the hoped for exodus out of Babylon, meaning Jamaica, to that country in which the hands of the inhabitant were stretched out to God and where that man "was born"; an exodus so excellently done, years after, by Bob Marley.

By late 1968, the government of the day was helping to invest "black" with revolutionary political power in society. It was making an all-out attack on "black". Immigration officers were charged, or felt charged, to prevent books dealing with black issues from entering the island – it was rumoured that even the children's novel *Black Beauty* had been proscribed. It was quite likely that radio and television programmes had been censored as reading material had been, and the word "black" with them. Anti-government sentiment was ventilated in songs such as "Everything Crash". This song depicts Jamaica as a place where all the essential services have gone on strike. The then prime minister's name was Shearer. Shearer pronounced "Shearoh" rhymed well with pharaoh. A culture which drew heavily on the Bible, which was imbued with the Rastafarian influence, which tended to see the current world as the fulfilment of the biblical prophecy and which was thinking about an exodus from Jamaica to Ethiopia, had a field day linking the prime minister and his government with Babylon and other evil conditions. Few of these, such as Prince Buster's "Pharoah's

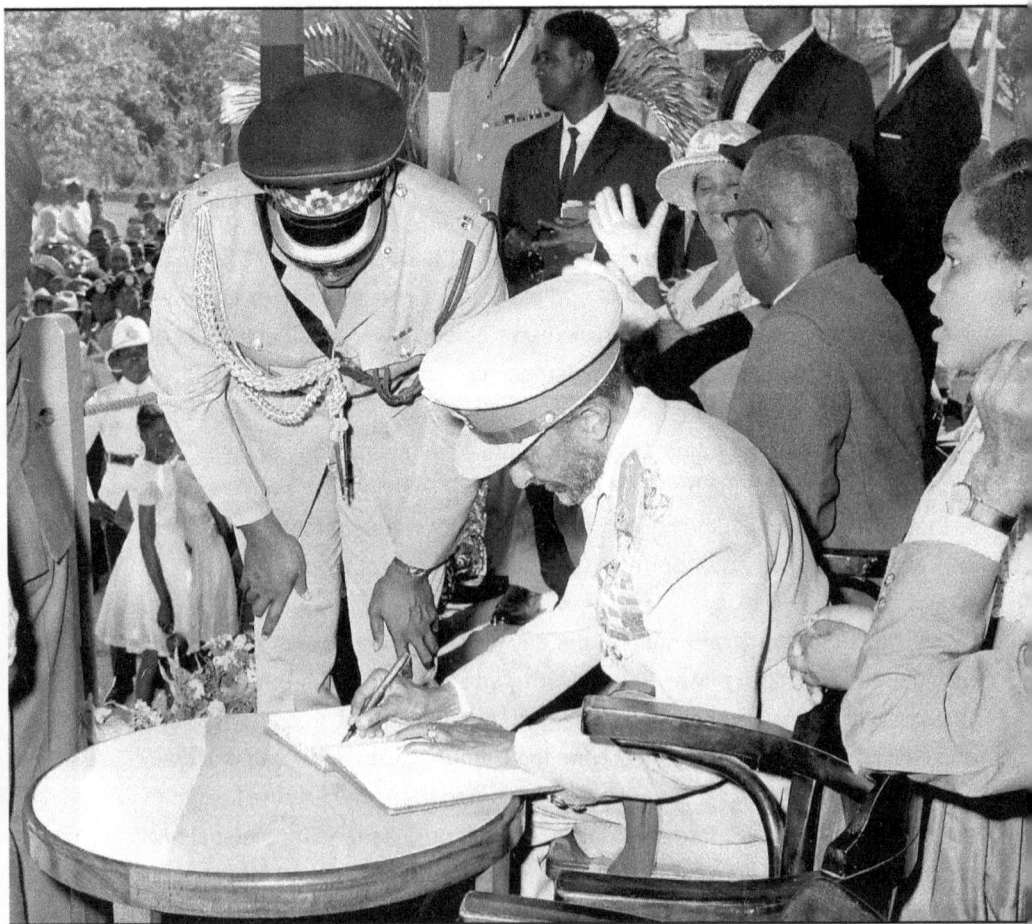

1.6 His Imperial Majesty Emperor Haile Selassie visited Jamaica in April 1966. On his arrival at the Norman Manley International Airport he was welcomed by thousands of Rastafarians. Courtesy of the Gleaner Company.

Army Get Drownded" were aired or reached the Top Ten, but, delivered in the attractive ska beat, they were heard in the dancehalls. "Everything Crash" commanded the chart in January of 1969.

"Look from you deh ya, you nuh know Bongo Nyah", Little Roy's "Bongo Nyah", holding its place in the charts for six weeks, seemed to be saying to recently graduated sixth formers eavesdropping on the culture from which most of these singers emerged: "Here you are peeping in, but Bongo Nyah has been around you and you around him all your life, why don't you know him?" "Lick it back Jah", Bongo Nyah continues. So the singer was now Bongo Nyah, the Rastaman, the old African, inviting the sixth former to throw off artificial blinders and look at black people and what they represented, threatening Jah's wrath on those who did not. Nina Simone's "Young, Gifted and Black" made the charts in February 1970 and stayed there until March. A funny thing happened, though, by mid-March. Prince Buster had, in today's terminology, "bought out" the argument of the African-American Simone and was with her in the charts until mid-April when he bought out the argument totally for he was there without her until early May, sending her message in the rocksteady beat. It was alright now to be called "black". Thanks to Simone, and even more so to our own Prince Buster, the word could now be associated with "gifted". An aspirant to the parliament, P.J. Patterson, later to become a prime minister, used "Young, Gifted and Black" as his campaign theme. The sixth-form graduate, knowing herself to be "young" and "gifted" need not be shy about putting a colour-coded adjective in the mix, making her "young, gifted and black". Indeed, she need not be afraid of being "black". Could young, gifted and black get into a hotel on the "naught coast"? He or she could if she cared to, for he or she was now a "Duppy Conqueror" – the name of a Bob Marley creation that stayed on the charts for twelve weeks.

What is a "duppy conqueror"? People wanted to know what they were buying and what the singers were saying. Answer: For a black person, the spirit is as potent as the flesh and, in fact, most potent after the body had passed away. Every sixth former's parents knew about this and they tried to shut up grandma when she came in from country with news of what duppy had done to whom. They knew that to be able to be the conqueror of another's spirit is really a mark of great power. But this was a "country" and lower-class belief. The sixth-form graduate now learned about the power of the spirit and that this faith was part of an authentic system of beliefs, translatable into the following: "You young, gifted and black sixth-form graduate, if you stick close to your black cultural under-standing of the world, and follow the paths of righteousness, you can have and exercise great power over others." Max Romeo's 1971 creation "Maccabee Version" appears not to have made the Top Ten at all. How could it be when Malcolm X's life story was banned? This poem/song complained about the negative effect of white culture and economic behaviour on black people. Being a song with a popular tune, this study in social and political history was more available than the works of George Beckford, who was punished during this period for his anti-colonial stand, as shown in his book, *Persistent Poverty*. The repeating chorus of "Maccabee Version", "Black man get up stand up on you foot / And give black god the glory", stimulated a lot of thought. I watched a dancing and singing mother forced by her six-year-old son's question – "Mummy what wrong with black man's foot?" – to give him a lecture on Caribbean history. Riding on the tune of a popular Christmas carol, "Good King Wenceslas", which described a king who seemed to be learning, too late, of the distressing conditions of his people, Max Romeo's "Maccabee Version", whether he intended this or not, juxtaposed the colonial condition with a new kind of independence for all to digest as they "tightened up" and "rocked steady":

> You gave I King James version
> King James was a white man
> Now give I Macabee version
> 'Cause I am a black man
>
> You stole the land God gave I
> And taught I to be covetous
> What other wicked deed
> Have you got in mind
> Tell me what are [you] going to do
> To stop these daily crimes.
>
> What other wicked things
> Have you got in mind?
> Tell me, what are you gonna do
> To stop these daily crimes?

Bring back Maccabee Version
That God gave to black man
Give back King James Version
It belongs to the white man

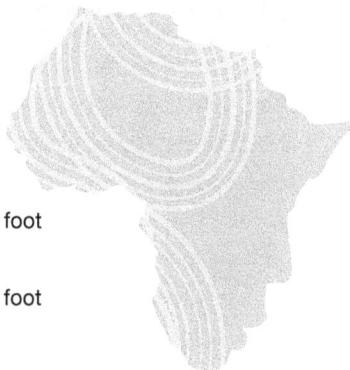

Black man, get up, stand up on your foot
And give black God the glory
Black man, get up, stand up on your foot
And give black God the glory, yeah

You suffer I and you rob I
You starve I then you kill I
But what are you gonna do
Now that your sword have turn against you?

Black man, get up, stand up on your foot
And give black God the glory
Black man, get up, stand up on your foot
And give black God the glory

Bring back Maccabee Version
That God gave to black man
Give back King James Version
That belongs to the white man

Black man, get up, stand up on your foot
And give black God the glory
Black man, get up, stand up on your foot
And give black God the glory

"Maccabee Version" taught you, as you tightened up or rocked steady, that there was a deity whom we ought to hail. The song begins by paying respect to Jah Rastafari, a deity at this time recognized only by black Jamaicans. Max Romeo's line in his first stanza, "I am a black man", was as declarative and as definitive as Martin Luther's seventeenth-century piece, his ninety-five theses pinned on the church door, *Here I Stand.* One of Max Romeo's theses was that there are versions of the Bible specifically given by the Almighty God to the black man for his empowerment, but this version had been hidden from him. This is the Maccabee version. Whether anyone could show him or her the Maccabee version or not, the graduate from sixth form could understand that black people were not only gifted and had particular ways of doing things and a particular view of the world, they were special to God: there was a version of the Bible written especially for them. The thoughtful did look to Old Dreads and to the University of the West Indies lecturers to help them to find the knowledge with the black man's name written on it, knowledge Bongo Nyah told them was within easy reach. Many bright sixth formers, by now about to graduate from universities here in Jamaica and elsewhere, left home to study at the feet of one elder or another. Max Romeo had said "Black man get up and know yourself", and they were off to know themselves.

The Melodians's "Rivers of Babylon" spent eight weeks on the Top Ten. The lyrics were borrowed from Psalm 137: "By the rivers of Babylon / where we sat down / And where we wept / When we remembered Zion." Who were these weeping people to whom the Melodians' song, referred? Black people, of course! That guy with the bad foot who had difficulty standing! Who else was taken away from their lands and transported elsewhere? The sixth-form graduate would sing and dance while better understanding her history and what it meant to be "black". It was Burning Spear who brought civics, taught in the lower grades of the school, into the mix. He created the song "Marcus Garvey", which was the most purchased tune in March of 1975. The sixth former knew Marcus Garvey to be an unequivocally black-skinned man and the country's first national hero. He was given prophetic powers in Burning Spear's creation; note the lyric "Marcus Garvey prophesy say". This is another thing that black people could do: see around corners. Apart from his prophetic ability, Marcus Garvey was a published author who had mesmerized the world. Here was a hero whom no one could escape from seeing as black. Here was a role model, even one that Babylon could not resist acknowledging and giving to the people.

"Reggae", translated by the most erudite of the eavesdroppers as the dative form of the Latin word "rex" for "king", therefore meaning "music for a king", was not the first time that black-skinned people, the descendants of Africans enslaved in Jamaica, were creating ways of defining themselves on the basis of their colour and their history; building and disseminating theories to explain their uniqueness, and designing theories to guide praxis. Marcus Garvey's Universal Negro Improvement Association had done this here and abroad. Others, not quite satisfied with the Bible, had published the *Holy Piby*, and there was *The Promised Key* written and published by Leonard Howell under the pseudonym G.G. Maragh. A little booklet eight by five inches and having just fourteen pages, it was inexpensive and easy to store: it could be used as a bookmark for the Bible. The author, interested in addressing a particular people, black people, seems to have wanted to offer a theory which explained their present status vis-à-vis people of other colours, to warn them against false ideologies and to present guides to healthy and holy living.

The book has on its inside cover those words quoted by black nationalists as early as the eighteenth century: "Ethiopia shall stretch forth her hands unto God." Also there is the charge, "Arise and shine for the light has come, and the glory of the Lord God of Israel is now risen upon us." The next page has a picture of His Imperial Majesty the Emperor Haile Selassie. The book is now divided into sections, the first of which is entitled "The Mystery Country". This describes Haile Selassie's coronation in all its majesty. The next section discusses "The False Religion" where we are told the following: "My dear Reader you can see that all the foundations of the earth are out of course. Allow me to say that there is no throne for the Anglo Saxon white people, they must come down and sit in the dust on the ground there is no throne for them. See Isaiah 47th chapter."

The next is *The Promised Key*. Here we are told that "His Majesty Ras Tafari is the head over all man for he is the supreme God", and his godly qualities are listed for us. We move on to "Ethiopia's Kingdom" where we are introduced to King Alpha and Queen Omega, Rastafari and his wife, emperor and empress of Ethiopia, and the author gets a chance to make a definitive statement linking blacks to this majesty: "King Alpha and Queen Omega are the paymasters of the world, Bible owners and money mint. Do not forget they are black people if you please." We move on to guides to righteous living in Jamaican society – what is a "balm yard" and how to approach the notion and the fact. Who are revivalists and how much of what they peddle should be accepted? We are told, also, how to fast. The section entitled "Department" is very difficult to understand. The section marked "Government" is easier: we are here introduced to the concept of black supremacy: "Instead of saying 'Civilization'", we are told, "Hereafter, we shall say Black Supremacy." It is further explained to us that "Black Supremacy has taken charge of white supremacy by King Alpha and Queen Omega, the king of kings". Herein we are also told that black must not marry white and white must not marry black; that we should not marry divorced persons and that wives and husbands must not "watch and peep on each other".

We move on to the "Eternal Law Office". Here there seems to be some biblical revisions: Adam, Eve, Abraham and Isaac have been given no books in the Bible, so "according to the clearness of this case there is nobody named Adam, Eve and Abraham". These, the writer seems to be saying, are figments of the imagination of "ministers and lawyers who have no part in the business of Queen Omega and King Alpha". The revision continues with the discussion of "Eve the mother of Evil". She and Adam and Abraham are "white people if you please" and are no family to King Alpha and Queen Omega, who have said "that they are our parents and keeper of the Tree of Life". The next section is "Rapers". The discussion here is of the Ku Klux Klan, who "committed boisterous fornication with the black women who were taken as slaves", so "both rapers and mob lynchers and Klu-Klux-Klan [sic] are to be shot from off the face of God Almighty's beautiful earth".

We come now to "the Ethiopian Question" where we learn that "we gave ourselves to be slaves for hundreds of years"; that we had given up King Alpha and Queen Omega and this was, it seems, the cause of our enslavement. "The First and the Last" is a "praise" paragraph in which King Alpha and Queen Omega are described as "the type setters for time and eternity". "Matrimonial Affidavit" is a section in which justification is made for treating King Alpha and Queen Omega as "the first and the last, the beginning and the end". The final section in this small pamphlet is entitled "Black People, Black People Arise and Shine". We are told here that "The white man's doctrine had forced the black man to forsake silver and gold and seek Heaven after death. It has brought us to live in disgrace and die in dishonour." But now that we have found out that "their doctrine was only a trick, and all their intention was to make themselves strong and to fool the black man", we must cleave to His Majesty Rastafari.

All the theses in *The Promised Key* were restated in the reggae: the existence of a person called the black man; the Bible, a gift to the black man but which had been polluted; the importance of Ethiopia to God Almighty; the authority given to His Imperial Majesty Haile Selassie by Almighty God to rule the world; the need of guides for righteous living for the black man in Jamaica;

and the expression that it was time for him to get up and assert himself in the society. Why did these theses need to be reasserted? No doubt Howell, this early elder, preached from his book, bringing his ideas near to his audience in this way. Reading the work by oneself is challenging as punctuation marks are few and far between, words are given peculiar meanings and a thorough editing is badly needed. The message of the writers such as Max Romeo, Prince Buster, Bob Marley, Burning Spear and the Melodians was easier to understand. One listened to words backed by a catchy tune. The philosophers of the days of reggae were gifted with radio and sound system as communication devices. Their oral messages did not need the intervention of the pen, print and punctuation marks.

E.N. Burke was a student at Mico College in 1929 when Garvey held meetings at nearby Edelweiss Park. He told me that he liked what Garvey was saying: "We who were Black like myself, were [in Jamaican society] down the bottom so it was something great to me, as a very black man to know that somebody was telling me that I could achieve, I could be somebody, that I am somebody" (Brodber 1984). He read Garvey's *Black Man* regularly and discussed it with others, but he was a Garveyite only "in spirit", "because in those days it was not 'the thing' for an aspiring young teacher to link up politically". Garvey's treatise could not be made into fact through the up-and-coming middle class in the 1930s because they feared loss of jobs. The reggae listeners of the 1970s "dreaded" their visage and turned their backs on their establishment homes and situation with amazing alacrity. Something had changed.

The sixth former or university student was not afraid of pennilessness or joblessness. So convincing were the arguments coming out of the lyrics of the reggae that he or she believed, indeed, that she had to take a stand with his or her life and that, like the lilies of the field in the Bible, he or she would be taken care of, and he or she was. Several have today found their places at the pinnacle of the society, having gone through this initiation. The reggae message to the black man, disseminated in sweet rhythmic music more effectively than the writings of the 1930s, provided a space for argument and counterargument, for learning that there is something called a black man and for teaching the initiate how to be a black man. Reggae of the 1970s created a black space; it was an incubator for a kind of knowledge that needed to work its way out of the ground and into the minds of the young descendants of Africans enslaved in Jamaica. Not just chatter among the platters, the early reggae allowed meditation while you danced and even if you did not want to be black, you could at least understand why others would want to be.

In 1922, the *Methodist Recorder*, published in the United Kingdom, announced that Jamaican cleric Reverend R.N. Parnther, "a highly honoured negro", had died. Some Jamaicans of his Methodist faith here were outraged at the description of the reverend by reference to his race, and even thought of ending their association with the church because they found the descriptor insulting. "A black man, educated, gentlemanly and successful", his defender the Reverend Geddes, head of the church in Jamaica, advised the church in Britain, is never referred to as a "negro". He is referred to by his place of birth. He added that only the apostles of Garveyism referred to themselves by this term.

Ninety years later, the people of the class of the Reverends Geddes and Parnther are willing to answer to terms which refer to them by race and ancestry. A great deal of this change has to be attributed to the reggae artists who, by a variety of literary and musical strategies, have pried the word "black" from "poor", "ugly", "stupid" and imposed other and more positive connotations upon it. Before the 1980s ended, we were told that " 'natty' was now the head one a UC". Black man was now pictured as the bright guy, the intellectual and administrator at the university level.

Reference

Brodber, Erna. 1984. "A Life of Service: The Rev. E.N. Burke". *Jamaica Journal* 17 (2): 10–18.

CHAPTER 2

FROM MENTO
TO SKA
& REGGAE
TO DANCEHALL

PETER ASHBOURNE

This chapter examines two important changes in the direction of Jamaican popular music: the change from mento to ska, and the change from modern reggae to dancehall. It is less important for this enquiry to follow the singers in either case, as the accompaniment did not change appreciably from singer to singer. Stylistic changes tended to occur more from studio band to studio band, with individual musicians having various effects on the sound and "feel" of the rhythm side. Just like the singers, musicians or groups of musicians enjoy their period of influence until someone else becomes fashionable or the trend moves on.

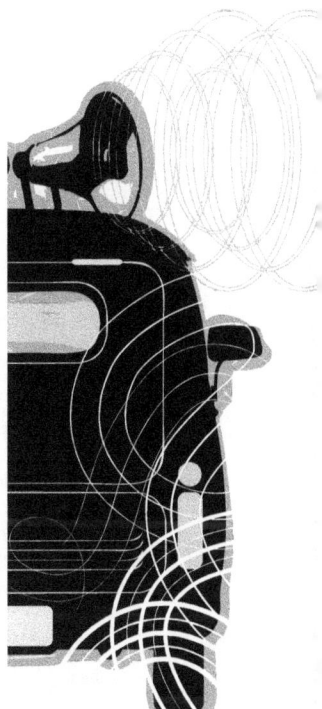

Mento to Ska

A rough definition of mento (and the most useful for this discussion) is the commercial version of Jamaican folk songs. This was the style of music that was played by mento bands and dance bands prior to the onset of recording in the island. The name eventually came to mean all types of contemporary Jamaican music and also the Jamaican version of Trinidadian calypso. Mento was the most significant style of Jamaican popular music, roughly speaking, from the 1920s until the early 1960s.

Like all forms of Jamaican pop music, mento is pattern music. That is, various instruments play

2.1 What is now referred to as the "traditional" mento band consists of anywhere from four to eight performers playing maracas, congas, guitar, banjo, rhumba box and some kind of wind instrument (clarinet or saxophone). Courtesy of the Gleaner Company.

together, each playing a short rhythmic pattern or riff that is repeated for the duration of the song, possibly with minor variations from time to time. In the case of pitched instruments, the chord progression is stretched over the framework of the riff. Recorded examples of mento generally come in two types – traditional mento band performances and those played by popular or jazz bands. The main features that differentiate these two types are instrumentation, repertoire and production value.

What is now referred to as the "traditional" mento band consists of any-where from four to eight performers playing maracas, congas, guitar, banjo, rhumba box and some kind of wind instrument (clarinet or saxophone). One of the players – often the maracas player – would be the lead singer, while the rest of the players provide the chorus. Analysis of the components of this performance reveals the following: the maracas play a constant sixteenth-note pattern. There may, or may not, be conga drums playing the appropriate pattern.

The guitar plays the standard mento guitar riff, the banjo can improvise freely in a manner complementary to the guitar rhythm and the singing line, and the rhumba box usually plays one of the standard rhythmic riffs for the bass instrument. The vocal component is usually a lead line that allows for call and response singing somewhere in the song. The saxophone, clarinet or violin function like the banjo in that they play in the instrumental breaks and supply complementary *obligato* lines, for example "Iron Bar" by Count Owen. The rhythmic "centre" of the music is with the bass line. The total sound of this type of performance tended towards earthiness and a not unpleasant rough charm.

When the urban bands played mento, the instrumentation was different. In this type of music, the four-note limit of the rhumba box was replaced by the double bass, and later by the electric bass guitar, so the harmonic range of the band immediately increased by a large factor. Maracas and congas were replaced or augmented by the trap set, so the percussive component changed in character. The element of the maracas could be effectively dupli-cated, while making available another type of drumming known as *bruck-ings* – a busy rhythmic improvisation on the snare drum. What was frequently used was a clave-type pattern that can be found all over the Americas. This model has become the mento template for any Jamaican band playing mod-ern instruments. There is a wider range of songs available for performance,

2.2 Seaford Town Mento Band. Courtesy of the Gleaner Company.

helping to widen the appeal of the style. The "cleaning up" of the sound and delivery is noticeable – this can be seen in "Hol' 'im Joe" by Lord Flea.

As is now widely known, the ska came out of the need by the owners of local sound systems for fresh and catchy recorded material that would promote the quality and uniqueness of their particular sound systems. Some of them made recordings, called *specials*, and this process is what started the experimentation and fusion that resulted in ska. The specials of the sound systems initially consisted of covers of boogie-woogie and other songs with a shuffle beat, as well as 12/8 ballads as in "Feel so Fine" by Shirley and Lee.[1] The Jamaicanization of these covers started to occur. The musicians and singers making these recordings were, consciously or not, adding, replacing, changing or augmenting elements in the music with elements from their own experiences. Mento, Cuban rhythms, and other elements from mainstream US and British pop culture were fair game. The end result of this experimentation was the ska beat. "Boogie in My Bones" by Laurel Aitken illustrates this fusion.

In technical terms, the alterations of boogie-woogie/shuffle beats resulted in the following: (1) a slower tempo; (2) a dramatic decrease in importance of the first or "down" beat; (3) the accenting of the off or "back" beat; (4) the reinforcement of the up beat. In practice, this meant more instruments played this attack, if necessary, and this approach simplified the chord progression. For most examples, this meant changing the swing feel to a straight feel. Some rhythms are swung to varying degrees, and some songs have both swing and straight lines playing together.

An important difference between ska and mento is that the former has a backbeat and the latter does not. Mento tends to feel rural and gentle whereas ska feels urban, urgent and more aggressive. The fact of the backbeat may have contributed to the appeal of ska outside of Jamaica, despite the fact that it was so "back-to-front" when compared to all other forms of pop music. Interestingly, the blues chord progression was largely ignored in ska and the evolutions following, even though much of the singing had a pronounced R&B slant. One of the few examples of a blues ska is "Easy Snappin".

Roots Reggae to Dancehall

The change from modern reggae to dancehall was quite different from that between mento and ska. In the late 1950s, once the "sound system" recordings started to be made, the music started to change. Ska emerged from its boogie-woogie origins in about three years. The evolution of dancehall was quite different. The sound systems always had a *toaster* – someone who would chat up the crowd, give some jive talk and generally entertain while the records were being changed on the turntable. Some of these toasters had such an engaging rap that they became a significant part of the sound system's appeal.

When some sound system operators started making recordings, it was only a matter of time before these toasters, or DJs, were featured. These early recordings can be thought of as precursors of the dancehall style. The early DJs – U-Roy, King Stitt, Big Youth and others – while being top DJs in their sound systems, also enjoyed success as recording artists on a fairly regular basis. So, in a sense, dancehall style was always part of reggae music.

Dancehall has two distinct periods: the first covers the material that uses contemporary reggae patterns and recycled rhythm tracks for accompaniment, with occasional departures from that formula. The second phase is demarcated by the accompaniment, which no longer uses reggae patterns but has a unique sound. Part of the new sound involved the use of electronic music instruments. Drum machines replaced the trap set, and synthesizers could substitute for any of the other instruments. Even when technology made sampled instruments a practical reality (this means more faithful duplication of acoustic instruments), the resulting sound was coupled with vocals that employed chanting and talking in rhythm. Dancehall therefore became a fully matured style.

One may now even be able to identify a third period of dancehall, as currently the trend is towards a "retro" use of the venerable one drop rhythm. Singers are making a comeback and some *riddims* (rhythms) – but not all, by any means – are sounding more and more like normal rhythm tracks for songs. All this is happening while the tempos for the regular dancehall are increasing even more, and riddims are appearing with great frequency.

In the late 1970s, when word started to spread around Jamaican society about this new type of music called dancehall, Sly Dunbar and Robbie Shakespeare were the most prolific and influential musicians. Their creations propelled Black Uhuru, Culture, Gregory Isaacs and others to reggae stardom, and it was not unexpected to hear their drum and bass at the vanguard of this new musical phenomenon. Their stripped-down-to-the-minimum drum and bass is evident in the recording of "Arlene". The primary components are the basic rock pattern on the drums; the reggae bass line; and the vocal performance that is a mixture of talking in rhythm, chanting and singing. In "Diseases", by Michigan and Smiley, there is more of the "sing-jay" approach to vocals.[2] The instrumentation has more components than the previous example: there is a guitar and an organ shuffle. But the stripped-down, dub-wise approach is very clear. The tempos here are in the range of eighty beats per minute.

"Sleng Teng" by Wayne Smith is one of the occasional variations to the evolution of dancehall music. Perhaps it can be said that it gave a foretaste of the highly electronic and machine-like productions to come. This one-bar pattern was never intended to be a reggae music pattern. The basic pattern is actually a pre-set pattern in a Casio-brand mini-keyboard of that time. The pattern was labelled a rock pattern and meant to be played at a much faster tempo than that used for the sleng teng series of recordings. The pattern consisted then of the Casio pre-set at a slower tempo, drum set and piano ska (or "bang", as it is now called) overdubbed – and *voilà!* – there was the rhythm with the most versions ever recorded. The last count was 117 versions.[3]

"Punany", originally by Admiral Bailey, is an important rhythm because many successful versions have been made and it has also managed to out-live many other rhythms. In "Punani", there is a new drum pattern, reinforced with a cowbell. There were many more like this from this point on. This is also another one-chord song with raunchy lyrics. In the track there is a section where the rhythm track makes a series of dramatic cuts to emphasize the lyr-ics. This is a technique called "mix" and is used frequently in recordings and extensively in dancehall performances.

"Duck" is the rhythm that heralded the ascendancy of Steely and Clevie and their status as important creators of dancehall music. Notice the, by now familiar, bass, drum and cowbell pattern; the bass line implies a one-chord progression as in "Duck" by Steely and Clevie. "Telephone Love" (1989) uses another Steely and Clevie rhythm. This song is a good example of the rela-tively few successes of the straight singers (meaning those singers who *only* sing) at this time. Both Gregory Isaacs and J.C. Lodge (the singer of "Tele-phone Love") had big hits with songs written on this rhythm. Clevie Browne (of Steely and Clevie) began making his drum rhythms more "busy" (meaning

2.3 Steely and Clevie (Wycliffe Johnson and Cleveland Browne) were important creators of dancehall music. They pioneered the use of the drum machine in dance-hall rhythms. Publicity photo.

with more components). This change in attitude had very little to do with the search for artistic direction. Clevie confessed to me that boredom with the current music was his motivation for adding more instruments in interesting places. It must be mentioned that, by this time, electronic equipment was more available, affordable and accessible. The advent of the drum machine, for instance, made many more instruments available for easy recording at a fraction of the cost of a musician for each instrument. Clevie very quickly embraced this technology, as it was the perfect complement for his new burst of creativity.

Clevie's tune "When" (performed by Tiger) is important for several reasons. This song marked what could be considered the second period of dancehall. At this point, the evolution was complete and dancehall was audibly different from its predecessors of ska and reggae. This song also established Steely and Clevie as preeminent dancehall musicians. Interestingly, on this rhythm track, Clevie dispenses with the bass entirely. The tuned drums at a low pitch were sufficient to provide the pitched bass component, and since the vocals were completely spoken – there was no recognizable melody – the pitch necessity was somewhat lessened.

Bogle, perhaps the most famous of all the dancehall dancers and dance creators, established, once and for all, the trademark rhythm of dancehall, as if it needed more emphasis! This rhythmic device is all-pervading and continues to today.[4] Steely and Clevie's dominance continues, although more producers have, by now, made creative contributions to the riddim landscape. Among this number are the producers who have limited or no skill on any musical instrument. Instead, they are naturally musical, very aware and conversant with current tastes and, most importantly, are very comfortable with the available technology. With these attributes, they are able to turn out successful and popular musical productions. Notable are the Kelly brothers, Dave and Tony, who are audio engineers and the earliest of the non-musician producers.

Dancehall gave rise to the concept of the "riddim", a passage of music (meaning the music and the audio) – anything from a two-bar pattern to an eight-bar chord progression – becoming a template for the creativity of the singer or DJ. The pattern, or "riddim", is used in loop fashion for the vocal-

2.4 In the dancehall era the straight singer played mostly in a secondary role to the deejay. A notable exception to this general rule was Beres Hammond. Photo by Adrian Creary; courtesy of the Gleaner Company.

ist to create a "song". The practice, itself, is not new. From as far back as the rocksteady era, producers were recycling the rhythm tracks of songs in various ways – instrumentals (not the same melody) using the track, "version", sometimes called "dubwise", and even new songs. The difference here is that a popular riddim will be used by all and sundry, while it is popular. This practice raises very complex copyright issues.

The one-chord song predominates in dancehall. It seems that the most important component is a good groove. The pitch component is treated differently. A tonality is established, if only in the bass. If the other pitched instruments are consonant with the bass, then that is okay. If the vocal is also consonant with the rest of the track, that is okay. If it is not, then that could also be okay, as long as the groove is good. Volume is also a major factor in dancehall music. Many recordings that sound mediocre and ordinary at a low volume level suddenly come alive and aggressively confront the listener when played at an ear-shattering level by a stack of eleven-foot speakers.

Dancehall marked the ascendancy of the DJ, as opposed to the singer. Singing was replaced by what could be roughly termed chanting: highly rhythmic singing using one, two- or three-note melodies. Singers were not completely silenced, but the singer was mostly in a secondary role to the deejay. Notable exceptions to this general rule were singers Beres Hammond, Bloodfire Posse and J.C. Lodge. The quality of singing, in this instance, was usually below that of the average singer, but most of the time it seemed to be adequate for the occasion. A popular song form is to have one performer chant or deejay the verses and another performer sing the choruses or else two line interjections in a "best of both worlds" situation.

Once dancehall found its own voice, it seemed that the tempos started speeding up. "Diseases" by Michigan and Smiley was at a stately 80 beats per minute. Compare this with 130 beats per minute, which was the average dancehall tempo in 2005. The song form was also changed. A much more flexible approach to forms emerged. The two main types of earlier forms were conventional pop song (verse and chorus) and call and response, usually corresponding with a two- or four-bar pattern and chord progression. There were flexible verse lengths.

Deejays now make extensive use of extemporization, creating on-the-spot lyrics. Topicalities and social commentary are the main subjects. The frequent misogyny, glorification of sex, violence, gun culture, and strident homophobia have been criticized in many quarters, but there has hardly been any change in the lyrical content. More recently, another stream of "conscious" lyrics has emerged. These lyrics have a more philosophical and less belligerent attitude.

One of the most attractive features of classic ska, rocksteady and reggae is the natural and live quality of the recorded performances. Many factors contribute to this perception, not the least of which is the timing of what is played. Practically all of the recordings up to the late 1970s were done without click tracks (this is the sound of a metronome counting time – all the musicians play to this track during recording), so the music runs on "human" time with minute variations in tempo and it "breathes". This phenomenon is what the listener perceives as a "live" quality. It is significant, then, to enter the world of sequenced recordings (sometimes referred to as "computer music") where the timing is perfect. It is more difficult to make this music humanly imperfect than to leave the timings in lock step with each other. When this is done with other styles of music, listeners describe it as robotic and cold. It is interesting that dancehall fans seem to have no problem enjoying it. Perhaps the deejay performance with the rhythm causes them to ignore the slightly unnatural timing situation.

There are several key developments in the evolution, including those from mento to ska, and from reggae to dancehall, which must be examined for a full understanding of the development of Jamaican popular music. Given the de facto demise of the recording industry,[5] and the fact that Jamaican popular music developed as a result of this industry, what then, will drive the next key evolution?

Notes

1. The easiest way to understand the various rhythmic styles is to listen to audio examples of them. For instance, a well-known 12/8 ballad is "I've Been Loving You too Long" by Otis Redding.
2. "Sing-jay" refers to those artists who combine singing and deejaying into a single performing style. Lovindeer ("Wild Gilbert") is a perfect example of a sing-jay.
3. The precise number of versions is not known as more than one producer recorded that pattern. It is probably safe to say that they number in the low three figures.
4. In the absence of audio, I could suggest recalling Jamaican folk songs "Slide Mongoose" and "Brown Skin Gal". The rhythm of the words "Slide Mongoo(se)" and "Brown Skin Ga(l)", repeated endlessly, constitute the central pattern of this type of dancehall.

5. The recording industry is changing in fundamental ways, chiefly because of changes in electronic and computer technology. The paradigm of recording sales being the justification for all other activities such as concerts and touring is no longer relevant. Concerts and touring constitute the core activity with recordings providing promotional support. Put another way, recordings are not as important as they used to be.

CHAPTER 3

THE IMPACT OF JAMAICAN MUSIC IN BRITAIN

AMON SABA SAAKANA

The popularization of Jamaican musicianship has been felt for a long time, going back to the 1930s with the development of Jazz in Britain. A significant number of musicians from the Caribbean came to Britain to establish themselves in a peculiar enterprise called the music industry. Racism, without over-emphasizing the point, characterized the victimized status of Caribbean peoples, and music was one of the rare professions where an individual could attain some level of marksmanship and prominence in spite of its visceral and brutal existence. This chapter examines the role of Jamaican musical ideas specifically as they impinge, impose and impress upon all areas of British popular life, whether in music itself, or television, or speech or lifestyle.

Music in a Toilet

The conceptual base of British mythographers was a mental separation between the so-called West Indian and themselves. This mythogram was constructed around ideas of primitivism and a continuously refined British modernity: thus a successful rebellion which ultimately led to the early nineteenth century overthrow of French enslavement in Haiti by the shapers of Haiti themselves led to an outcry of barbarism. This example can be replicated in the consequences of the Morant Bay Rebellion. Civilized reaction was modernized during the second major European war in which volunteers from Africa and the Caribbean were characterized and projected as rapists. Again, in the realm of culture in a period of vulnerable humanism, early Jamaican popular music was characterized in Britain by DJ Tony Blackburne (a successful R&B jock for the then highly popular Capital Radio) as "music recorded in a toilet". Blackburne, in the twentieth century, carries reverberations of the British cleric and landowner James Phillippo, whose conception of eighteenth-century Jamaican music was equally pejorative and ignorant: "discordant sounds", and "the most hideous yells from the whole party by way of chorus" (1969, 242–43). One can also compare the then critical reaction to Beethoven's work in early nineteenth century Vienna. Sidney Finkelstein expresses it as follows: "As is always the way with reactionary critics, who recognize the cultural threat to their patrons, they try to destroy the new realism by accusing the work of poor craft, bad taste, ignorance of the correct rules, vulgarity" (1976, 56).

In reconstructing the prism through which these statements were made, one can see a modernist continuity of the Haitian and Jamaican examples alongside the development in recording studio techniques and technology in which many successful recordings in the United States of America and Britain were recorded in the toilet of a one, two and four track studio. At no time in the history of Jamaican popular music was there a great disparity between the recording standards of Britain and Jamaica. The difference in time was no more than twelve months. By the early 1960s, many of the successful songs by African Americans, as well as British and American pop and other genres of music, were recorded on mono, then stereo in two-, four- and later eight-track studios.

To paraphrase Ernst Fischer, one can, a posteriori, apply a theoretical structure to the assigned role of the Jamaican artist in British society: the illumination of social relationships in society, the enlightening of the racist in an opaque society, of assisting the dominant to recognize and change social reality, and finally, to dramatize the notion that social contradictions cannot be passed off as the rational process of mythologizing (1971, 14). The Jamaican artist set standards in refashioning the sonic properties of instrumentation and moved the boundaries of limited lyrical content. By so doing, in his Jamaican stubbornness and nationalism, he was attackingly transforming the genetically limited DNA of the British sound environment from mythogram to a new sensoform.

I have already indicated that African-Caribbean musicians were significant voices in the development of jazz in Britain. I would, however, like to add that they also played a powerful role in transforming British military music from as early as the eighteenth century, and those who have always suspected that the drumming in European military music had its roots outside Europe, would be correct.

A Personal Note

Before 1965 I had met one Jamaican, an athlete in Trinidad. On the boat to Britain I encountered a Jamaican brother who ate daily at the table with us and shared cabins with six women. I also met an ambassadorial postee to Africa, a very tolerant and patient man. My supervisor on my second job was a Jamaican lady who became a fast friend. My first introduction to Jamaican music was in the same year at the home of a now deceased Trinidadian social worker, Norton McClean, who was playing "Put It On" by the Wailers. This was my first encounter with Jamaican music, very different from kaiso and other black musics I already knew. Because of the numerical superiority of Jamaicans within the Caribbean populations in Britain, and their characteristic stubbornness in the pursuit of their music, as well as its widespread popularity in all areas of Caribbean entertainment, whether in the nightclub or at a party, I became more and more drawn to not only appreciating and loving the music but also to writing and reflecting on it.

My younger brother was convinced that his love, Alton Ellis, was much greater than my own, Ken Boothe. I came to appreciate and admire Ellis as a very special and gifted singer and his *Sunday Coming* album as a standard in popular music. Many years later, in interviewing him, I was to understand why that album was so special not only to my brother and me but to Ellis himself. I am interjecting this testimonial to confirm the extent of my interest in things Caribbean and, in particular, Jamaican popular music. Interestingly, the people who were writing intelligently about the music in the late 1960s and early 1970s were non-Jamaicans: Patrick Griffith, now dead, Trinidadian; Imruh Caesar (now Bakari), Kittian; and myself. Jamaican Carl Gayle was not yet publishing. We constituted an intellectual defence of Jamaican music against the barrage and excesses of the rantings and ravings of the dominant society. In so doing, we were authenticating our Caribbean culture regardless of source or location.

Iconic Appropriators/Cultural Influence

Curiously, simultaneous with the reactionary tide were the early appropriations of the music's rhythm by the most iconic of the British pop groups. "Ob-la-di, Ob-la-da" by the Beatles is a case in point. Another curious sight was the *David Frost Show* on London Television in which each commercial break was introduced by Frost pointing his finger and saying, "Soon come." For those who are not aware, Frost was a Cambridge man and quite upper crust in his speech and demeanour. But he was obviously very socialized, as he was once engaged to a Jamaican lady. The word "crucial" became widely used even in radio news programmes. Today, the most middle-class of British speakers use the phrase "nuff respect" or simply "respect" in everyday application. This is an imitation of their former yard boy, now canonized.

With the coming of Channel 4 television in 1985, African-Caribbean–led campaigns and position papers resulting in contracts being given, for the first time, to African-Caribbean directors and producers. The Jamaican accent, as well as others of the Caribbean, became a weekly cultural disseminator until they were progressively axed. When David Rodigan hosted a deep roots reggae programme on Capitol Radio, the language of Jamaica was weekly being inserted into the consciousness of British listeners with words like "dress back", "wicked", "I man", "Yes, roots/natty", "inna yard", "forward" and so on.

These examples are important because they represent the most prestigious icons in British entertainment: the Beatles were undoubtedly the biggest

band in British popular music history and Frost was the definitive interviewer of the cream of British and international personalities. These examples also portentously indicated, in an almost subtle, surreal and subterranean way, that the normative imperviousness of British society was being secreted and impregnated with a new set of genetic cultural markers which already heralded the profound cultural alterity that British society was destined to experience.

3.1 Alton Ellis, a special and gifted singer, was among the pioneers popularizing reggae in Britain. Courtesy of the Gleaner Company.

3.2 David Rodigan hosted a deep roots reggae programme on Capitol Radio which he used to sensitize British listeners to the Jamaican language with words like "dress back", "wicked", "I man", "forward" and so on. Publicity photo.

C.L.R. James liked to say that African captives brought themselves to the New World. In so doing they brought a civilization, and in the brutal circumstances of plantation slavery there was an inevitable mediation of adjustment or accommodation. This is not unique to conquered peoples, but to all those who have experienced migration. Jamaicans are no different in this regard. Just like Jamaica itself, where the pioneers and entrepreneurs of the Jamaican sound were cane cutters and other low-paid workers, so too in Britain did the Jamaican working class constitute the pioneers and activators of the music. The importation of Jamaican recorded music was first conducted by Jamaicans themselves; the avenues through which this music was played were located in flats, illegal clubs (commonly called "shebeens") and other nightclubs. An entrance fee was paid and one was regaled with the latest sounds, food and drink.

Entrepreneurial Firsts: Jews and Jamaican

Here the question of entrepreneurship comes into play: the marginalized Jew, who may be characterized as vulturous in his relationship to African-created sounds, has to be acknowledged as sharing a history of oppression and marginalization. Thus the Jew's understanding of a publicly unacknowledged identification with the circumstances of the African-Caribbean migrant, as well as the vision of a limited business opportunity, saw him as a pioneer in bringing the music before British and, by extension, European audiences.

Thus, as early as 1946, Emile Shalet, who later collaborated with Siggy Jackson, both eastern European Jews, founded the Melodisc label specifically to fill the gap of imported jazz records from the United States, but later entered the arena of kaiso in 1951 and, still later, African continental music. This final type constituted, as export, one third of all the sales of their records. Two of the early recordings of Jamaican vinyl on Melodisc were "Worried over You", by Keith and Enid, and "Dumplins", performed by Byron Lee, a Jamaican version of an African-American R&B instrumental. It was stated that sales could reach three hundred thousand to five hundred thousand singles for a hit of any of the genres delineated above, and interestingly one-third of these sales were based on the export markets in West Africa and the Caribbean. This was not only phenomenal but of comparative mainstream achievement for sales in any genre from that time.

Finkelstein, writing about the foundational element of European popular music, says that both Europe and America exploited Africa and Asia through colonialism and robbery and in the last five hundred years they made an indelible contribution to popular music which drew heavily upon Asian and African music: "The folk music of eastern, central and southwestern Europe, which infused the (European) classic musical creations of the last five centuries, was itself built on a heritage of Asian and African music" (1976, 15). How does this influence begin? It begins with imitation, characterized by both awe and contempt: the former because of the brilliant, innovative traditions inherited and ingeniously adapted, and the latter because of the position of servility of the innovators. This, naturally, led to large-scale rip offs, claiming music that they did not write, receiving unwarranted praise, and the indignity of performance segregation in America, while in Britain it was confinement to small clubs and a ban from radio and television.

Melodisc, Blue Beat and Ska

The marketing of the early music, inevitably and predictably, encountered obstacles and resistance, particularly from BBC radio and television producers. Jackson describes the experience of Melodisc and Blue Beat labels: "Wherever I went, all our records were played [in the discos] but we had a hell of a battle to get them played on the BBC. They didn't want to know. Our records sold more than other hits in the charts, and yet we couldn't get into the charts. Nor could we get the plug. There was terrific prejudice against black music" (Clarke 1980, 140).

Melodisc later formed a specialist label, Blue Beat, for Jamaican music and ska when it came into being, this appellation serving the music upon which the label was issued. The major mechanism through which Jamaican rhythm and blues and later ska records was popularized in Britain was through the sound man. Just as in the Jamaican context, the innovation, after new trends in popular music in the United States in the early 1960s became fixed in the American preoccupation with rock 'n' roll, was channelled through the sound man. It was the sound man who popularized the early nascent acetates and later vinyl that incubated in the masterful musicianship which ska axiomized. The concealment of label and artist identity was deliberately executed and exclusivity was the norm. Parties or clubs would have two sound men battling it out with the secret weapons of new sounds.

Early Pioneers

Sonny Roberts, a Jamaican carpenter, and Lloyd Harvey, a record enthusiast, formed Planitone Records in 1961, fulfilling the same thirst for rhythm and blues. With an ambition to own his own record label and studio, Roberts rented premises on the Edgware Road, established a one track studio and bought his own disc cutting equipment. Distribution was through friends, parties and clubs. Among those recorded were Dandy Livingstone, Tito Simon and saxophonist Mike Elliot. Chris Blackwell, after initial involvement in Jamaica with the R&B phase, came to London and visited Roberts. He listened attentively to his experience and then also visited Melodisc Records and the distributor Lugtons where he met Dave Betteridge, who later became a limited shareholder in Island Records and later the managing director of CBS Records in the early 1980s. Roberts introduced Blackwell to Lee Goptal, a Jamaican accountant of Indian heritage. Roberts moved offices from the Edgware Road to Cambridge Road in Kilburn, now renting from Goptal with whom Blackwell was now a tenant. Blackwell offered to distribute and promote Roberts's records. Blackwell, like Jackson and Shalet, was the pioneering Jamaican Jew, whose bold approach to understanding the Jamaican music business in London, led him to form temporary liaisons with fellow Jamaicans. Now that Blackwell had control of distribution and promotion, the competition for Roberts became disadvantageous. Blackwell, instead of recording in London, focused on licensing record masters from Jamaica. While Planitone floundered and eventually went out of business temporarily, Blackwell's Island Records made ascending strides in controlling the Jamaican music market.

It can be clearly seen that the impetus for Island Records' intervention in the British Jamaican music business was a direct result of Blackwell first interrogating Roberts and then distributing his product. In this way Blackwell could test the market without financial risk. A similar strategy was to be employed by Virgin Records in the late 1970s. Another by-product of the fated meeting of Roberts and fellow Jamaican Goptal was that the latter, originally distrustful and hesitant about Roberts's quest for success with his label, collaborated with Blackwell to form Trojan Records in 1968, Blackwell later selling out his interest to Goptal. By the middle 1960s Blackwell had already expanded his financial horizons beyond Jamaican music to include rhythm and blues and soul and later rock, a strategy Goptal was to emulate with great success but also tragic consequences.

Blackwell's cadre of artists included Owen Grey, Laurel Aitken, Kenrick Patrick, the Blues Busters, Derrick and Patsy, Jimmy Cliff, and Jackie Edwards, among others. Blackwell also created management, concert promotion, and publishing companies, so that he was making money from all angles of the business. Jamaican music provided the bedrock upon which his music industry experience was built. From there he successfully launched Island as an important label for the new rock music as well as British imports and British versions of rhythm and blues. Blackwell's management of Millie Small resulted in her number one hit in the British charts, "My Boy Lollipop" (the arranger being seminal guitarist Ernest Ranglin) in 1964. Along with the Spencer Davis Group, he licensed both of their music to more mainstream and successful labels. An offshoot of the Spencer Davis Group was Steve Winword's rendition of Jackie Edwards's composition, "Keep on Running", which became a Top Ten hit. Thus, Jamaican music provided the bedrock upon which his music industry experience was built.

Prince Buster's Breakthrough

Jamaican popular music, confined to parties, shebeens and small Caribbean-owned clubs, simultaneous with supplying the British Jamaican population with sonic cultural insurgency, was also radiating out onto the larger British population in peculiar ways. Prince Buster, an early sound man, business man (who owned a shop and label), and proactive articulator of early Black Power, became a British and European sensation with his "Madness" single which sold over half a million records. The new British post-war generation, searching beyond the skiffle groups that abounded in Britain, was looking for new and exciting avenues of expression. With Prince Buster they found a master, and Buster had a cult following among the Mods, who were, paradoxically, known for racist behaviour, abuse and violence on people of colour. This is, however, no different from the meeting and incorporation of mixed cultures that abounded in Britain.

Racism, Incorporation and Culture

It is interesting to note that in most circumstances in which racism flourishes there is an interdependent relationship between the oppressed and the oppressor. There are sizeable racial minorities in Germany and France – and just as the politics of the National Front are constitutionally racist, so too in these nations. But there is an element of incorporation by these dominant societies by their genuine friendship with some mixed-race Germans, French or British. There are instances of mixed-race spokespeople being incorporated into the body politic of racist and facist groups that are objectively racist in their policies but reserve this hostility for the unknown racial mass.

A brief note should be inserted here. Outward racial discrimination functions in a society in which legislation is almost absent and politicians aggravate the chasm between contending groups in order to ensure their election. In this context, whether racial differences were exploited by politicians and others before World War I or after World War II – and between – the undeniable fact was that racial division also promoted racial attraction and cultural magnetism in terms of the seemingly weaker culture enduring the weight of social discrimination, while paradoxically influencing the dominant society. This meant that social relations were forged in the dens of the shebeens, illegal parties and dingy nightclubs where Jamaican music and culture drew a cross-section of the British class system. It was not only the youth who were influenced by the subaltern culture, but men and women in unequalled pyramidal social occupancy. Ackee and saltfish, rice and peas, Guinness punch, spliff smoking (introduced by Noel Coward, a British expatriate to Jamaica, and his coterie), language and the penchant for colourful clothes, all had an indelible impact on the British consciousness. The "rivers of blood" surrealistic nightmare that Enoch Powell foresaw, and the later cultural "swamping" xenophobia of Margaret Thatcher, both reflected the groundswell of the continuing births of the children of immigrants and their expressed dissatisfaction with their condition of racism in the classroom, in the work place and the limited opportunities opened for self-expansion.

Thus when the Lord Profumo scandal burst on the tabloid press in the mid-1960s, exposing the illicit exotica of relationships between the lord and the serf, the serf and the "slave" – Christine Keeler and Mandy Rice Davies being the modern serfs and Lucky Gordon the modern "slave" – the exposure merely unearthed a trend that had moved from the master's plantation in the Caribbean to his urban centre of the metropolis. A popular, unknown sexual proclivity was characterized by the late Lord Mountbatten's wife, who hired working-class Caribbean men for sexual copulation. Another is the now published thirty-year romance between Grenadian balladeer Hutchinson and the late Princess Margaret, the sister of Queen Elizabeth II. Yet another is the jailing of a Trinidadian jazz pianist Wilfred Woodley, for a bank robbery he was accused of and sentenced to eight years in prison. His crime was being married to Juliet Duncombe, whose family inherited an earldom. They produced a daughter, Karin Lee. For the middle and upper class, power and exotica had been the bilateral ingredients of cohabitation in both geographical localities. The European working-class had also enjoyed this position of cohabitation – normatively characteristic for men but taboo for women. The war years, however, intoxicated with American swing music and the African-American GI, as well as his Caribbean counterpart, showed that the woman was no longer nailed to Mary's cross, but bit, with relish, into the black apple in gardens of Jamaican musical culture.

It was this climate which produced the readiness with which people gravitated to Jamaican music. In personal relationships between the British and the Jamaican, there has been, and continues to be, the spectacle of complete mastery of the Jamaican language by some British people, and not always young people. I know instances in which after the relationship had ended between a Jamaican and British person, the latter continued to live, work and socialize among Jamaicans and other Caribbean people. Sometimes the mastery of the language does produce astonishment: one such being a cockney speaker having a conversation with a Jamaican nation-language speaker and both articulating themselves in their own languages with total mutual comprehension. I, a Caribbean national, had to struggle to understand the Jamaican. In this culturally burgeoning context, the independent Jamaican record entrepreneur continued his assault on British music culture in order to create a standardized platform for the acceptance of a black face in the record business.

Trojan Records and Small Labels

Because of deregulation in radio application licences, there was increasing sales competition between the majors, which operated a closed-shop policy and the small, independent labels that were previously excluded from competition. Listen to Jamaican Chips Richards, a former sales manager of Trojan Records who later became a business partner with Miss P (Sonia Pottinger) through her label High Note:

> I was pushing a record called "Everything I Own" by Ken Boothe, which finally became No. 1 [on the British pop charts], and I was in the BBC offices when it was being played over the radio by Tony Blackburn. Then halfway through playing the record, he stopped it and said something like: 'Oh, utter rubbish! How can anyone in his right mind go out and buy something like this, after listening to the David Gates real version? . . . I no longer used the soft smiling attitude. I began to demand. I used to compile scrap books showing them the demand for Reggae. I wrote letters showing them that our records were in the breakers of the British Market Research Board, and that our records used to outsell a lot of pop records. (Clarke 1980, 152)

It was common practice, according to Richards, that when pluggers of reggae records (sales reps seeking airplay and television exposure for said records) delivered copies to the BBC, the rock or soul records would be taken by the radio producers while the reggae ones would be dropped in the rubbish bins. It should also be noted that the few sincere British pluggers also experienced the same racist treatment meted out by the BBC. Capitol Radio reversed that, and the fortunes and visibility of reggae slowly began to make an impact, one that was feared and resented by the majors.

British Market Research Board's Control of Hit Music

From the 1950s, the British Market Research Board was the official organiza- tion that monitored record sales from a selected list of shops they called "chart returns". This simply meant that a number of mainstream shops were selected on the high roads of major cities throughout Britain and sales returns were calibrated from them. There have always been, however, alternative markets or shops outside the mainstream considered non-chart return. Because of the problem of distribution and radio play from the African-Caribbean–derived companies, the mainstream shops would not stock records which were not played on radio or featured on television. So records that became popular in the discos or nightclubs sold in sometimes large quantities, but these sales were outside the jurisdiction of the industry's monitoring body. They some- times outsold highly charted records without the benefit of a single airplay or sales achieved from a chart return shop.

Pirate Radio: The Change of Fortunes

By the late 1960s, with the deregulation of the methods of radio licence appli- cation, there was a plethora of pirate as well as legitimate radio stations. By far the biggest and most successful was Capital Radio. I have stated that BBC radio, monopolizing what should or should not be heard, operating a clearly racist policy, was now challenged by this successful new station. More impor- tantly, Caribbean-owned companies, including Lee Goptal's Trojan, grasped the opportunity of buying time on radio, just as advertisers bought time. This released a Pandora's Box of competition among the majors characterized by increasingly bold attempts to undermine Capital Radio by making representa- tions to parliamentarians to institute a new set of regulations that would make it illegal. This finally became a success and reggae's success or failure was now in the hands of the majors.

Desmond Dekker and Skinheads

In 1968 Desmond Dekker had a number one hit with "The Israelites" on the Trojan label; previously in 1967 he reached number sixteen with "007/Shanty Town". It is interesting that "The Israelites", though largely difficult to understand lyrically, received massive airplay on the radio as well as significant television exposure. This may well have to do with the extent to which Jews themselves were important cogs in the wheel of the different aspects of the recording and entertainment industry.[1] It also became number one in Israel, which caused Israel to become attached to the reggae phenomenon. It should be mentioned here that Tony Cousins and Bruce White, two English music agency operators with a company called Creole, recognized a hole in the loop and filled this by combining touring and record releases while achieving several hits. They toured the Ethiopians with their Top Twenty hit, "Train to Ska-ville", and brought over Desmond Dekker, who now signed to and had six Top Twenty hits on the Creole label. Dekker became a sensation, like Prince Buster before him, with his sartorial splendour: tight pants cut four inches above the ankle, closely trimmed hair and spectacular dancing moves. Dekker's model precipitated the skinhead movement, again, like the Mods, a colour-bashing, beer swilling, unemployed youth sector that apotheosized Dekker and reggae while espousing racist diatribes.

Turning New Fortunes

It would not be until the late 1970s, after years of African-Caribbean organizational structures to combat racism, several modern "slave" uprisings in the modern British urban centres throughout the country, the growing exposure of this experience in small magazines and journals, the rise of Bob Marley and the Wailers, the increasing visibility of reggae, its new-found model for relaunching recumbent careers as with Eric Clapton's Bob Marley–penned song, "I Shot the Sherrif", that British youth, already rebelling against the staid social *mores* of British life, now moved, visibly, to form structures such as Rock Against Racism and the Anti-Nazi League. Linton Kwesi Johnson, the dubsonic poet, whose career took him to Virgin Records as an advertising writer, was the first to benefit from the activities of British youth campaign-

ing and university as well as college circuit rallies and events.

Interestingly, Virgin Records, which saw the export market as a distinct source of revenue, soon saw Richard Branson, by 1978, in Jamaica offering big contracts to Jamaican artists. An astute business man who was known and convicted for criminal activities in the record business, he recognized the disparity between paying in the British pound and the Jamaican dollar. He

3.3 Desmond Dekker became a sensation with his tight pants (cut four inches above the ankle), closely trimmed hair and spectacular dancing moves. Ironically, his model precipitated the skinhead movement, which apotheosized Dekker and reggae while espousing racist diatribes. Courtesy of the Gleaner Company.

3.4 Dubsonic poet Linton Kwesi Johnson (*left*) with Rex Nettleford (*right*). Johnson was awarded the Institute of Jamaica's Silver Musgrave Medal for poetry in 2005. Courtesy of the Gleaner Company.

offered contracts to Jamaican artists based on the declining Jamaican dollar and had the facility to elude the limited exchange rate of the mainstream banking system by buying through specialized foreign currency companies. He was winning on both fronts, but when Nigeria, its biggest export market, closed its doors to imports, Virgin dropped the flaming chalice and bolted out of the reggae business as though pursued, as Chris Blackwell was by the machete-wielding Peter Tosh. Just as Blackwell kicked the recording business bucket to pursue the hotel-hospitality business with £200 million in his back pocket, so Branson pulled out, selling his record company for £600 million to EMI. Having outwitted his American introducer Randolph Fields (who later died in 1997) of Atlantic Airlines, he formed the highly profitable Virgin Airlines. Branson is now a multibillionaire.

The fortunes of waning careers in the pop business were revived by the utilization of reggae as the basis for exploration. Paul Simon is the best American example with "Mother and Child Reunion" in 1971. He later said, having asked the Jamaican session musicians what they wanted, that he paid them ten pounds per track. The Police, which featured Sting as lead singer and bass player, featured reggae rhythms in almost all of their successive hits worldwide. Lee Perry's ingenious experimentation with technology, gadgets and the science of recording techniques produced amazing soundscapes that ricocheted profoundly in the pop world. The list of international artists who openly acknowledge the influence of the Perry sound is best characterized

by Madonna, who brilliantly imitated his methods on her album *Ray of Light*. Anti-racism activities produced the climate for the synthesizing of sounds: the punk rock movement, centred in London, was revived by the utilization of reggae as the basis for exploration. The 2 Tone movement, based in the north of England, best expressed this mixture. The Clash's Joe Strummer was keenly aware of the Jamaican musical sound and successfully experimented with it in the production of

3.5 Richard Branson of Virgin Records saw the export market as a distinct source of revenue, and offered big contracts to Jamaican artists. Branson is here pictured with Amanda Wills, managing director of Virgin Holidays, at the official opening of the Branson Centre of Entrepreneurship. Photo by Janet Silvera; courtesy of the Gleaner Company.

3.6 Chris Blackwell focused on licensing record masters from Jamaica, and his label Island Records made strides in controlling the Jamaican music market. Photo by Carlington Wilmot; courtesy of the Gleaner Company.

3.7 The Birmingham-based UB40 became an international institution after their initial success with the Neil Diamond composition "Red, Red Wine". Courtesy of the Gleaner Company.

the Clash's first album. He included a version of Junior Murvin's Lee Perry produced "Police and Thieves" and later versioned Toots Hibbert's 1968 scorcher, "Pressure Drop". But it was Don Letts, an Anglo-Jamaican reggae DJ and later pioneer in the video business, who gave exposure to punk and reggae in his Harlesden residency at the Roxy in northwest London. The Specials, a Coventry-based group, was an opening act for the Clash and their preoccupation was revival ska. The group spawned a massive trend and had enormous success, not only with their own music, but also with other bands they produced. Their leader, Jerry Dammers, was an art college graduate, as were many of the British pop stars of the 1960s including John Lennon and Paul McCartney of the Beatles, Keith Richards of the Rolling Stones, and Ray Davies of the Kinks. With art as a background, and with an understanding of European art history, and its many Africa-centred movements, they were conscious, cross-cultural insurgents.

On the other side of the nation, the Birmingham-based UB40, an appellation derived from the unemployed card one was given to sign on at the dole on a weekly basis, became an international institution after their initial success with the Neil Diamond composition, "Red, Red Wine", which appears to me to be an imitation of the Jamaican version. UB40 was the only British band that generated a following in Jamaica itself and, with a profound love for Jamaica, attempted to build a house and studio in Jamaica. Their leader, however, relegating the responsibility to one of his spars, experienced the Brer Nansi duplicity that many foreign-based Jamaicans have experienced – even with family members – the loss of serious money.

Conclusion

The journey is long and detailed and seemingly inexhaustive, but we must not lose sight of the major thesis of this work: the Jamaican working class, a class beaten, jailed, killed, shut away in mental asylums, maligned and denigrated by the Jamaican ruling class, is now in the United Kingdom confronting racism but having the opportunity, in whatever limited area, to make cultural and material progress. As they bore the brunt for being stubbornly nationalistic to their African-Jamaican origins, the Jamaican working class has honoured the memory of his ancestors who were bodily buried in the earth with their heads bathed in molasses and ants feeding off them; who, pregnant with babies, were whipped mercilessly; who were subjected to massa's lustful eyes and the power to enforce his wishes; who washed massa's clothes and entertained him although receiving his verbal abuse; who abandoned the plantation to work for themselves, and has been no betrayer of his history. After Emancipation did the African not abandon the plantation and forge a living for himself, and is this not in keeping with the independent line he developed, to be freed of the white slavemaster, as can be seen with the many higglers today, as well as the philosophy of the Bobo Shanti to work for himself? All these philosophical orientations were reinforced by the Universal Negro Improvement Association's and Marcus Garvey's espousal of the black man's desire to forge an independent economy despite the pressures of colonial and postcolonial governments to assign him or her to the margins of society via a dependency syndrome and facilitate self-destruction through state-sponsored violence.

It is these men and women who are responsible for the international acclaim of Jamaican popular music. It is their lives that were sacrificed to creating, out of this complex, complicated and ambiguous road to so-called independence, the cultural powers that are searingly represented by the radically altering paths to restating riffs, developing rhythmic patterns, melodies and harmonies, and using technologically engineered imaged soundscapes, all of which axiomize Jamaican popular music.

Note

1. David Betteridge, former Island co-owner and former CEO of CBS Britain is Jewish, Chris Blackwell is Jewish, Emile Shalet was Jewish, Lew Grade, founder of London Weekend Television was Jewish. This is not an attack but a description that has its own validity for Jewish involvement with black music having themselves been historically and contemporarily persecuted.

References

Clarke, Sebastian (Amon Saba Saakana). 1980. *Jah Music: The Evolution of the Jamaican Popular Sound*. London: Heinemann.

Finkelstein, Sidney. 1976. *How Music Expresses Ideas*. New York: International Publishers.

Fischer, Ernst. (1959) 1971. *The Necessity of Art: A Marxist Approach*. London: Penguin.

Phillippo, James M. 1969. *Jamaica: Its Past and Present*. London: Jon Snow, Paternoster.

CHAPTER 4

THE EVOLUTION OF
REGGAE
IN EUROPE
WITH A FOCUS ON GERMANY

ELLEN KOEHLINGS
AND PETE LILLY

We would like to start with a statement from the German reggae artist, Gentleman, from a 2003 interview in *Riddim* magazine, that shows where reggae in Germany stands: "Take this riddim 'Doctor's Darling' based on Gregory Isaacs's 'Night Nurse' that was created in Berlin by the reggae band Seeed, then voiced by the Jamaican singer Tanya Stephens in London and then her song 'It's a Pity' became a No. 1 hit in Trinidad. What's that? German reggae culture? Okay, it was created in Germany, but it's a global thing. Everything is getting closer, even on the level of production" (Gummersbach, Koehlings and Lilly 2003, 28). The "Doctor's Darling" selection was released on the Germaica Records label, whose name not only expresses

4.1 Gregory Isaac's "Night Nurse" riddim was the base of the popular Germaica Records' riddim "Doctor's Darling". Here Isaacs is pictured at Rebel Salute 2007. Photo by Claudine Housen; courtesy of the Gleaner Company.

the global nature of the music, but at the same time embraces Jamaica as its epicentre. Their logo shows the Jamaican flag combined with the colours of the German flag.

Gentleman's explanation shows that pop music in general, and reggae in particular, cannot be fenced in by national borders, and not even by language barriers, even though it is true that Jamaican and English have remained the main languages of reggae. Five years after Gentle-

man made his statement – he has become an internationally accepted reggae artist in the meantime – we can talk about a flourishing European reggae scene characterized by an ongoing exchange with Jamaica, the United Kingdom, the United States of America, Canada, Africa and, of course, other Caribbean islands. Today it is no longer surprising that artists such as Million Stylez from Sweden, Ziggi from the Netherlands, Ill Inspecta from Germany or Alborosie from Italy

4.2 German reggae musician Gentleman is an internationally accepted reggae artist. Publicity photo.

can be found sharing a selection with artists from Jamaica, Bermuda, London or Gambia.

How did it come about that youths from European countries without significant Caribbean communities are able and motivated to re-create something that is genuinely Jamaican in origin and can, to a certain extent, even compete with what is happening in Jamaica today? The ease with which information from the reggae motherland can now be accessed through the Internet has certainly helped a lot. But a lot of other things had to happen beforehand.

In order to understand the changing parameters, this chapter provides a brief, but by no means complete, account of the reception and production of reggae music in Germany. First of all, though, our sincere apologies to all the important people who helped to shape reggae in Germany, whom we will not be able to mention. If we did, we are afraid we would bore you all to tears with names that could mean nothing to you. We will place the focus on Germany, not only because it is our home country and we experience first-hand what happens there, but also because – next to France – Germany is the most important European reggae market today. Actually, it has become a kind of trailblazer for other continental European countries. While in the early days, England functioned as a reggae role model for Germany, reggae fans from Italy, Spain, Portugal, Poland and so on, now look to Germany. This is not so much due to Germany being home to better music, but rather to the well-developed infrastructure that has grown over the years. We should qualify that by saying that the evolution of reggae in France and certain parts of Spain differs from other European countries, a fact that may be explained by their respective colonial histories in the Caribbean and the associated cultural exchange. Whereas the Spanish so-called *mestizo* (meaning "mixed") genre that incorporates various musical styles – such as reggae, ska, salsa, rumba, cumbia and rock elements – is quite widespread in the rest of Europe, the French more or less like to do their own thing, which means that the French version of reggae does not get much recognition outside of French-speaking countries.

But how is it that, of all countries, Germany could be of any importance for the development of reggae in continental Europe? How do you marry such allegedly German traits like punctuality, diligence and tidiness, as well as a

4.3 Alborosie, Italian reggae artist.
Publicity photo by William Richards.

tendency towards stiffness and restraint, with the laidback, vibes-laden atmo-sphere, spirituality and explicitness of reggae that is supposedly driven by a soon-come attitude?

Popular Music Post–World War II

Ever since the rise of popular music after World War II, which started with swing in the 1940s and rock 'n' roll in the early 1950s, Germany has been importing foreign musical cultures. There are two main reasons for this. First, any kind of German folk music that could have been a blueprint for post-war popular music had been discredited by the Nazis, who abused these musical traditions as part of their propaganda; and second, musical genres like Jewish klezmer or Gypsy music were silenced, either because those who performed the music were killed during the Holocaust or, if they were lucky, they had fled the country.

Therefore, musical styles had to be imported from other countries, and they came mainly from English-speaking nations. In each case, the "adoption process" began with a passive reception of the respective genre. With a grow-ing desire to become part of a certain musical culture, there was the formation of bands that simply tried to copy the English or American original and make it sound as "authentic" as possible. But since a copy is never identical to the original, uniquely German versions of the respective genres were created quite unintentionally. Acid rock evolved into Krautrock, new wave into Neue Deutsche Welle, hip-hop into Deutsch-rap and so on.

When the Allied Forces took over Germany in 1945, they also established their own radio stations, like American Forces Network or British Forces Broadcasting Service, where you could listen to their respective forms of pop-ular music. In contrast, it took German radio stations until the mid-1970s to discover the value of pop music in gaining audience ratings. A large segment of the post-war generation totally rejected anything German, anything that was associated with the war, anything that – however remotely – smacked of the dictatorial regime and the Holocaust, and everything the parental genera-tion stood for. This brings us to a typical German feature of popular music: the generation gap. More so, perhaps, than in many other countries, popular music allowed the young to set themselves apart from their parental generation, a generation that lacked any understanding of what their children were listening to. Indeed, the older generation of the day habitually referred to rock 'n' roll in an extremely derogatory, racist way as "Hottentots" music. Kids spoke of *Vatermord*, meaning patricide, which fortunately remained on a symbolic level. This attitude exploded in 1968 with the student revolts. Yet, to a large degree, even the German student revolts were "imported" and had their blueprint in American student revolts.

This generation gap has remained essential throughout the development of pop music right up to the present day, except that now it is not only about the gap between parents and children, but rather between one pop generation and the next. Today, it is more of a "cultural clash" of younger kids that do not want to listen to the music of their older siblings. It is always about distinction or disengagement from established forms. Despite these generation gaps, the music industry soon figured out that it could make a lot of money by selling records and merchandise. Therefore, the industry had to water down the subversive aspects that tended to go along with pop music, be they of a political, cultural or sexual nature. This led to another development, the distinction between so-called underground versus mainstream music. Mainstream meant polished, consumer-friendly music courtesy of the recording industry. This music was even capable of gaining the approval of the parental generation. Raw and unpolished underground music was often made by kids themselves. The reason for making this music was not necessarily to become rich but rather to express their rejection of the status quo, anger and inner feelings. This kind of underground music usually sold considerably fewer units, but it was often regarded as innovative and rebellious. Some even felt it was emancipatory in a hazy sort of way: it seemed to be leaning to the left. It was the real thing.

Marley Mania in Germany

Enter Bob Marley. Even though there were a few Jamaican artists that had made the German charts before, like Millie Small's "My Boy Lollipop" or Desmond Dekker's "Israelites", the German reception of reggae started with Bob Marley. And first and foremost, this is a story of misunderstandings. When Marley entered the German market with the album *Rastaman Vibration* in the mid-1970s, his audience mainly consisted of rock listeners. White, middle-class kids with long hair and torn clothes were looking for a new Jimi Hendrix. Since there was no Jamaican community in Germany, Marley fans did not have much knowledge about Jamaica, the Jamaican language, Rastafari or the living conditions in a post-/neocolonial country.

Even though, from a Jamaican perspective, Marley's music of the mid-1970s might have seemed polished, in Germany, as well as in other predominantly white countries, his music was identified as "authentic" reggae – the *real* deal. It was perceived as raw, energetic and unedited. His appearance played a part in his success, too: the dreadlocks, the relatively simple stage gear as well as his love of ganja. Hippies identified Marley as one of their own. Rock stars from the 1960s or 1970s, like Jimi Hendrix, Jim Morrison, Janis Joplin, Bob Dylan and Mick Jagger were either dead or had sold out. In 1980, the sophisticated German rock magazine *Sounds* described Marley as follows: "Bob Marley adjures his listeners to join him on the Zion train, Bob Dylan boarded another train and the Stones waited ages for their train and then switched to private jets" (Schwaner 1980). Marley embodied rebelliousness. He *was* underground.

While his music was aimed at rock-influenced listening habits, his lyrics spoke of black emancipation, religion, and a mystic worldview that had nothing to do with the lives of his white audience. But, despite the Jamaican language, which can be hard to understand for the uninitiated, Marley's use of unknown proverbs and biblical references, as well as his universal approach, left enough space for free interpretation. Rock fans were fond of picking out familiar slogans like "Revolution", "Burnin' and Lootin'" or "Get Up Stand Up" – everything that Jagger, Dylan or Lennon promised but never delivered. They interpreted Marley's lyrics according to their own needs, all the while ignoring the fact that Marley was referring to a black revolution. Most of his audience only had a vague idea of social resistance against the principles of a technocratic society as well as a general affront against the bourgeois establishment. At the time, Marley's songs were a popular choice for chanting at demonstrations against military armament or nuclear power plants.

The white rock audience, intent on escaping the confines of their rationalist society, was also good at incorporating the religious aspects of Rastafari as

4.4 Bob Marley's appearance – the dreadlocks and simple stage gear – led to his attraction for the German youth in the 1970s. Here he appears in concert, 1976. Courtesy of the Gleaner Company.

an esoteric retreat that promised to fulfil an "alternative" hippie utopia. Marley's Rasta messages embodied a long-lost "authenticity", credibility and a contemplation of "true" values. The world promised by Marley was a mythical Africa as a symbol of black identity. But this world simply could not be translated into a "white" lifestyle. Therefore, Marley's audience simply ignored the central aspects of his message.

In the wake of Marley mania, many other Jamaican roots bands toured Germany; for instance Black Uhuru, Burning Spear, Peter Tosh and Inner Circle, as well as British acts like Aswad or Steel Pulse. At the end of the 1970s and at the beginning of the 1980s, reggae was understood as being synonymous with Rasta music, and Rasta was misunderstood as the Jamaican equivalent of the US Black Panther movement. At least that was what the blurb of the book *Rastafari* by German author Peter Michels said in 1979.

A few years earlier, Britain had witnessed the rise of another pop cultural movement: punk rock, which formed a liaison with reggae, as documented in the Marley and Lee Perry song "Punky Reggae Party". It did not take long for the punk rock movement to reach Germany, one more example of imported pop culture. On British Forces Broadcasting Service radio, German kids would listen to John Peel's punk radio show as well as *Rodigan's Rockers*, on which David Rodigan would play the whole gamut of reggae music – and only reggae music. He was the first DJ on European radio that provided the necessary information on the country and the culture the music had emerged from. Rodigan succeeded in cracking cultural codes by giving history lessons and explaining how Jamaican sound systems operated. He played a central r ole in the spread of reggae music in Germany from the late 1970s onwards, and lots of young listeners regularly taped his shows. But this was still very much an underground phenomenon. It only attracted a handful of die-hard reggae fans who had had to endure a decade of cheesy reggae productions by white producers and somewhat nostalgic roots reggae bands, all trying hard to keep the Marley myth alive. When Marley passed away, the German music press even summarily proclaimed the death of the whole genre (Jakob 1993).

4.5 David Rodigan played a central role in spreading reggae music in Germany from the late 1970s onwards. Lots of young listeners regularly taped his shows.

Reggae in Germany

Information on what was happening in Jamaica was still scarce in 1980s Germany. The rise of dancehall reggae in Jamaica went hand-in-hand with a focus on local rather than universal issues. It was, therefore, no longer possible to sell reggae as a mouthpiece for an oppressed "Third World" and its black population. Instead, the German mainstream pinned reggae down to a sort of "swaying cruise-ship wanderlust dream" (*"schunkelnder Kreuzschiff Fernweh Traum"*), as in "happy-go-lucky sunshine music" (Jakob 1993, 131). The relaxed nature of reggae vibes, which originated from a disengaging from the capitalist rat race, was confused with the weariness of a hard-working man who sinks into his armchair to watch television after an exhausting day (ibid., 131). This sentiment was reflected in the success of, for instance, "Sunshine Reggae" by the Danish duo Laid Back, or "Sun of Jamaica" by the Goombay Dance Band. It was later projected onto crossover-hits like Eddy Grant's "Electric Avenue", UB40's "Red Red Wine" or Inner Circle's "Sweat (A La La La Long)".

Among the few international artists that helped to establish reggae as a serious genre in Germany were the dub poets Linton Kwesi Johnson and Mutabaruka, as well as the deejay Yellowman and later Macka B, all of whom toured Europe on a regular basis. But since Rodigan was still the only person who provided information about Jamaica, a Xerox-copied reggae fanzine called *Trenchtown*, the first German reggae publication, was launched in 1986. A quotation from the first issue's editorial may explain why only six issues came out within three years: "This magazine is not done by journalists, but by reggae fans hampered by a lack of information" (1986, 3, author unknown). The later fanzines *Dread* and *Mix Up* were barely more successful.

The year 1986 also saw the birth of Europe's biggest annual reggae festival, the Summerjam, which was first called Reggae Sunsplash, but had to be renamed after two years due to legal problems with its Jamaican namesake. What started out as a one-day roots reggae festival with Black Uhuru, Dennis Brown and the Wailers has by now turned into a three-day mega-happening that attracts more than thirty thousand people – many of whom pitch their tents on the festival grounds. On two stages and in two sound system tents, the festival covers all aspects of reggae music, from ska to dancehall, and also incorporates world music acts.

4.6 Summerjam, Germany's biggest three-day reggae festival. Press photo.

4.7 Rototom Sunsplash is a ten-day reggae festival including live performances and sound systems, as well as workshops on dance, drumming, health issues and Rastafari. Press photo.

Before we continue with our chronology, we want to briefly explain a general change in the way German pop culture now functions: while the music industry had always been behind pop cultural developments from the underground, it shifted into turbo-gear in the late 1980s. It got closer and closer to what was produced underground. Therefore, the underground had to come up with a strategy to escape the all-embracing clutches of the mainstream music industry. The result was an immense diversification of musical styles, which no longer tried to attract a generation of youth as a whole, but rather led to the formation of countless musical subcultures. The members of each exclusive subculture came to know the music and its codes by heart. It was like being in possession of arcane knowledge, because people outside of any given subculture did not necessarily have access to this knowledge, and it was not readily shared.

Back to reggae: In the early 1990s, dub experiments by reggae pioneers such as Lee Scratch Perry and King Tubby were held in high esteem as the big bang of German and European club culture. The rise of techno and house, strictly instrumental and technically created music styles, led to a new interest in Jamaican music. Only this time, the interest had shifted from artists to producers and from lyrics to technology (Wynands 1995, 114). The pop discourse that celebrated dub as a strategy of deconstruction separated the music from its political and religious background. But, since dub was not produced in Jamaica at the time, people either searched for old Jamaican dub records or they looked to England, where, among others, Adrian Sherwood of On-U Sound and Mad Professor produced what was called neo dub. Bands like Dub Syndicate, Zion Train and Revolutionary Dub Warriors, all heavily influenced by the late-1970s Jah Shaka, frequently toured Germany at the time.

With the international success of Shaggy and Shabba Ranks – only a year or two later – Jamaican-style reggae re-entered German pop culture. After hip-hop artists like KRS-One, Queen Latifah and Just Ice, as well as the UK-based deejays Asher D and Daddy Freddy (on their album *Raggamuffin HipHop*), had combined hip-hop and dancehall elements in the late 1980s, ragga became *the* sound of the summer of 1993. Suddenly people were dancing to Chaka Demus and Pliers's "Murder She Wrote", Snow's "Informer", Shabba's "Mr. Loverman" and Shaggy's "Oh Carolina". Various music and city magazines explained the meaning of dancehall idioms like "booyaka", "punany", or "slackness". But, it was a short summer! The ordinary German listener was still utterly clueless about what was going on. With the exception of tunes with a certain crossover appeal, such as the ones just mentioned, people were not ready for dancehall. As a matter of fact, most people did not enjoy listening to dancehall at all. They did not know how to dance to it, nor did they understand the humour and the irony of the deejays. The popular stop-and-go technique, with all its rewinds, was the exact opposite of what people in Germany were accustomed to as dance music (Jakob 1993, 142). For other dance music styles of the time it was crucial that you could dance non-stop and could not tell where one song ended and the next began.

And this was also about the time that the concept of political correctness entered the pop discourse. When Buju Banton sang "Boom Bye Bye", people were shocked. A song that was probably not even meant to be heard outside of Jamaica was suddenly being judged in a foreign context. More to the point, the culture doing the judging had itself only recently discovered homosexuals as a group worthy of protection from homophobia. We would like to add that homophobia is still very much alive in Germany, even if it is not expressed as explicitly as in Buju's song.

The Sound System in Germany

Therefore, after a brief period of hype, dancehall seemed to disappear again but, of course, it only disappeared on the surface. There were still those who felt the energy, got the bug and delved head-first into dancehall culture. Given the scarcity of music and media information, they had little choice but to teach themselves about the meaning of a riddim, a sound system, a deejay and so on. At this time the first German sound systems that had been founded at the beginning of the 1990s recruited small but loyal followings. Pow Pow Movement from Cologne, Concrete Jungle from Berlin, Silly Walks from Hamburg and, later, Soundquake from Detmold held their "lawns" in old, disused, and often dilapidated industry buildings. Their massives were made up of small circles of insiders who knew about dancehall culture either from trips to Jamaica or from Rodigan's radio show and his dances in areas where British soldiers were stationed. These German sound system dances were always attended by the same set of people, and it is important to note that nobody outside of this select group had the vaguest idea of what was going on at these events. It remained a strictly underground phenomenon for quite a few years. Even though the first selectors, mike chatters, deejays and singers emerged at these early sound system dances, the shows were extremely amateurish. But the intimacy of this scene provided enough time and space for the protagonists to improve their respective skills.

With dancehall events slowly becoming more successful and financially rewarding, these early soundboys were able to afford trips to Jamaica and experience the culture on site. Deejays such as Gentleman, Tolga and D-Flame, who were to become successful later on, as well as sound system mike chatters started to learn the Jamaican language. Selectors cut their first dub plates and, in general, German sound systems modelled themselves very much on their Jamaican counterparts and tried hard to be as "authentic" as possible. As sound systems slowly began to draw bigger crowds, they soon entered the club scene, which was a novel development at this time. Only two years earlier, music critics had predicted that dancehall could never work with a German audience (Jakob 1993, 142). But here it was, definitely working! The Petit Prince Club in Cologne, where Pow Pow resides on Friday nights up to the present day, was the first of its kind to host a sound system regularly. Thousands of miles from Jamaica, German reggae dances now had MCs chatting in Jamaican as well as people yelling "pram pram", blowing tin whistles and igniting spray cans and lighters to shoot flames in the air. Add to this lickshots, rewinds, deejays riding over riddims with ad hoc rhymes and the wine and grind of eager hips, and you begin to get the picture – a picture that Germany had never seen before! By 1997, Friday nights at the Petit Prince Club had become notorious all over Germany for supposedly "authentic" reggae vibes. But still, on a trip to Jamaica in 1996, we met a group of Germans with whom we went to a dance and they were hugely shocked. They had expected to hear Bob Marley and Burning Spear. To them digital dancehall beats had more in common with techno than what they believed Jamaican music to be.

From that time on, though, everything began to happen very quickly. Sound systems increasingly succeeded in freeing Jamaican music of its former clichés. Having grown up with hip-hop, the up-and-coming generation was especially up for the dancehall experience. Rap music had already informed them of urban poverty, police brutality and black history. In a similar vein, they were equally accustomed to songs that revolved around bragging and boasting about talent, strength and, of course, sexual prowess, as well as the topics of homophobia and misogyny. This is a highly interesting example of cultural transfer. An art form whose origins lie in the American inner cities and whose deep roots connect to the history of African-American culture has become a central part of German pop culture. And, over the years, this generation of young, German hip-hop protagonists managed to create an independent hip-hop culture with its own traditions, styles, topics and, especially, language. Some of these German hip-hop heads then began to defect to dancehall music, especially since US hip-hop was increasingly being "mainstreamed" and the record output of its German counterpart, Deutsch-rap, was taking on inflationary proportions. The defectors thought the German rap scene was losing its vitality and credibility; they were therefore looking for something new. Dancehall was an obvious choice, because it had not been exploited commercially. This led a few clever promoters to become aware of dancehall as a profitable niche market. More and more artists from Jamaica started to tour Germany with great success: Bounty Killer, Buju Banton, Anthony B, Tony Rebel, Luciano, Beenie Man, Morgan Heritage and so on. The aforementioned Summerjam included all these artists in its festival line-up.

German Reggae Artists

In 1998 the popular German hip-hop group Freundeskreis released a song featuring the German reggae artist Gentleman. This tune, "Tabula Rasa", even entered the national charts. The bald-headed Tillmann Otto, otherwise known as Gentleman, from Cologne, was already well known as a sound system MC and deejay within dancehall circles. But in the wake of that record release, he became the talk of the town or, rather, the country. It was then only a matter of months before he released his own debut album, *Trodin' On*, in 1999. Here, for the first time, we had a German artist who was successful with his "original" Jamaican style. Gentleman never strove for cultural independence, but rather sought to copy the original as faithfully as possible. His success inspired other artists, like the Afro-German D-Flame or the Turkish-German Tolga, to voice dancehall riddims. In contrast to Gentleman, however, they also began to incorporate German as a usable language. But, like Gentleman did before them, they started to travel to Jamaica where they voiced for Jamaican producers and did combinations with Jamaican artists.

Meanwhile, many German hip-hop releases included dancehall or reggae tunes. Because of this fruitful connection between the two musical genres, the successful German hip-hop magazine *Juice* began to publish reviews and articles on Jamaican artists. Other music magazines followed suit. But, despite this, basic terms like dub plate, riddim, sound system, clash and so on still had to be explained over and over again.

Still, things were changing. More and more reggae artists were entering the national charts. The Afro-German Patrice, whose roots reggae could have been produced in Jamaica, was chosen to support Lauryn Hill on tour in 1999. Another well-respected artist who contributed to the phenomenon of hip-hop heads deserting to reggae and dancehall was Jan Delay. As a leading figure of Deutsch rap, his German-language roots reggae offshoot album *Searching for the Jan Soul Rebels*, entered the charts and his video went on heavy rotation. This was the first reggae album that not only featured German-language lyrics, but also talked about German political issues. In contrast to his predecessors, Jan Delay did not even try to be "authentic", but intentionally addressed a German audience. Musically he – and to some extent Patrice – brought traditional one-drop reggae to the forefront again, and even hardcore hip-hop kids approved of it.

Around the same time, the Berlin based band Seeed helped to advance the "Germanyfication" of dancehall. Their debut album *New Dubby Conquerors* and hit tune "Dickes B" (meaning "Capital B") – an homage to their hometown – soon climbed high in the national charts. However, the band's excellent live concerts proved to be the real marker of their success, even leading to their performance at the opening ceremonies of the 2006 football World Cup with millions watching worldwide. Consisting of eleven people from something like eleven countries, Seeed is representative of a modern, multicultural Germany.

With an increasing number of artists at their disposal, it was only a matter of time for German producers to come up with their own riddims. Although there are countless German names in the field of reggae production by now, we only want to mention four representing different approaches. Ingo Rheinbay from the Pow Pow sound system tries to be as "authentically" Jamaican as possible. Most of his riddims were played by the Jamaican Firehouse Crew and voiced, at least at the beginning, almost exclusively by Jamaican artists.

4.8 Jan Delay, a leading figure of Deutsch rap. Press photo.

And with tunes like Junior Kelly's "Blaze", Richie Spice's "Blood Again" or Gentleman's "Superior", his productions were even successful in Jamaica. At one point when we were at the Aquarius record store in Kingston and asked for the latest releases, the shop assistant played the latest Pow Pow selection, unaware of its German origin. We had to tell him that we wanted to listen to the latest *Jamaican* stuff and not releases from our hometown.

A similar, yet also different, approach is taken by the German Brotherman, who operates his Minor7Flat5 label from the Spanish island Gran Canaria. Even though his riddims incorporate elements of hip-hop and house music, he voices only Jamaican artists, and mostly focuses on singers and deejays that are virtually unknown in their homeland. Interestingly enough, in doing so he has helped artists like Turbulence, Lutan Fyah and Ras Myhrdak to break in Jamaica. He even produced *Biological Warfare*, by Cocoa Tea, a singer who is more usually known for sticking to a set of Jamaican producers that he has worked with for a long time.

Teka from Rootdown Records in Cologne takes quite another approach, even though his productions do not sound all that different from Pow Pow's. Thanks to his focus on German artists, his label has become synonymous with a German version of reggae. Just like record labels in other musical genres, Rootdown puts a lot of effort into artist development and can now boast various artists that almost exclusively release on Rootdown: Nattyflo, Mono and Nikitaman, Nosliw, Maxim, and others. In contrast to common practice in the reggae world, Rootdown Records mainly puts out albums instead of seven inches. The Nosliw album *Mehr davon* (meaning "More of That") was highly

4.9 Rootdown Records
crew. Press photo.

appreciated within reggae circles. Nosliw proved German can be made to fit a reggae groove even though it has always been said the German language lacks musicality.

Along with a growing number of new artists on the scene, sound systems were and still are mushrooming even in small towns. From 1998 onwards, a second generation emerged – spearheaded by sounds like Supersonic and Sentinel – playing out every weekend and familiarizing their ever-growing massives with Jamaican reggae culture. Towards the end of 2000, Germany's number one juggling sound system, Pow Pow Movement, took part in the World Clash in New York along with Kilamanjaro, Bass Odyssey, Tony Matterhorn and Mighty Crown. And although they were eliminated in the first round, they managed to convince the highly critical clash audience of their quality dub plates. This paved the way for Sentinel, who set forth from their home base of Stuttgart – the place where Mercedes Benz is situated – to win the famous World Clash in 2005 against Black Kat, Bass Odyssey, Mighty Crown and others. This was taken as a sign that German dancehall had finally gained international recognition.

While in the 1990s, dancehall was restricted to a certain set of well-informed insiders within Germany, the new millennium not only ushered in an era of much easier access to information about the culture, but also generated a measurable, more lasting success for reggae in the German mainstream. Gentleman's 2002 album *Journey to Jah* went gold and the follow-up *Confidence* even went platinum, having hit the number one spot in the German pop charts in the first week after its release. Backed by the Far East Band, Gentleman now tours the world to sold-out venues and has even made an impression in Jamaica. In the meantime, he has become a role model for other European artists like Ziggi from the Netherlands or Million Stylez from Sweden. Along with the huge success of Sean Paul, this equally impacted the previously strictly underground sound system dances and began drawing the uninitiated. These were people who were unfamiliar with what was going on and would have left the clubs straight away again just a few years earlier.

Riddim Magazine

The situation at the beginning of the new millennium was perfect for launching a magazine like *Riddim*, the first high-gloss magazine for reggae music in Germany, with a current circulation of forty-five thousand. In addition to featuring reggae and dancehall artists from Jamaica, Germany and other countries in equal measure, the policy of *Riddim* is also to mediate Jamaican culture as a means of raising awareness of the genre's historical roots and the society in which the music is so embedded. Even after six years' worth of publications, we find people are still hungry for a deeper knowledge about Rastafari as well as Jamaican history, folklore, language and *politricks*. The response we have received to date has proven our concept to be on the right track. People from all walks of life and of almost all ages read *Riddim* – we know of readers from ten to sixty years of age. Although this sometimes makes it difficult to cater to the full diversity of tastes, it also keeps our work fresh and exciting. Aided by an international cast of contributors from Germany, Jamaica, the United Kingdom, the United States of America, France, Austria and Switzerland, we try to offer a subtle blend of stories that are just as heterogeneous as our readership. Content ranges from short, light pieces in the warm-up/news section to in-depth, analytical features or interviews that are up to ten pages long, exclusive picture spreads and an extensive review section. As an added extra, a cover-mount CD graces each issue and serves as an aural illustration of the magazine's content. After the first issue of *Riddim*, sceptics questioned how we would ever fill further issues. Evidently, they were ignorant of both the genre's long and rich history as well as its vivid and vital present-day forms. Others criticized the length of some of the stories, saying that today's youths do not like reading. But after seven years we feel safe in claiming that reality has proved them wrong. Subscriber numbers are still growing and kids have let us know that it was through *Riddim* that they started to enjoy reading and – in quiet defiance of the generation gap we spoke of at the beginning of our talk – some even share a copy with their parents.

Having long lacked a suitable platform upon which to promote their products to their core audience, the recording industry also welcomed the appearance of *Riddim*. While we would of course not claim *Riddim* was solely responsible for the commercial success of reggae in Germany, we did help the genre to find its market. By now, the summer months are dotted with more than thirty open-air reggae festivals each year in Germany, Austria and Switzerland. The magazine even succeeded in attracting the interest of book publishers, resulting in the publication of a book on Rastafari, dictionaries on reggae terminology and, most recently, a book on reggae in Germany (Barsch 2003; 2006; Bratfisch 1999; Karnik 2007). In addition to *Riddim*, the Internet has, of course, also helped a lot to spread information on the music and its culture. While working in our editorial office, for instance, we can listen to IRIE FM or watch a live stream of the Sting festival. And, just as importantly, the Internet has also made formerly hard-to-find music readily available – whether legally or not. As a spin-off of the successful sound system of the same name, the German mail-order service Soundquake.com managed to liberate the seven-inch format from its previous strictly urban confines and spread it around the world. Recently, they were the first to establish an MP3 shop exclusively for reggae.

But even though it is hard for *Riddim* to compete with the pace at which information is distributed through the Internet, the English offshoot of *Riddim* received a warm welcome all over the world. The English edition was published from May 2005 until March 2007 and was mainly distributed in English-speaking countries, while still being available in virtually all parts of the world. Although we ourselves had a lot of scruples publishing a magazine that we felt should come out of Jamaica, we were encouraged by people from the industry, artists, fans and even our dear friend Carolyn Cooper. And the reactions to the first issue proved them right. We received handwritten letters from as far away as Zimbabwe, where people long for any information on reggae. Unfortunately, we had to put the English edition on hold after seven issues due to distribution problems, but are ready to revive it any time we find a sponsor that is willing to invest in this worthy project.

The European Reggae Scene

We could, of course, go on forever, but, before we come to an end, allow us to broaden the perspective a bit more. While some parts of Europe only began establishing a regional reggae scene relatively recently, things have developed at a much faster rate in the last few years than the German crawl of the 1980s and 1990s. Nevertheless, a lot of people are still looking to Germany, be it for sound systems, record outlets, artists like Gentleman or a magazine like *Riddim*. The development process of other continental European countries mirrors the one seen in Germany in that they began by first copying the Jamaican blueprint before turning initial misunderstanding into something productive, something that is Jamaican in form, but European in content. All this goes hand-in-hand with the gradual building of local infrastructures that include prosperous sound system scenes, a healthy live circuit, a recording industry, the existence of artists and producers and, most importantly, a strong massive. All of this becomes most visible in the summer months when, for example, thousands of people from all over Europe travel to the Rototom Sunsplash Festival in the north of Italy. This ten-day festival not only includes live performances and sound system dances, but also various workshops on dance, drumming, health issues and Rastafari, as well as movie screenings, exhibi-

4.10 "Reggae University", where journalists, scholars and musicians teach different aspects of reggae culture.
Photo: Luca d'Agostino, Phocus Agency.

tions and a "Reggae University", where journalists, scholars and musicians teach different aspects of reggae culture.

While European reggae scenes have traditionally taken Jamaica to be their first focal point and produced mimetic versions of the "original", the subsequent development of these scenes has generally tended towards an increasing emancipation from the reggae motherland in favour of a more or less independent pop culture. This is because, as soon as the music is established to a certain degree, new approaches, experiments, fusions with other genres and distinctively own styles of expression are possible (Karnik 2007). This is not to say that Europeans do not regard reggae from Jamaica as the real thing – they do. But next to Jamaican artists, we are witnessing a rising presence of European acts in the various reggae charts. And there are even a few artists, like the Italian Alborosie, who are shoulder-to-shoulder with their Jamaican colleagues.

References

Barsch, Volker. 2003. *Rastafari: Von Babylon nach Afrika. Geschichte, Hintergründe und Werte der Rasta-Bewegung*. Mainz: Ventil Verlag.
——. 2006. *Rasta Chant. Das Who-Is-Who des Roots-Reggae*. Mainz: Ventil Verlag.
Bratfisch, Rainer. 1999. *Reggae-Lexikon*. Berlin: Schwarzkopf and Schwarzkopf.
Gummersbach, Gerd, Ellen Koehlings and Pete Lilly. 2003. "Gentleman: Straight from the Backyard". *Riddim* 4: 26–28.
Jakob, Günter. 1993. *Agit Pop. Schwarze Musik und weiße Hörer. Texte zu Rassismus und Nationalismus, HipHop und Raggamuffin*. Berlin: ID-Verlag.
Karnik, Olaf. 2007. *Reggae in Deutschland*. Ed. Helmut Philipps. Cologne: Kiepenheuer and Witsch.
Michels, Peter M. 1979. *Rastafari*. Munich: Trikont Verlag.
Schwaner, Teja. 1980. "Bob Marley, Eierkuchen und Kulturschocks". *Sounds,* August.
Wynands, René. 1995. *Do the Reggay: Reggae con Pocomania bis Raggamuffin und der Mythos Bob Marley*. Munich: Piper Verlag.

CHAPTER 5

REGGAE IN CUBA
AND THE HISPANIC CARIBBEAN

SAMUEL FURÉ DAVIS

I vividly recall when, in 1993, I was introduced to a small group of Rastas in a suburban and apparently poor and marginalized neighbourhood in the southeast of Havana.[1] That was the first of very frequent contacts with that group. Around the block from the house of one of the Rastas was a small so-called amphitheatre, which would later become an important centre of community cultural activities. This group of Rastas would play a prominent role in the organization of such activities. One event took place at this small venue on 31 October 1999; a major reggae and rap concert was organized. It was jam-packed with a very heterogeneous, and primarily young, audience of approximately two hundred people. It was one of a series of cultural events structured around reggae music and the social contribution of the Rastas to the cultural life of that community, combined with the frequent participation, lifestyle and expressive needs of the rappers. However, none of these events was free from a number of restrictions and regulations imposed by the local authorities in terms of when, how long, and why the activities were organized, and they were conditioned upon the usually excellent public discipline and order.

Unlike the rest of the Hispanic Caribbean countries during the period of the mid- to late 1990s, socialist Cuba was undergoing a serious economic crisis – known as the "special period" – resulting from national and international political circumstances that reflected the long economic dependence of the nation upon the Eastern European socialist bloc. The consequences went far beyond the economic boundaries: its effects were, in the long run, more visible in society and culture. This period shook the grounds of Cubanness (called *cubanía* or *cubanidad* in Spanish). Some intrinsic values, such as egalitarianism and collectivism, took new meanings and adapted to the new circumstances. The individual had to face new and different personal problems. Individual and collective identities, reshaped mainly around religion, race and the re-emerging notion of class, became more diversified. Many small- and medium-sized private businesses were legally owned by Cubans for the first time since the revolution. National agri-food market reforms created unexpected negative impacts. New markets and foreign investment were urgently sought as a solution to bring the country out of the crisis. The "smokeless" international tourist industry replaced the sugar industry as the foremost source of hard currency in the country. The noxious effects of the mass introduction of international tourism into Cuba (class differences, prostitution, dual currency, and others) created class and social divides experienced at unprecedented levels by the predominantly young population born after 1959. It is this population that suffered from these consequences more than ever before and more than anybody else.

The works by José Moreno et al. (1998), Robin D. Moore (2006) and Sujatha Fernandes (2006) are a few examples of the extensive and critical studies of this period both *a yard* and abroad; the last two illustrate the ensuing cultural changes, mainly in the music industry. Moore, in his chapter entitled "Music and Ideological Crisis", makes a drastic point: Cuba before the 1990s "bears little resemblance to that of the present" (2006, 225); the special period left a mark in the musical changes and the cultural politics. Moreover, Fernandes's objective and critical understanding of the consolidation of the hegemonic socialist ideology in the Cuban society during the post-revolutionary period leads to an analysis of how "new cultures" are emerging. These "new cultures" embody cultural diversity, contestation and protest as new forms of revolutionary attitudes. In a nutshell, this period was one more "critical event" in the historical development of revolutionary Cuba, which "altered relations among specified sets of elements" (Sawyer 2006, 3).

The state's exercise of control and hegemony to save the nation from the ideological attacks of the powerful enemy is evident in the nationalist discourse intended to counteract the effects of the emerging class inequalities. Therefore, state control of cultural politics is accurately defined by Fernandes as "a process of partial reincorporation . . . to assimilate counter-dominant expressions and practices into official discourses and institutions" (2006, 26) by using mechanisms to control, not to prohibit, cultural production and dissemination to the public. This explains the co-option that many artistic expressions have experienced during the 1990s and beyond.

Two clear examples of how alternative contesting expressions were recently assimilated and incorporated in Cuba are rock and hip-hop cultures, and primarily the musical styles associated with them: rock and rap. The process of incorporation as a political response to contestation by hegemonic forces is frequent in Caribbean musical history: pan in Trinidad and Tobago, calypso in the Eastern Caribbean and reggae in Jamaica are all now cultural symbols, but they have all been, since their beginnings, anti-colonial weapons used by the poor and lower classes. Cuba and the rest of the Caribbean display a lot of similarities and differences not to be fully discussed here, but it suffices to say that the historical and cultural connections of people (as a result of migration) and ideas between Caribbean countries during the late nineteenth and early twentieth centuries have generated common ties of cultural – more specifically musical – brotherhood that are stronger than linguistic differences.

Both Cuba and the rest of the Caribbean are, similarly, the result of ethnic and racial mixtures, but the ingredients in these "melting pots" mixed differently during the relative asynchronic formations of our nationalities. The changes suffered by Cuba during the 1990s have driven the country to implement capitalist market economy strategies and have triggered social class divides between rich and poor that are similar to those existing in the capitalist neoliberal Caribbean nations. However, there is still a major distinction marked by the ruling social system that strives to preserve essential benefits. The socio-economic condition in Cuba is much different from the increased privatization and the decreased government assistance to solve social, educational and cultural problems in many countries of the region during the same period. Moreover, in Cuba, the prevailing nationalist discourse has led to a very cautious official recognition of cultural diversity and foreign cultural influences, to the extent that the Rastafari culture is still disapproved of, and reggae music is marginalized and regarded with contempt. By contrast, in the Hispanic Caribbean, the more limited social integration of migrant groups since the first decades of the twentieth century as well as the contemporary governments' indifference to some social, cultural and community problems in neoliberal societies during the last three decades might have facilitated the more independent development and local organization of unfamiliar or foreign cultures such as Rastafari and reggae.

As the "special period" went by in Cuba, with its complex dynamics of economic, political and cultural changes, some social minority groups, such as the Rastas mentioned at the beginning of this chapter, increased in number, became more visible and acquired new meanings and roles; consequently, this foreign cultural expression was adopted and transformed within the new context.

Reggae has not been much of a victim of co-option in the Hispanic Caribbean partly because it has continued to be a resistant, marginalized, independent, Maroon lifestyle when it is related to the Rastafarian worldview. It is a type of music with little or no official mainstream broadcast in Cuba. Nevertheless, it has also been commercialized worldwide, sometimes even alongside representations of Rastafarian symbols and attributes that have been co-opted and distorted to meet market demands in the music industry.

In this chapter, I will compare the ways in which reggae serves the interests of youth both in Cuba and in the rest of the Hispanic Caribbean as the most important social agent in this cultural dynamic, in particular in the relationships between reggae and Rastafari in assuming a Rasta identity, and in the representation of racial and ethnic identity. An essential point here is that, whereas reggae both in Cuba and in the rest of the Hispanic Caribbean serves the same spiritual and commercial purposes, no academic study of both contexts can follow the same analysis. I will then concentrate on Cuba in order to explain in greater detail the interaction between the reggae scenario and another cultural expression that appeals to the youth today: rap and hip-hop culture.

Cultural Hybridity

In a 1994 lecture, Joseph Pereira identified Panama, Puerto Rico, as well as other Latin American societies, as the cradles of reggae in Spanish.[2] Pereira noted several significant factors in the spread of reggae in the region. These include the role of the Miami- and New York–based communities that were very influential given the high incidence of Spanish in the commercialization of popular music, and the financial prospect of the Spanish Caribbean market (Pereira 1994). Cuba did not count as part of the flourishing Spanish-speaking market created by the music industries in Central America and the Latino communities in the United States. The origin and development of reggae in the Spanish-speaking, socialist, Cuban cultural context is attributed to three sets of causes. First, a series of political and cultural developments took place after the 1970s, namely newly created political, economic and diplomatic links, closer cross-cultural contacts regionally and globally, and the organization in Cuba of a number of remarkable cultural events in different cities, such as the Carifesta and the Fiesta del Fuego (a festival of Caribbean culture organized in Santiago de Cuba). Second, Jamaican and other Anglo-Caribbean students, workers, and trainees, as well as an important number of Cuban workers, travelled back and forth to Cuba after 1972 as a result of newly established diplomatic relations. Third, a concurrent and decisive development was the ability of Cubans to tune into some Caribbean (specifically Jamaican) and Floridian radio stations, particularly in the east and northwest of Cuba. This was a most covert, but direct, contact with the reggae world. This sort of "clandestine" reception of airwaves, as well as the first recordings of these radio broadcasts, made reggae a new, if still marginal, musical alternative. These recordings were commonly played at reggae parties or *bonches*[3] arranged during weekends in private homes of particular neighbourhoods in, mainly, Havana and Santiago de Cuba, and attended by an increasingly large number of mostly black youth. These *bonches* triggered a significant and growing appetite for reggae music which was not exclusive to the Rastas; these parties also developed a conscious knowledge and consumption, as well as a keen enthusiasm and devotion to the music made by the booming reggae bands and singers from all over the world. The *bonches* are still an essential mechanism in keeping reggae an integral part of the music diversity in Cuba today.

Other factors, not fully explored in Pereira's 1994 lecture, are historically determined. Before focusing upon specific characteristics of this process of musical acculturation in Cuba, characteristics common to many Hispanic-Caribbean countries should be identified. First, these societies were destinations for thousands of Anglo-Caribbean migrants at different moments during the early twentieth century. Panama, during the period of the construction of the Panama Canal, was the primary destination. The endogenous nature of the generational evolution in the urban settlements of these migrant communities facilitated the continuation of the musical tradition of the anglophone Caribbean, especially that of Jamaica, in such a way that reggae, when it emerged by the end of the 1960s, easily became part of a cultural hybridity that had been developing in these communities for decades.

Second, as noted by Pereira, the assimilation of reggae in the new Hispanic-Caribbean context was not "a one way process". Jamaican singers started to make, he said, and I add "they still make", versions in Spanish of their hits. One example is Tony Rebel's "Si Jah está a lado de me [*sic*]" ("If Jah is standing by my side"). He not only uses lyrics in Spanish but incorporates a distinctively Cuban (some would say Latin), danceable rhythm. In this sense, language was not the only target of the Spanish Caribbean influence in the Jamaican reggae scenario, but also Latino music.

Cuba did not escape the impact of Caribbean migration and cross-cultural influences. Therefore, we must take into account the cultural relations, enhanced in some cases by the political links between Jamaica and other countries of the region, mainly with Cuba. Some artistes in Jamaica echoed the significance of the Cuban presence in the English-speaking island, especially during the post-independence Manley years. It was common to hear songs of socio-political commentary; for example, mentioning the construction of schools in Jamaica by Cuban workers or the popular reaction when Jamaica broke diplomatic links with Cuba (see Badoo "Diplomatic Links" on *The Sound of Channel One*). One more example of this border crossing is the use of Jamaican rhythms by the pioneering Cuban reggae band Tierra Verde

(Green Land) in a reggae version of a well-known bolero popularized decades ago by the famous Benny Moré entitled "Alma mía".

We must not forget the important presence of West Indian migrants and descendants in Cuba; however, I argue that this has not been a key factor in the introduction of Jamaican popular music and the later assimilation of reggae in Cuba, due to historical and cultural circumstances. During the first four decades of the twentieth century, the Jamaican (in general, the West Indian) immigrant found himself in a different society as compared with those of Central America. Besides their pride as British subjects and their conservative cultural traditions, some West Indian immigrants felt comfortable with the idea of whitening their skin in response to beliefs that had gained force in Cuba since the nineteenth century. A significant number of the country's high and middle classes had also developed a certain anti-black fear despite the gradual recognition by Cuban popular culture (in religion, music, theatre, and literature) of its African cultural heritage. In this context, those "British subjects" slowly became acquainted with the idea of "being and living like Cubans" (Chailloux 2005, 2); their integration became more significant in the formation of the Cuban nation. Therefore, unlike the rest of the Hispanic Caribbean, the West Indian culture in Cuba could not play an active role in facilitating the entry of reggae music in the 1980s because it was both "frozen" in time and integrated into the Cuban nationality. Only recently, some West Indian associations, such as the Asociación Caribeña de Cuba (Caribbean Association of Cuba), are co-opting the reggae cultivated by the Cubans as an example of the Caribbean culture they represent. These dynamics worked differently in the West Indian diasporas of the Spanish-speaking Caribbean, as in Colón, Panama, for example, where reggae was welcomed by these communities since its early years, the 1970s.

Characterizing Hispanic Reggae

"Reggae in Spanish" sometimes is not the best designation for these creative actions in Latin America and the Hispanic Caribbean. Groups like Bamaselo (from Costa Rica, founded in 2001) used to write most of their music in English, the language of their lead singer and composer Michael Livingston, even though they are trying to please their fans by writing more in Spanish today.[4]

Consequently, the term *reggae Latino* (Latin reggae) is more comprehensive inasmuch as it makes reference not only to the language but also to the musical fusion with the distinctive sounds of the region.[5] However, as the focus here lies only on the socio-historical characteristics, I will refer to it by the more general term "Hispanic reggae", in other words, the reggae music created in Spanish in the Caribbean and in Latin America, but this usage of the term is free from the hegemonic or derogatory connotation that the word "Hispanic" suggests when it refers to the Latin minorities in the United States. This reggae Latino is not merely nurtured by the social contradictions of minorities in the metropolitan, hegemonic environment in the United States (the "American Dream") or in Europe (specifically Spain); it stems from the social conditions of the (neo) colonized, marginalized and materially impoverished people in the South, Latin America and the Caribbean. Therefore, to limit the scope of this paper, instead of stating a focus on "reggae made in Spanish", this definition of Hispanic reggae or reggae Latino does not include reggae made in Spain.

A succinct review of the characteristics of Hispanic reggae must include at least three elements: the language issue, the use of translations and versions based on known "riddims" as well as background music, and regional consciousness.

First, one significant characteristic in the assimilation of reggae in the Spanish-speaking Caribbean is the different kind of articulation of the "nation language" (Brathwaite 1984) to transmit the anti-colonial and nationalist feelings it has in the non-Hispanic Caribbean. The Creole languages, the vernacular mother-tongue for everyone in these territories, have been very instrumental in conveying a traditional folklore by combining popular beliefs, sound and rhythm of the folk poets, entertainers, performers and deejays such as Louise Bennett, Bob Marley, Mutabaruka, Michael Smith, Buju Banton and myriad others. This choice of the Creole language as an oppositional tool against the dominant language and culture of the metropolis conveys the extra message of what Louise Bennett called "Colonization in Reverse" in a homonymous poem (Bennett 1966).

We are all mindful of the historically determined circumstances that led to the absence of a Patwa or Creole language in the Hispanic Caribbean. "Aquí todos hablamos español" ("Everyone here speaks Spanish") despite the language variants or accents, different vocabularies and registers that character-

ize the language of every country in Latin America and the Spanish Caribbean. Thus, Hispanic reggae loses, in part, that flavour of the "nation language". The anti-colonial – anti-Babylon, for the Rastas – folk spirit that is easily found as an intrinsic element in the English subregion is only transmitted in Spanish by the message conveyed in the lyrics and the rhythm itself, not only by the language choice. Other common and unifying language-related features of reggae in the Hispanic Caribbean, and even in Latin America, are the use of cultural elements that came to the region with the Rastafari culture

5.1 Dub poets such as Mutabaruka have been instrumental in using the Creole language as an oppositional tool against the dominant language. Photo by Mel Cooke; courtesy of the Gleaner Company.

as well as expressions denoting some other typical attitudes and spaces of Jamaican society, such as "the chauvinist rude boy" and "the dancehall". Therefore, phrases and exclamations like "Jah Rastafari!", "Selassie I!", "Fire Burn!", "Lord a mercy", and many more abound in the reggae lyrics in a sort of mixture of English-based Creole and Spanish language (it can also be called "Spanglish"). For example, the lead singer of the Havana-based band Paso Firme (Firm Step) introduces the song "La que pasé" ("How Hard It Was") with the short speech: *"Fire to Babilón! Paso Firme te canta con amor pa' que me acabes de entender que somos cubanos y nadie nos puede parar, no. Aborrezco la obra de los que se desvían. De Cuba y para el mundo – Jah Rastafari!"* ("Fire Babylon! Paso Firme sings for love so that you can finally understand that we are Cubans and no one can stop us. No. I abhor the work of those who have led themselves astray. From Cuba to the world – Jah Rastafari!").

Seen from this point of view, the language acts to instil some fundamental Rasta religious ideas in the Hispanic Caribbean. This snobbish reproduction of the Rasta language or "dreadtalk" is typical of most reggae music performed in Spanish, not only in Cuba, since the "musical migrations" (Aparicio and Jáquez 2003) were generated first by mere reproduction and assimilation, then followed by a gradual cultural authentication, that is, the resemantization and adaption to the national popular culture and the mainstream. Fans simply started to make meaning out of the music rather than out of the lyrics in an English or Creole language that they initially did not understand, although eventually learning some English words helped them to comprehend the message. Thus the language barrier is overcome by the action of the accompanying Rastafarian ideology. Finally, different languages – the Jamaican English, the Spanish and the dreadtalk – are useful in conveying a broad thematic spectrum. In terms of themes, the lyrical messages generally cover the Rastafarian worldview as summarized in the motto "Peace and love", as well as common references to nature, denunciation and critical comments on socio-economic problems, as well as on the historical roots of the Latin American and Caribbean ethnic diversity including, of course, the African ancestry.

Second, in addition to making covers and versions, one effective form of producing reggae is the use of "riddims" and the so-called backgrounds (the instrumental tracks of prior hits) to back up lyrics originally composed in or translated into Spanish. This is especially effective in Cuba where the lack of resources makes it difficult to create a fully equipped band. Therefore, burned

CDs with dub music, riddims, and instrumental tracks pass from hand to hand to accompany solo singers in their public presentations. The song "No hay noche en Zion" by Hijos de Israel, a Nyabinghi Rasta band created in 1997 in Cuba, is partly a translation from Culture's (Joseph Hill's) "No night". The hook of the song is literally translated, but part of the text was originally developed in Spanish. You can see this below. The Spanish version is a direct translation from the English until the final line of the chorus, translated as "Zion is blessed. Evil will not get in."

"No hay noche en Zion"
by Hijos de Israel

Noche en Zion, no hay noche allí
Jah Rastafari es la luz, no queremos otra luz
Aleluya no hay noche allí
Zion es bendito. El mal no entrará

"No night"
by Culture

No night inna Zion, there is no night there
Alleluia, there is no night there
King Rastafari is our light and we no need no other light
Alleluia, there is no night there

Third, the other characteristic of the reggae music in the Hispanic Caribbean is the expression of a regional consciousness perceived by the unity of interests among the roots reggae makers. Several Latin American brethren have invited reggae singers and deejays from other countries in the region to participate in their musical productions. The Mexican reggae artiste Ras Fabio, for example, on his album *Rasta Para Tí* works with a variety of Latin American voices and messages from Mexico to Chile, including Cuba. Moreover, Kaweskar (Chile) on his album *Taksu* (2006), features performers from Cuba such as Principe Carlos from the band Insurrectos (The Insurgent) – now renamed Herencia (Legacy). This also serves to break down the relative isolation of Cuban reggae in the region. Similarly, the increasing number of websites with music samples and general information about Latin or Hispanic reggae adds to the regional dimension of reggae in Latin America.[6]

In general, the Cuban contribution to the regional dimension of Latin or Hispanic reggae is restricted by the limited possibilities for commercial promotion of the creative talent of the few national reggae artistes and bands through free access to official record and distribution labels. These labels operate under a controlled cultural policy which tries to balance the extensive variety of musical production in the so called "island of music". The development of reggae in Cuba is proportionally very small as compared to dominant or popular musical styles; it even compares unfavourably to other alternative cultural manifestations like rap and rock. Therefore, it has not gained general acceptance as a result of these and other factors, including the fact that Rastafari culture is not institutionalized or visibly organized and is still officially regarded with disdain. This is due to the association of Rasta with the sacred use of cannabis – severely punished by Cuban law. The above contributes to the unstable development of Cuban reggae; some bands have appeared and disappeared from the scene in less than a year, such as Punto Rojo (Red Point) or Magia Negra (Black Magic). Moreover, there are no financial resources at hand for private production. More peculiarities of the Cuban context will be explored later on.

The Makers and the Audience: Identity Representations

With these preliminary ideas about the historical regularities and the general characteristics in mind, it is possible to discuss identity issues intrinsically related to the reggae enthusiasts (both the makers and the audience), both to the bands and the dancing and listening public, neither of which is exclusively Spanish-speaking nor exclusively Caribbean. In other words, reggae in Spanish has reached beyond the geographic borders of Latin America and the Caribbean. My focus lies on representations of identities. It is useful to characterize reggae fans and their interests based on three characteristics, namely the generational cultural expressions (the youth); the main concerns regarding racial self-recognition and affiliation; and Rastafarian religious expressions and beliefs.

In explaining this, I am aware of one fact: some risky generalizations have to be made based upon field research in Cuba and Panama, and upon conclusions by other scholars regarding the social context in which reggae emerged and developed in the Hispanic Caribbean. First, commercial and popular reggae is primarily one of several cultural expressions of one segment of the population, the youth, which cannot always be defined simply in terms of age. Other characteristics come into play, such as "being spontaneous, energetic . . . venturesome [which I interpret as "revolutionary" not only in the political but also cultural sense of the word, meaning a call for changes in the settings, conditions and situations that control creative expression], disrespectful [which I interpret as 'transgressive'], . . . and erotic" (Berger qtd. in Wulff 1995, 7). Moreover, the study of reggae in this social context must not only be done from outside with concepts like marginalization, deviance, transgression, or opposition which are typical of the subcultures; it must also be conducted from inside to facilitate recognition and social inclusion of cultural diversity (Zúñiga 2003). This social context plays an essential role in shaping a cultural process because in matters of globalization and cross-cultural connections, "youth cultures are in the forefront of theoretical interest; youth, their ideas and commodities move easily across national borders, shaping and being shaped by all kinds of structures and meanings" (Wulff 1995, 10). Therefore, in Hispanic Caribbean societies, reggae cannot be assessed separately from other youth cultures and musical forms, such as rock and rap.

Second, there is the question of class, race, and racial identity. We know that roots reggae has a solid ground not only in the ideas of emancipation, freedom, and love, as presented in the music of Jimmy Cliff, Dennis Brown, Bob Marley and others, but also in the pan-African tradition and blackness (Burning Spear, Peter Tosh and more). In our Spanish subregion, reggae is mainly preferred and cultivated precisely in communities mostly inhabited by underprivileged people who are deprived of opportunities for upward mobility. Therefore, as in the rest of the reggae world, the study of the emergence of alternative cultures and musics in reaction to hegemonic politics, as well as marginalization, exclusion and similar concepts, is an essential methodological tool in the study of the social contexts of reggae music in the Hispanic region. Additionally, this area of the Caribbean is a laboratory of historically determined racial and ethnic mixtures. At present, in truth there is no "purely" white or "purely" black person. The ethnic diversity of Africa and Spain disappeared under the unifying notions of class and race; skin colour means nothing in the analysis of ethnic ancestries in Cuba and the Hispanic Caribbean (Morales 2007, 87). Moreover, being white generally became a symbol of wealth and authority while blackness implied dependence and lower social status. Consequently, whiteness became a symbol of betterment in society, and the one-drop theory, as well as other considerations that determine racial-ethnic ancestry in non-Caribbean societies, does not apply here. Instead, I argue that a more practical position is to consider blackness as awareness of the African heritage rather than just the amount of melanin in the skin. It is particularly valid in the insular and continental Spanish-speaking Caribbean where ethnic diversity has generated unprecedented levels of racial mixtures and denominations for every shade of colour.

Any analysis of reggae from a class–race perspective in the Hispanic Caribbean, as in other parts of the world, must distinguish between ideology-oriented roots reggae and the market-oriented commercial reggae.[7] The differences in their messages, lyrics, appeal and social response are clearly apparent. The former is commonly, but not exclusively, associated with small groups of black lower class, and therefore marginalized, groups of fans who are, in addition, conscious of the Rastafarian ideology and way of life. Reggae was able to spark a strong awareness of the common social, historical and racial situation among these groups. To these people, reggae music is not only a way of life, it also adds meaning to life. On the other hand, "the music business"[8] of commercial and roots reggae has made reggae and its symbols fashionable for larger crowds of non-Rasta youths in Panama, Puerto Rico, Costa Rica, and many other Latin American and Caribbean countries including, of course, Cuba.

This phenomenon has driven reggae music in general along the same routes to the same destiny: a wider consumption not only limited to black or poor social sectors. In a case study about reggae in Puerto Rico, for example, Giovanetti noted two kinds of identification with reggae: one located in the mixture of Jamaican dancehall with Puerto Rican rap that imitates the gangsta rap culture of some African-American youth; the other is characterized by the consumption of original, pure, roots reggae (1995, 28–29; 2003, 85). The former is typically found in the lower-class communities, and features some so-called underground, contesting lyrics and messages; the latter has been adopted by more "well-off" groups in Puerto Rican society, called *blanquitos* or *riquitos* (white or rich youths in a pejorative sense), who can afford expensive tickets to quality reggae shows, among other luxuries. This is understandable in this context because Puerto Rico, in the early decades of the twentieth century, did not have a large influx of Anglo-Caribbean migrants, unlike many Central and Latin American countries including Cuba. Large communities of roots reggae fans in Panama, for example, are to be found on the Caribbean coast in towns like Colón and Portobelo, where many West Indian immigrants and descendants still reside in large numbers. Reggae in these places is usually accompanied by Rastafarian symbols and ideology. However, in the capital city on the Pacific coast, despite the fact that the Anglo-Caribbean community also has considerable cultural influence, reggae is under the influence of the music market, fused with national styles but also with a more cosmopolitan folk music in a blend that projects the "slackness" (Cooper 2004) – the materialistic worldview – of the Jamaican dancehall culture (with its preoccupation with impressive clothing, luxuries and sex), the hip-hop lifestyle and reggaeton. One example is to be found in El General's tracks "Get Down" and "El Bomper".

This kind of reggae is especially welcome by a larger and more diverse audience which is, nonetheless, predominantly young. The racial and class divides within this audience are not as visible as in Puerto Rico. As to the message, there is an explicit appeal to female sexuality echoed by young females. Nevertheless, not all lyrics are exploitative of women; the band Raíces y Cultura (Roots and Culture) from Panama uses the same dance-appealing style to denounce how girls with a "good body" abuse their beauty for personal benefit as a subtle kind of prostitution. In this case, the use of reggae is very commercial, but it stays away from slackness to promote good behaviour among the youth.

Another important dimension of this analysis concerns the unique sociopolitical situation in Cuba. As compared to other Hispanic Caribbean countries, expressions of class and racial differences and marginalization were reduced to a minimum during the first decades of the Revolution. The resulting discourse around national unity was made a paramount priority to the detriment of a fair and necessary assessment of racial and class differences and cultural diversity. Not until the twenty-first century did the social sciences in Cuba have the necessary support to promote interest in studying policies of cultural diversity, including those concerning race and class in a society which has always promoted equality as an essential component of the social system. In general, racial consciousness – the basis of roots and Rasta culture

– was regarded as merely another folkloric contribution of the African heritage to Cuban culture. Moreover, negative factors like violence, high school drop-out rates and drug addiction were virtually invisible. Educational opportunities developed to increase the cultural sophistication of the population. Furthermore, there was a feeling of official disapproval or at least careful evaluation of foreign, mainly anglophone, cultural and musical influences before permitting their transmission by the national media. I emphasize these features because, in the characterization of the social context of the major Hispanic Caribbean, foreign specialists take into account the exposure of reggae fans to live concerts, the media, academic research and other mechanisms of cultural diffusion. In Cuba, there was no major international reggae event during the last three decades of the twentieth century – the period when reggae became a global phenomenon. The exception were isolated performances by Jimmy Cliff, the Fab Five, and Eddy Grant in Cuba as part of a programme of more comprehensive cultural celebrations, such as Carifesta and the Varadero International Music Festival. However, in the twenty-first century, the situation has gradually changed, and some international artistes from Jamaica and Europe have recently performed in Cuba. The leading Jamaican singer, Luciano, for example, was applauded by a crowd of high-spirited Havana sympathizers during the May 2004 Cubadisco Fair (dedicated to the Caribbean) when he performed without his band. Meanwhile, the lack of exposure to reggae by means of the national media and the scarcity of live reggae events[9] has generated alternative forms of cross-fertilization by means of international tourism, and by tuning into international radio stations from Jamaica or Florida. This parallel exposure to reggae has nurtured both the musical production of national artists who have incorporated reggae into their repertoire and the preference for reggae among the young fans during the 1970s, 1980s and early 1990s – just before the boom of the Rastas and their music.

Finally, in considering how and which identities are represented by reggae in the Hispanic Caribbean, I should briefly mention the adoption or acceptance of the Rastafarian worldview by both reggae fans and performers or singers. As in the global context, it is through reggae that some people in the region, especially the youth, start to engage with Rastafari, its ideology and religious beliefs. The links between reggae and Rasta are common in the global context, but in the Hispanic Caribbean, as previously noted, this connection is most common in poor and predominantly black communities that

5.2 The band Remanente is Cuba's leading reagge group. They have been active since forming in 1995 and only three of their original members have changed in that time. Photo courtesy of Remamente.

are excluded from the mainstream. These sectors of the population take on Rasta philosophy in a serious, orthodox manner, inspired by the communication possibilities of reggae, whereas commercialization and the music industry may not be a priority for them. I mentioned before the examples of Puerto Rico and Panama, and no major differences are found in this respect within the wider Hispanic Caribbean. However, the different socio-political context and state-controlled cultural policy in Cuba have exposed Rastafarian reggae makers to other problems.

Rastas generally acknowledge the importance of reggae in their lives, as a music that contributes to the "inner peace" and "control" which they see in the Rasta way of life. Reggae is for others the most effective means of communication; they can sing what they cannot freely say because they are not given a space or opportunity in which to do so. This is one cause for concern. Other worries are related to the nature of the Rasta philosophy itself or the specific political and legal context in which the Rastas act. Some elements of the Rastafarian way of life in Cuba have stigmatized reggae, so it still maintains negative associations as a result. One of the reasons is to be found in the sacred use of cannabis sativa by many Rastafarians worldwide. This is a serious social problem in Cuba, but it is not exclusively associated with reggae; nevertheless, this connection indirectly affects the social credibility and cultural institutionalization of the music. Additionally, reggae became visible in Cuba only in the late 1990s, following the government's official acceptance of all religious practices and the relaxation of the ban on people congregating for religious purposes in 1993. Later, the creation of the first institutional (and therefore legal) Rasta organization, the "Bob Marley Association", in Santiago de Cuba a year or so later opened up opportunities and spaces for the spread of reggae. Several reggae groups were born in Havana, and more spaces were slowly opened, though some were also closed immediately after the authorities detected any "irregular" behaviour.

An illustration of the ambivalence shown to this religious and musical subculture is provided by a Rasta from Camagüey who observed that he saw in Rastafari and reggae a refuge to escape from the hostility of neighbours who rejected him because of the colour of his skin. The longer he grew his hair, the greater the rejection he experienced in his native village, and the more acceptance he found among other Rastas. He told me this while grabbing his locks and pulling them strongly, "Here, there is a message!"[10] The "dreadful" physical appearance of the Rastas and its evident and essential connection to blackness and Africa reinforced the marginal conditions out of which Rastafari and reggae started to develop in Cuba. Therefore, the Rasta image, way of life, ideology, and music were not welcomed by the wider society. In the early years (late 1970s to early 1990s) there was no Cuban-made reggae, so the music performed by the Jamaican and international superstars was fundamental in the promotion of this new revolutionary and religious message.

In the larger Hispanic Caribbean, some other noteworthy identity reactions using the Rasta culture and its music have been recorded. A recent study about youth cultures in the region noted that "in continental Latin America, roots reggae has been adopted by juvenile individuals who use it to vindicate the native ethnicities in their respective countries, such are the cases of the *rastecas* in Mexico or the *rastaínos* in Puerto Rico . . . who claim a nature-related life style, denying the values of modern capitalism (urban life, waged labour, fast food, etc.)".[11]

We must remind ourselves that cultural resistance to colonization and slavery is an intrinsic component of the Rastafarian worldview and its music.[12] Therefore, it is not surprising that such an interesting interpretation of reggae is found in Hispanic Caribbean countries. The Aztecs and the Tainos, both peoples being exterminated by Spanish colonization during the fifteenth century, have become a symbol of resistance. In this case, reggae becomes a means of escape back to the roots, the early roots of resistance in the pre-Columbian Caribbean, long before enslaved Africans were brought on the scene.

Reggae versus Rap in Cuba

Reggae and rap are commonly found in a symbolic interaction because both address similar expressive needs and both communicate messages shared by diverse social groups that are organized around analogous identities, even though each represents a different lifestyle. In the larger Hispanic Caribbean, the commonalities and symbolic cross-fertilization between these musical structures exist in various countries, such as Puerto Rico (Giovanetti 2003), Cuba (Fernandes 2006; Fernández 2003 and others) and Panama.[13] How racial identity is lyrically expressed in Cuba by these two musical styles is discussed below.

Rap and reggae coexist in the "alternative"[14] music scenario. They sometimes contain bluntly irreverent messages in their interactions with the mainstream, being very critical of the most pressing social problems; other times they seek access to commercial distribution and more time on the airwaves. They share individual and collective identities. For example, the imaginary "borders" that characterize or identify fans and sympathizers of either musical style are usually non-existent or imperceptible. Both are concerned with the experiences of young, mainly black, men and women who, marginalized or partly excluded from social spaces or opportunities for upward mobility (as a result of the cyclic reproduction of marginalization), try to secure some visibility by their own means. Their critical discourse is embodied in their lifestyle and more specifically in their music. Reggae and rap have proven to be very effective socializing agents for these youth and also for some adults from the same communities. Both are rooted in one way or another in cultural resistance to Eurocentric and hegemonic attitudes and in the struggle to achieve social acceptance within the nation's diverse population. Even now that the rapper is institutionalized, and thus is in a better position to criticize openly and publicly, both rap and reggae artistes are "subaltern subjects" (Zurbano 2005, 9) who fight against cultural hegemony and occasional exclusion. Therefore, these musical forms have been very instrumental in enabling these young people to construct an identity that is distinct from that of the mainstream. Their emergence and development in Cuba is asynchronic but similar. This has been explained using the conceptual frameworks of transnationalism or cross-cultural connections, either as a result of spontaneous transgressive attitudes and the alternative development among those sectors of the Cuban youth (men and women alike) or as a form of resistance.

Despite the common characteristics of reggae and rap, rap in Cuba is more popular than Cuban reggae. Reggae is less significant in terms of the number of its fans, and is less representative of a popular, commercial culture. It is full of ups and downs and inner conflicts among its fans and musicians. But while we should remember that reggae emerged in Cuba earlier than rap, these differences, along with others, have been essential in the institutionalization of rap in Cuba, the opening of some spaces and opportunities for its commercialization, and the co-option of hip-hop culture, as well as some reggae-based cultural expressions, such as reggaeton and the black-conscious "spoken word" poetic expression by the Agencia Cubana de Rap (Cuban Rap Agency). Whereas this "if-you-can't-beat-them-join-them" philosophy rules among policymakers, a brief assessment of the connections between rap and reggae reveals the emergence of evolving attitudes as well as fluctuations of identity among these musicians and their fans. Some are drawn to reggae or reggaeton from rap; for others, the reverse is true. According to research data, some of the earlier reggae sympathizers were rappers and break-dancers, and vice versa.

Although many agree that Tierra Verde (Green Land), the first all-reggae band in Cuba, was formed in 1988 and first performed that same year, the boom of this music in the island did not occur until the mid-1990s. During this decade, there was an explicit interest in revitalizing reggae in Spanish, especially in creating a reggae made in Cuba reflecting "an instinct of preserving the African legacy that runs through our blood".[15] It is not a coincidence that this is the same period of the rap boom. The rap context consolidated itself since the early 1990s with a great and increasing creative production of music, posters, street-shows, television and radio shows, recordings, newspaper articles, academic studies, and many more initiatives that account for the perception that the birth of the "movement" occurred in 1995, the year of the first National Rap Festival in Havana. The hard years of economic crisis, the "special period" that started in 1991, transformed the whole cultural scenario: music, religious expression, literature and visual arts. There was the need to communicate new ideas with fewer resources and opportunities.

Moving along the thematic plane, we can easily identify some shared interests in the contesting, rebellious and alternative messages of both rap and reggae. These interests cannot be viewed apart from the ideas, values, and symbols that support these musical expressions and lifestyles. In Cuban reggae, there are basically four thematic issues: (1) the definition of ideological and religious foundations, (2) the nature of racial identity and race relations, (3) the impact of marginalization and social exclusion, and (4) the chronicling of common social problems – in which the reggae singer describes everyday life, drawing attention to social problems of individual and collective concern including issues of identity, prostitution, poverty, economic hardships, inequality, international politics, sexism, love and so on. Cuban rap also examines the last three of these concerns. The recurring presence of these ideas reflects the correspondence between everyday experiences (the message) and their expressive means (their songs, their lyrics). This combination is an alternative proposal of constructive criticism of the Cuban social context but bearing in mind the differences between Cuba and the rest of the Caribbean and Latin America. The rap duo Anónimo Consejo (Anonymous Advice), one of the performing groups that led the boom of rap since the 1990s, explained the difference in an interview: "Cuba is one of the Spanish-speaking countries with a high cultural level and more language resources. Many Latin rappers are copying the Americans in everything, lyrics referring to drugs, violence, and material things. I think that the positive messages in our lyrics are a result of the Cuban context as a country of revolution and struggle" (Fernández 2003, 9).

The second of these thematic concerns – race issues and consciousness – is worth particular attention for it is an essential theme in these lyrics, and certain interpreters are consistent with their manifestations of racial affiliation and identity. From this viewpoint, there are no fluctuations or shifts from the underground to the commercial styles of both Cuban rap and reggae in order to sell more and to be more popular. This topic has a radical importance to both Rasta and hip-hop philosophies. Both identify strongly with Africa's culture and history and the prolonged suffering to which the black race has been subjected; some reggae and rap artists think that it is important to portray their moods, sense of reality, and life experiences in their lyrics in order to provide a credible idea of their day-to-day life. For example, interracial marriages in Cuba are as common as the conflicts they stir up in prejudiced relatives and families. Topics like these are not new in Cuban popular music. What is relevant in the treatment of this issue in rap is that the taboos are destroyed by presenting characters and situations that contradict, constructively, the "supposed" absence of racial prejudice in Cuba so that more and more people, mostly young people, understand and appreciate their messages of harmony and love regardless of skin colour.

Moreover, the lyrical possibilities of reggae are enhanced by the use of drums and bass in a combination that corresponds to the contesting and rebellious message of the rhythm and to the environment in which it has developed. The reggae drum and bass beat was evidently unfamiliar to many in the early 1990s before the reggae boom. It was precisely at that time when the Cuban songwriter Pablo Milanés, shortly after the release of his album *Proposiciones*, responded in a televised interview to a question as to why he chose reggae as the rhythm of the song "Nelson Mandela, sus dos amores" ("Nelson Mandela, his two loves"); he commented, "It's a rhythm strong enough to express the feelings of freedom."[16]

The common themes of rap and reggae (anti-racism, racial pride, marginality and more) make the rapper and the reggae singer appear to be one and the same sometimes. Songs like "Hip-Hop for Jah", by the Cuban reggae deejay Cocoman, or "Hip-Hop Reggae", by the Havana-based reggae band Paso Firme, illustrate this relationship. The following is one example that illustrates the importance of the African heritage and the need to expand one's knowledge of the history and culture of the mother continent.

"África, la musa y yo"
By the reggae band Paso Firme

Expreso lo que siento y no me detengo porque soy
Un afrocubano 100% al nivel
Construyo líricas baratas para decirte todo lo que puedo hacer
Mi mente está conectada a salvar a la África FIRE
Esto da pa' más, mucho mucho más, África mía
. . .
África, ven que en tu ser el dolor está reinando
Y me cansé, me cansé de tanto sufrimiento
Ya me cansé de tanta suciedad

English version:
I express what I feel and I can't stop because I am
An Afro-Cuban 100 per cent

I compose inexpensive lyrics to tell you all I can do
My mind is focused on saving Africa Fire
More should be done, much much more. My Africa

. . .

Africa, your person is in deep pain
I am tired, tired of so much suffering
Tired of so much dirtiness
(Transcribed and translated by the author)

If these reggae lyrics try to raise awareness about the diverse problems in Africa, and the poetic persona makes a very explicit declaration of racial affiliation by defining him or herself as Afro-Cuban, the hip-hop philosophy also contributes to this interest by increasingly drawing attention to antiracist ideas expressed by Cuban heroes of the late nineteenth and early twentieth centuries. The rap duo Anónimo Consejo pays tribute to Pedro Ivonnet and Evaristo Estenoz, the national leaders and martyrs of the Independent Colour Party, and thousands of other Cuban blacks massacred during the first half of 1912 in the eastern provinces of Cuba. These rappers may at first appear to represent two different social or cultural identities. Adeyeme and Sekou, the members of the duo, are bound by the same radical philosophy of hip-hop and their African roots; their names illustrate this. However, Sekou identifies himself more with Rastafarian ideas, values and symbols, including the reggae music that was an important part of his adolescence in the late 1980s and early 1990s. Adeyeme is more radical, projecting a rapper's fashion and lifestyle (for example, wearing a baseball cap and playing basketball). Nevertheless, these are not two different manifestations of hip-hop or reggae; the duo presents the same message based upon two different life experiences. Their identities mark no contradictions in their lyric making.

Another example of the fusion of rap and reggae was recorded by Hijos de Israel (Children of Israel): the song "Canta Rastaman". This group identifies itself with the radical Nyabinghi music and lifestyle of Rastafari, but some of its members have been very active rappers and break dancers since the late 1980s. They have progressively moved from rap to reggae, even if their music is performed on hand-made drums and by the sound of their voices, which reflects Rastafarian expressive values. In this shift, the radicalization of blackness remains the same; what is more, it incorporates a strong recognition of Cuban cultural heritage and African origin in the difficult times of the 1990s.

"Canta Rastafarian"
By Hijos de Israel

El Rasta con orgullo envuelto en su manta
Cuidando mi garganta
Expreso lo que siente mi raíz cubana ante sus antepasados
Con fuerza en este caimán barbudo
Sin avergonzarme de mi trascendencia africana
Tengo mi religión yoruba afrocubana
Esta es la historia de mi raza . . .
En este mundo yo he vivido
Tratando de ocultar
El sufrimiento de mis seres más queridos
Es la piel blanca que ha acabado con la negra
En la tierra negro con blanco ya se dan la mano

English version:
Proud Rasta wrapped on my blanket
Watching my throat
I express the feelings of my Cuban roots for the ancestors
With strength in this bearded Cayman
Without a shame of my African transcendence
I have my religion Afro-Cuban Yoruba
This is the history of my race . . .
In this world I have lived
Trying to hide
The suffering of my most beloved ones
White skin has destroyed Black skin
On the Earth black and white now shake hands
(Transcribed and translated by author)

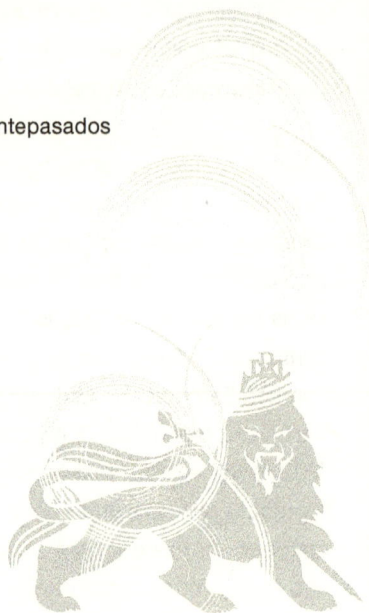

This song also raises noteworthy issues that highlight the ways in which reggae has been appropriated by some in Cuba, in contrast to Jamaica. The reference made by this Nyabinghi group to "my Afro-Cuban Yoruba" religion clearly addresses the multi-ethnic and mixed roots of Cuban culture. What the poetic persona here calls "Afro-Cuban religion" is a complex of various religious traditions of African origin that were recreated in Cuba by blacks, both free and enslaved, during colonial times. The Yoruba component, called Santería, is the result of a mixture of African-originated divinities and Catholicism that persisted underground, hidden from the hegemonic culture and colonial domination and resistant to it. The continuing spread and evolution of these beliefs and religious practices gradually transcended colour and class boundaries to become tradition embedded within Cuban popular culture, which has always confronted the conventional and hegemonic standards of the empowered elitest social sectors. Therefore, it is not surprising that a Cuban group which reproduces the conservative rituals of the Nyabinghi order of Jamaica accepts the Yoruba religion as a major tenet of individual identity, in spite of Nyabinghi's rejection of spirit possession and Christian (Protestant) interpretations of sacred writings as distortions of the truth. In fact, many Cuban Rastas are also practitioners of Santería, Palo and other Afro-Cuban religious traditions; moreover, some were Protestant or Catholic believers before accepting the Rastafarian faith or became Jehovah's Witnesses after cutting their dreadlocks. These different religion-based identities are not contradictory inasmuch as recognition of the African ancestry understood as a proud racial affiliation marks a common point.

However, the commercial representation of these identities in music (both in reggae and rap) is not as uncompromising. For example, the deejay Militar Dread from Havana makes a contradictory argument in "Excepción de Raza", a rapped text that appeals for unity and peace between human "races", but that lacks a proper assessment of the historical past.

"Excepción de Raza"
By Militar Dread

Negro no significa malo, blanco no significa bueno
Es nuestra raza
Y la defiendo porque buena sangre por nuestras venas pasa
Es nuestra raza
Que representa amor y lealtad

A diferencia de otras que representan amenaza

Y hablando de amenaza, ¿por qué me tiras tú?

Ven, siéntate en mi mesa a compartir este menú

Compartiendo para tumbar esa apariencia negativa

Hay muchos hombres esperando que llegue ese día

En la unión está la fuerza y el pasado es bobería

English version:

Black does not mean bad, white does not mean good

It is our race

And I defend it because good blood runs through our veins

It is our race

Which represents love and loyalty

Unlike others which represent threat

Talking about threat, why do you attack me?

Come, sit at my table to share this menu

Sharing to destroy that negative image

Many are waiting for that day to come

Union is strength and the past is foolishness.

(Transcribed and translated by author; the emphasis added by author)

As previously noted, reggae and rap developed simultaneously in the 1990s Rap, however, appealing to a wider mass of youth, attained a more consolidated position with institutional support. But the social background of both reggae and rap fans were the same – mainly black, marginal(-ized) youth. This explains why many reggae fans performed rap before they devoted themselves to reggae, or vice versa, as they constructed identities of their own. In general, despite the conflicting views regarding commercial concessions, they have declared that both reggae and rap are essentially the same forms of expression.

The sociocultural process surrounding the emergence and development of Cuban reggae reflected its subcultural nature. In overcoming the language barrier; in facing social rejection or marginalization and racist thinking; in reaffirming blackness, African roots and racial pride; in listening to and recording from "foreign" radio stations a "foreign" music downgraded in the national media, and therefore developing alternative modes of subsistence; and in conquering social and public spaces beyond the suburban or marginal context from where they stemmed, these self-taught singers and lyric makers created a transgressive way of life which is now easily observed. The result of these expressive efforts is found in two forms of musical expressions. The first is Cuban rap which can now stand on its own, autonomous and strong in its development, and diverse in style and subject matter, but which has also been appropriated by commercial interests that make it serve different purposes. The second form of musical expression is Cuban reggae, popular with only a minority of the population, in which the adjective "Cuban" does not yet represent the same degree of independence and autonomy that the rap has already attained. Reggae has faced serious setbacks in the form of ideological, social and political prejudices which have constrained its own development possibilities. Therefore, the consciously created Cuban reggae still survives only as a "marooned" culture.

Conclusion

Reggae in the Hispanic Caribbean is usually considered one part of a major subcultural or countercultural phenomenon of post-modernity. It is usually regarded as one of the musical genres in which development has occurred in a manner typical of Maroon cultures. It is a medium of rebellious contestation rising from the underground, from marginalized positions, to permeate the formerly dominant aesthetic orders. Rock music and culture, for example, reached all the way from America to Europe; in its transnational and globalizing evolution, it embraced forms of exotic – even the erotic (as in Elvis Presley's performances) – styles never seen before. Jazz is another example of music that travelled from the United States to the Hispanic Caribbean, including Cuba, where it was initially regarded as foreign and, therefore, marginal. It later acquired "Latin" characteristics that elevated it from this initial position of inferiority. Reggae music, originating in Jamaica as a genuine expression of popular culture, spread throughout the Hispanic Caribbean as a foreign genre. Therefore, it had to evolve either as a subculture conveniently appropriated by social groups such as the upper-class whites or "blanquitos" of Puerto Rico (Giovanetti 2003, 85) or as a counterculture consciously adopted by social groups or individuals to represent their identity such as the "rastecas" (Reguillo 2000, quoted by Zuñiga 2003) of Mexico or the Nyabinghi band in Cuba.

Reggae in the Hispanic Caribbean is also certainly related to rap. What is common between reggae and rap music can be found not only in the social conditions in which they developed in the region, but also in the characteristics of social sectors and classes that welcome these two types of cultural production. In this relationship, racial affiliation is an essential concern in the lyrics of both reggae and rap.

Neither Cuba nor the Spanish-speaking Caribbean has escaped the globalization of reggae music. Nevertheless, an analysis of the different social circumstances of the wider Hispanic Caribbean as compared to those in Cuba leads to an understanding of the slower cultural evolution of reggae in Cuba. In general, just like the name of the Costa Rican group Mekatelyu (Spanish pronunciation of the Jamaican phrase "make I tell you" or "let me tell you"), reggae in the Hispanic Caribbean has still a lot to tell.

Notes

1. The presence of Rastas and reggae in Cuba started in the late 1970s and early 1980s. Although the reasons for that growth will not be explained *in extenso*, some abridged reference to these will be made later on.
2. In addition, we cannot forget the role of alternative cultures in Spain, where reggae has been simultaneously made in Spanish for the last two decades. For example, in 1984 the group Jah Macetas (meaning "Jah Flowerpots") recorded some songs in Spanish and the reggae-making tradition has gained force in the European country until the present time. Chulito Camacho released its CD *Kinky Music* in 2006. However, this chapter is not focused on the discussion about where and when reggae was first made in the Spanish language.
3. The word is derived from the mispronunciation of the English word "bunch" – a "bunch of" friends who meet to have fun as they listen to music, generally rap or reggae. This kind of music is itself called *moña* (something entangled or complicated, difficult to understand probably because of being new, foreign and in English).
4. See the track list and lyrics of the album *Natural* (2007) by Victor Montes, "Un tributo a la libertad" at http://www.salvareggae.com/index/index.php?option=com _content&do_pdf=1&id=89. Accessed 15 November 2007.
5. A musicological analysis of what is also called "Latin reggae" would reveal other elements, such as the fusion with the national genres and rhythmic structures despite

the fact that the covers and the versions of Jamaican or Western hits as well as the imitation of the Jamaican style, that is, to sound Jamaican, may also be an evident interest. However, this part of the analysis of Hispanic reggae is not the main objective here.

6. The site www.reggaelatino.com is a giant "information centre" that houses a large variety of links to other more specific webpages about the situation of the music in most countries.

7. This corresponds to the commonly used dichotomy between the dialectics "integration" and "opposition" (Aparicio and Jáquez 2003) or "transgressor" and "popular" (Furé Davis 2005).

8. Tanya Stephens, the leading contemporary Jamaican female voice, ironically uses the phrase "the music business in Kingston" in the lyrics of the song "Rebellution", from the 2006 album of the same name, to criticize the control and the indiscriminate commercialization of reggae music in the Caribbean and its appropriation by the transnational music industries in the United States and Europe. Here is my transcription of the lyric in context:

> Fake leaders claim thrones
>
> throughout their guilds and kingdoms
>
> same as the music business in Kingston
>
> when you defy for the future
>
> for all the daughters and sons
>
> instead of . . . your brothers fighting for crowns.
>
> But we will not be deterred by knives or guns.

9. Additionally, in Havana, for example there is no permanent space, such as a nightclub dedicated to reggae music (which is common in most countries). This can certainly be officially explained with arguments about the relative disproportion of the number of reggae fans and bands with respect to the cultural mainstream. However, there is no explanation from the point of view of respect to cultural diversity.

10. A personal interview by the author, Havana, November 1997.

11. The terms *rastecas* and *rastaínos* are quoted by Zúñiga (2003) from a study by Rossana Reguillo (2000). The emphasis and the translation is mine.

12. A similar movement of claiming the relevance of the indigenous populations is commonly found in other artistic manifestations, such as the visual arts and literature all over the region.

13. One example in Panama City is the young *reggaesero* (reggae singer-composer or deejay) known as "El Emperador". He effectively mixes the body language of the rapper with the dreadtalk of the Rasta thus appealing to a larger audience's attention to his uncompromising, critical lyrics in defence of the working class and the progressive ideas of SUNTRACS (the largest construction workers' trade union).

14. "Alternative" is here understood as being other than the traditional or commercial mainstream.

15. Felix Pablo Viltres, director of the Remanente reggae band, answered the question of why reggae is now in Cuba. This is taken from an interview on the radio programme *Oasis de Domingo*, Radio Taíno, Havana, 14 March 1999.
16. Although I am unable to quote the exact date and place of the interview, the launching of his album took place in Havana in 1988, when Rastafari and reggae were still far from gaining the visibility they have now in Cuba.

References

Aparicio, Frances, and Cándida Jáquez, eds. 2003. *Musical Migrations: Transnationalism and Cultural Hybridity in Latin/o America*. New York: Palgrave.

Bennett, Louise. 1966. *Jamaica Labrish*. Kingston: Sangster's.

Berger, B.M. 1971. *Looking for America*. Englewood Cliffs, NJ: Prentice Hall.

Brathwaite, Edward. 1984. *History of the Voice*. London/Port of Spain: New Beacon.

Cooper, Carolyn. 2004. *Sound Clash: Jamaican Dancehall Culture at Large*. New York: Palgrave Macmillan.

Chailloux, Graciela, ed. 2005. *¿De dónde son los Cubanos?* Havana: Ciencias Sociales.

Fernandes, Sujatha. 2006. *Cuba Represent! Cuban Art, State Power and the Making of New Revolutionary Cultures*. Durham, NC: Duke University Press.

Fernández, Ariel. 2003. "Identidades e interiores de ciertos consejos anónimos". *Movimiento: Revista Cubana de Hip Hop*, no. 1.

Furé Davis, Samuel. 2005. "Lyrical Subversion in Cuban Reggae". *Image and Narrative: Online Magazine of the Visual Narrative*, May. http://www.imageandnarrative.be.

Giovannetti, Jorge. 1995. "Del campo de batalla al salón de baile". *Revista Universidad de América* 7 (1): 28–29.

——. 2003. "Popular Music and Culture in Puerto Rico: Jamaican and Rap Music as Cross-Cultural Symbols". In *Musical Migrations*, ed. Aparicio and Jáquez, 81–98.

Moore, Robin D. 2006. *Music and Revolution: Cultural Change in Socialist Cuba*. Berkeley and Chicago: University of California Press and Center for Black Music Research.

Morales Domínguez, Esteban. 2007. *Desafíos de la problemática racial en Cuba*. Havana: Fundación Fernando Ortiz.

Moreno, José A., et al. 1998. *CUBA. Período Especial: Perspectivas*. Havana: Ciencias Sociales y Centro de Estudios Latinoamericanos de la Universidad de Pittsburgh.

Pereira, Joseph. 1994. "Translation or Transformation: Reggae Goes Spanish". In *Reggae Studies Series* (recording), 25 November. Library of the Spoken Word, University of the West Indies, Mona, Jamaica. (Transcription by the author.)

Reguillo Cruz, Rossana. 2000. *Emergencia de las culturas juveniles: Estrategias del desencanto*. Buenos Aires: Grupo Editorial Norma.

Sawyer, Mark. 2006. *Racial Politics in Post-Revolutionary Cuba*. New York: Cambridge University Press.

Stephens, Tanya. 2006. *Rebellution*. VP Records, VPCD1691.

Wulff, Helena, ed. 1995. *Youth Cultures: A Cross-Cultural Perspective*. London: Routledge.

Zúñiga Núñez, Mario. 2003. "Cartografía de los mundos posibles: miradas de protesta a la sociedad desde el rock y reggae costarricense". In *Informe final del concurso: Movimientos sociales y nuevos conflictos en América Latina y el Caribe*. Buenos Aires: Programa Regional de Becas CLACSO. http://bibliotecavirtual.clacso.org.ar/ar/libros/becas/2002/mov/zuniga.pdf. Accessed 28 January 2008.

Zurbano, Roberto. 2005. "Se buscan: Textos urgentes para sonidos ambrientos". *Movimiento: Revista Cubana de Hip Hop*, no. 3.

CHAPTER 6

REGGAE IN THE FRENCH CARIBBEAN

TEDDY ISIMAT-MIRIN

And if the future of Reggae in France was in the French West Indies." This 1999 statement from Gilbert Pytel, chief editor of the French magazine *Ragga*, illustrates the specific position held by the French Caribbean (Guadeloupe, Martinique, French Guyana) in the elucidation of the reggae movement in the French- and Creole-speaking worlds.

Very little literature has been produced about reggae music in the French West Indies as the main contribution of those islands in Caribbean music genres and their worldwide recognition has been mainly through zouk music. Although the band Kassav' remains the major music act from this region, the local reggae movement has evolved significantly over the past three decades, creating a vibrant scene that has consistently promoted its dynamism but which is presently in search of its own authenticity and viability as an industry.

The French West Indies: A Specific Context

Located in the heart of the Caribbean Basin, the French West Indies comprise the twin islands of Guadeloupe and Martinique, which are designated as Caribbean both through their geographic location and their culture. From an administrative and political point of view, Guadeloupe and Martinique are not independent but French Overseas Departments (since 1947) and regions (since 1981). The population of the area numbers some one million people, with Guadeloupe having 455,000 inhabitants, Martinique 420,000 inhabitants and French Guyana about 300,000 inhabitants.

Despite various waves of immigration which led to the settlement of some Indians, Europeans and Arabs (Lebanese and Syrians, for example) in Guadeloupe and Martinique, the population is made up mainly of African descendants. French is the official language, even if Creole is widely spoken.

The language barrier between the French West Indies and its Caribbean neighbours, as well as the relatively small population, has limited any significant development of overseas markets for culture through a relatively modest France-based diaspora (estimated at about one million people) when compared with English and the Spanish Caribbean ones.

Our Caribbean neighbours, independent states, have traditionally found it difficult to understand these young societies, but context is quite important in appreciating the development of cultural expressions as these vary according to the environment, from historical, sociological and political perspectives. So far, the French West Indian culture is known internationally mainly through sports and literature. In the area of sports there are celebrated ambassadors such as top football players Thierry Henri and Lilian Thuram, and Olympic champions such as Teddy Riner and Marie José Perec.

In literature, the *Négritude* movement led by Aimé Césaire and his companions Frantz Fanon, Leon Gontran Damas, Patrick Chamoiseau, Raphaël Confiant and Maryse Condé set the foundation and paved the way for later developments in popular culture. In the same way that the works of activists and thinkers like Marcus Garvey have pushed forward Jamaican music, the ideas and directions set by those writers, philosophers and poets have clearly inspired, directly and indirectly, generations of artists and musicians from Guadeloupe and Martinique.

Music production from Guadeloupe and Martinique can be divided into two major themes: folk and modern urban genres. Traditional genres have been, most generally, derived from African or European influences since slavery days.

1. *Gwo-ka* (most popular drum genre – Guadeloupe)
2. *Bèlè* (folk traditional drum genre – Martinique)
3. *Biguine* (derived from European genres – Guadeloupe)
4. *Mazurka* (derived from European genres – Martinique)

Since the 1980s, among modern genres, zouk has been recognized internationally. And Kassav' are genre ambassadors. Zouk remains, so far, the most prominent and popular music style in the French West Indies. In addition, due to the administrative and political relationship of those islands with France, all major popular cultural expressions have been underexposed for decades. The use of the Creole language was forbidden, folk musical expressions (such as *gwo-ka* and *bèlè*) were banned, and it was only relatively recently, since the early 1980s, that all that energy has been progressively freed. As a consequence of that delayed process of cultural appropriation, since the 1990s public opinion has been focused mainly on the conservation and valorization of heritage, local folk music and dance rather than on "imported" trends that are primarily supported by the youth. A clear understanding of this context is important in demonstrating how reggae has emerged in a market largely dominated by other local music genres.

Early Days of Reggae in the French West Indies

From a historical perspective, reggae penetrated the French Caribbean from the days of roots reggae music when the anthems of worldwide ambassadors, such as Bob Marley, Peter Tosh, Bunny Wailer, Third World, Jacob Miller, Jimmy Cliff and Burning Spear were first aired on local radio. Later in the 1980s, the London scene achieved recognition with bands like Steel Pulse and

Aswad. The favourable reception of this music in Guadeloupe and Martinique was mostly due to the quality of the music produced then and the themes that had great appeal at the time: the Third World order, equality and justice, black consciousness and repatriation to Africa. The first local reggae nights date from the 1980s with the Rasta communities in Guadeloupe and Martinique. In Martinique, RBR radio was already broadcasting reggae programmes with pioneer artists like General Tcho, Daddy Harry and Ruben Pat.

Among the first local productions in the early 1980s was the Martinique band Sixth Continent led by musical icon Kali. In anthems like "Reggae Dom-Tom", the themes related to French West Indian cultural identity, the need for strengthened Caribbean links and the limits of the political relationship with France were already being laid by these pioneers of Creole reggae. The popular success of Sixth Continent even led to a major deal with the CBS label in 1983 and opened the way for several major live performances in France and Europe. The main impact of those early local productions was to raise the consciousness among those who wanted to use reggae music as an instrument of expression for the French West Indian social and political context. Besides themes of repatriation to Africa, themes specifically related to Guadeloupe and Martinique emerged, such as pride in Creole culture and recognition of a French Afro-Caribbean identity.

Beyond the aura of Bob Marley, one of the main lessons from that period was that reggae had a negative image among the local music industry players and audience because of its close association, in Guadeloupe and Martinique, with the "unwholesome" image of dreads and Rastafarian communities. In those days, due to negative stereotypes, reggae was seen as related to crime and violence. Reggae was also linked to the illegal immigration of some gangsters and drug dealers from nearby Dominica. That harmful image has been exaggerated by the local media for years and has also tarnished the image of reggae.

The Sound System Era and Birth of Local Production

The popularity of reggae music can be traced back to the late 1980s and early 1990s when the deejay style was booming in Jamaica with artists like Yellowman, Fathead, Toyan and Eek-a-Mouse. That movement also led to the

6.1, 6.2, 6.3 Reggae ambassadors such as Peter Tosh (6.1), Bob Marley (6.2) and Jimmy Cliff (6.3) were first aired on local radio French Caribbean from the days of roots reggae music. Courtesy of the Gleaner Company.

explosion of local Creole production because this music was easier to produce for sound systems and DJs than that of the heavy, live, roots reggae
bands. In the 1980s, Jamdown, a record shop located in Pointe-à-Pitre, Guadeloupe started to distribute reggae records imported straight from Kingston.
I remember how entering that shop was like diving into Jamaica and the reggae culture, thanks to a broad selection of brand new releases, albums, posters, crafts and so on. This distribution outlet, along with independent imports
in Martinique, started fuelling the growth of a vibrant fan base and apprentice
deejays. Like its Jamaican model, the development of the reggae movement
in the French Caribbean islands emerged from the sound systems, and that
period launched the era of the reign of sound systems and the deejay style.

In Martinique, the first discos appeared in the late 1980s in downtown areas
like the Texaco district. At the same time, in Guadeloupe, the birth of a local
reggae scene came out of the emergence of the first local discos such as King
Majesty with pioneer King Charly in the ghetto area of Boissard. The music
played was essentially Jamaican, even if local artists like Ragga Bolo and
Daddy Yod started then by deejaying on seven-inch B sides. Local production
emerged when the Guadeloupean band and sound system Freedom Fighters
(with Ras Abbya) made waves with the first local hit "Corine", released in 1992.
Between 1990 and 1995, the band Neg Radikal and three major sound systems emerged in Guadeloupe: 3 Dom, Influence Sound and Karukera Sound
System (KSS). The sound system 3 Dom was led by MC Dalton, who was also
a member of Freedom Fighters. Influence Sound originated in Pointe-à-Pitre
and promoted a generation of artists including Tiwony, Boubou and Kulcha B.

Karukera Sound System was formed by Brother Jimmy (a performer who
returned from France and who was active through the Stand Tall sound) and
Pupa Alain (former selector for the King Majesty sound) and myself, on my
return from my first trip to Jamaica in 1995. *Karukera* was the Carib name for
Guadeloupe and the symbolism was clear. The sound system had the largest
crew in those days with twelve deejays who hailed from all over the island
and two selectors who played an important role in promoting the use of dub
plates. It was the first Guadeloupean sound to play both Jamaican (Buju Banton, Anthony B, Capleton, Sizzla) and local acts in French and Creole. Thanks
to a rich reggae culture and a clear strategy for development, KSS is credited with promoting many local artists in those years in Guadeloupe. Other
crews like Neg Radikal were very active both as sound systems and groups of

6.4 Daddy Yod. Photo: Sidney Kwanone.

recording artists. Neg Radikal, in particular, was led by Laion P. At the same time, in Martinique, King Kalabash and Baron Black for Big Family Sound were some of the pioneers along with Mc Far I. Ac Tone sound system was also ruling with Daddy Harry and Don Miguel, who also went into music production.

One difference marked the development of reggae between the two islands in the French Caribbean. Martinique developed a live tradition with numerous backing bands while Guadeloupe concentrated more on sound system units. The live tradition in Martinique and the better organization of the music market paved the way for a more active reggae scene. In Martinique, production really boomed after 1992 and 1993 when Daddy Harry and Don Miguel released the first local dancehall album, and compilations like *Martinique Dancehall*, *Dancehall Party* and *Dancehall News*. These were followed by numerous compilations like *Ragga Sun Hit* (1993) which revealed artists like Princess Lover and Master Mx, Janik and Metal Sound. Among other influential productions we can name *Dancehall Party* (1994), *Daddy Pleen and Doctor Charly* (1995) and ABM crew, who released the local hit "Marco". Above all, another local band, Metal Sound (with Guy al Mc, Skanky and Prince Radikal), set the trend over a period of eight years in the 1990s. The first album sold about twenty thousand units, and the crew will go down in history thanks to their great use of Creole, catchy riddims and promotion of themes that spoke to the public. These pioneers set the foundation for the development of the local reggae movement and the act that authenticated the movement was the use of Creole language (patois) and lyrics adapted to the local context. In the late 1990s and early 2000s came the domination of Ruff Neg crew with Kulu G, Daddy Pleen, Matinda

6.5 Karukera Sound System, 1995, featuring Neg Radikal, Influence Sound and Slykee. Photo: Daniel Goudrouffe.

and Ras Daniel (Dons Music Production), who sold over forty thousand singles and released three popular albums. They were followed by another famous producer, Laurent Leduc, whose productions "Red Zone" and "Maxi Dubplate" introduced artists like Papa Tank.

Martinique confirmed its supremacy with artists like Lord Kossity and Yaniss Odua buzzing in France. The role played by sound systems was crucial to the development of a real generation of local artists and a local reggae movement, as the artists linked to those discos have been dominant for years. The use and adaptation of Jamaican riddims was the rule, particularly those derived from the *bam bam* riddim (produced by Jamaica's Sly and Robbie).

After the leadership of the Martinique scene and thanks to an efficient management, links with some of Kingston's best studios (Arrows, Jammy's), music distributors together with a strong reggae culture, KSS exploded as the most popular sound in Guadeloupe. Without any media support and thanks to innovative concepts, KSS produced underground shows with audiences of over a thousand people. In 1995, in celebration of the abolition of slavery in the French West Indies, KSS invited "the outlaw" Terry Ganzie to perform at one of the best dancehall nights ever produced in Guadeloupe. After a memorable sound reunion in Guadeloupe between KSS and Ac Tone, the leading Guadeloupean sound won its first album deal with Don's Music label from Martinique. In 1995, *L'album* was released and launched a new generation of artists who are still active. At the same time, rival sound, Influence Sound, was also launching its first album (Riko Records) but with a more limited echo.

All those references testify to how active the 1990s were, particularly for the Creole reggae movement in Guadeloupe and Martinique; one justification is that all sound systems and bands were managed by real fans driven by a strong reggae culture. Despite some differences between those local music crews, there was a clear will to promote local artists from those days. I remember many shows in which reggae or dancehall acts gained more reaction from the public than zouk artists, and this was often not welcome from the perspective of the media and local promoters. We were still suffering from a ban on local radio stations of the so-called raggamuffin music despite the fact that Shabba Ranks and Chaka Demus and Pliers were conquering the air waves at the same time. Despite increasing popular support, I remember one day in 1995 when I was thrown out of a major FM radio station, Sun FM, where I had gone to propose the submission of some reggae for broadcast – dancehall singles straight from Kingston. And even though there was growing public recognition, there was still a long way to go as Creole reggae could not reach any mainstream market because it was seen as a community movement.

Migration to France

In that difficult context, despite a local dynamism, the lack of a positive local image and absence of viable producers and musicians led most of the first generation of French Caribbean artists to leave for France, traditionally the country of migration (like the United States for the rest of the Caribbean countries). Over the years, these artists have also contributed significantly to the dynamism of the French reggae market. At the same time, France is recognized as one of the most important global markets for music, particularly reggae music, and that position has enabled some positive developments for talented artists from Guadeloupe and Martinique. Local acts such as Guadeloupe's "King" Daddy Yod and "Martinique child" Mc Janik left early in the 1990s for France. Daddy Yod promptly released his first single "Rock en Zonzon" on *Rapattitude vol. 1* which sold over one hundred thousand copies in France. Born in Guadeloupe, Yod established his talent among French sound systems like Youthman Acadamy (with African DJ Pablo Master) and launched his first successful album *Redoutable* in the late 1980s. It was followed by the LP *King Daddy Yod*, which included the popular hit "Faut pas taper la doudou" ("Don't Hit the Girl"). Over his career, Daddy Yod released six albums and still appears as a veteran of the Creole scene. Another significant initiative came from Ragga Dub Force Massive (both backing band and sound system) when they produced, in 1991, a compilation with French Caribbean acts like Féfé Typical, Nuttea, Jah Mike and Daddy Yod.

After 1994, Groovin, a sound system and record label, started gathering artists from among French West Indians in France, such as Straika D, Guy Al and Mc Janik. Janik was one of the best deejays that had worked with Martinique sound systems, but he had left the island. In 1998 he released his successful album *Mc Janik* with a major company (Delabel), on which he included the Secteur Ä, who are a famous crew of hip-hop artists. This work was fol-

6.6 MC Janik. Photo: Dublivity.

lowed by the LP *T'inquiète* in 2002. Janik has been very productive and always maintained his Creole identity even on the French market. A few other inspirational acts, such as Ragga Bolo, also paved the way for the next generation.

Daddy Nuttea and Lord Kossity

Born in Guadeloupe and raised in France, Daddy Nuttea is, so far, the best-selling reggae artist in France. After years of operating sound systems in France (High Fight, Stand Tall), Nuttea became a key figure in French reggae music in the late 1990s as he brought the reggae and dancehall culture into the mainstream. He first appeared on some compilations (such as *Ragga Dub Force* and *Rapattitude*) and released four major albums: his single "Elle te rend dingue" went gold with 1.5 million singles sold in 2001; his album *Un Signe du Temps* sold over 450,000 copies but his last album, *Urban Voodoo*, came out in 2004 and had less commercial success. And then there is Lord Kossity. Initially a deejay and radio personality, he appeared in 1995 on a compilation entitled *V.I.P.* and exploded with his appearance on the local hit "Vanessa" (featuring Don Miguel and Fabien). Kossity then moved to France and has been very prolific. He has released nine albums thus far. He made waves very promptly with a hit single alongside hip-hop band NTM. The song "Ma Benz" sold over 150,000 copies. In 2002, he won a French music award for best reggae-ragga artist. Then, in 2005, an album named *Booming System* was released, with collaborations featuring Shaggy, Elephant Man, Toots and Vybz Kartel. He also recorded the hit "Hey Sexy Wow" featuring Chico. The video was widely aired, even on Jamaican channels. Another artist, Yaniss Odua, emerged as one of Martinique's favourite sons. He started with Daddy Harry in sound systems, left for France where he collaborated with the Mek it Happen label (linked with Lord Kossity), and then gained popularity. He signed a deal in 2002 with major record company, Small, to produce his first album *Yon pa yon*. All these artists are still active and touring in the French Caribbean, France and some European countries (Switzerland, Italy and Germany).

Despite recognized artistic talent, beyond the few big names listed above, most of the artists from the French Caribbean have never really succeeded in gaining mainstream success in France. To go mainstream, artists from the Caribbean have to sing in French and avoid Creole expressions, but in doing so they are in danger of losing their initial fan base as well as support from the

6.7 Nuttea on the cover of the French magazine Ragga. Photo: Ragga.

French Caribbean and from our diaspora in France. That search for a balance between an authentic Creole influence and constraints created by media and music labels whose aim is to penetrate the French market has been the hurdle of the past decade.

Connections between the French West Indies and Jamaica

Reggae artists from Guadeloupe and Martinique have traditionally established and maintained links with their Jamaican counterparts. For those who have travelled to each of these islands, it is clear that they share many cultural and human similarities. Many artistic exchanges have occurred over three decades. Kassav' diva Jocelyne Beroard was called on by Lee Scratch Perry of the Black Ark Studio in Kingston for some backing sessions. Sound systems like KSS and Ac

6.8 Caribbean Xplosion
tour poster. Photo: KSS.

Tone were pioneers in cutting Jamaican plates with top Jamaican artists. Presently, most newcomers record specials exclusively via the Internet.

In terms of production, MC Janik set a precedent when he left Martinique in 1993 to record his first LP, *Mc Beaucoup,* in King Jammy's studio in Waterhouse. His album *T'inquiète* was produced by Tyrone Downie in 2002. Nuttea also had numerous collaborations with Steely and Clevie, Handel Tucker, Luciano and Richie Stephens, among others. Kossity has also collaborated on albums and singles; for example, recording with Shaggy, Vybz Kartel and Chico. There have also been several singles including Saël and Bounty Killer (2007), and Admiral T and TOK (2006). Tiwony and Féfé Typical have worked with Determine, Future Trouble and Anthony Red Rose (Revolution, 2005). Fashion and Model icon Mounia also went to Tuff Gong for some 2002 recordings for her first album, entitled *Groovin.*

From an artistic and technical point of view, those collaborations have been mostly effective and quality projects. However, we do deplore the difficulty sometimes experienced in getting Jamaican artists to open up to other Caribbean and international acts. Even though Jamaica will forever be credited with giving birth to reggae music, they need to understand how some selected collaborations can open new avenues for the music. From the French Caribbean perspective, the time has come, also, to move away from the Jamaican model.

Society, Language and Identity

In comparison with the Jamaican model, some peculiarities can be identified in the so-called Creole reggae scene. First, the social context in Guadeloupe and Martinique is totally different from Jamaica as, instead of a dual society constructed mainly of high and low classes, the middle class is dominant. After the first generation of local artists, the reggae music fans and production base have moved from some depressed areas (so-called ghettos) to other parts of the island and various social classes. Moreover, political tension, which is the source of many additional evolutions of the music in Jamaica, was not present in the same way in Guadeloupe or Martinique. Reggae is not the domestic musical genre in the French West Indies. In short, reggae music in the French Caribbean did not benefit from the same sources of inspiration as in Jamaica.

The use of Creole reflects another vision, considering that each language has its own dynamics. In an interview released in the French music magazine *L'Affiche* in December 1994, Skanky (the lead singer of Metal Sound) said: "We sing in Creole because we think in Creole before thinking in French and because everybody understands Creole." As with Jamaican musicians and patois in some international markets, French Caribbean reggae artists have faced huge hurdles due to the use of Creole language in markets largely dominated by the French. From the early days, even top-selling artists from the region (such as Metal Sound and Ruff Neg) failed to reach a wider audience in France. It is notable that even Kassav', the creators of zouk music, have also faced this problem. But since the 1980s, they have never stepped back in terms of the use of Creole in their music production. As has been mentioned previously, all artists who found success in mainstream French markets (for example, Daddy Yod, Nuttea and Lord Kossity) had to sing in French. It is also true that some of them tended to avoid Creole in order to get contracts. It was hard to imagine that a Creole artist could get a major response in France.

In the year 2000 there was a tight opposition from France to West Indian reggae, considering the "creole invasion" that culminated when Big Red, a member of well-known band Raggasonic, declared that he did not like West Indians. The cornerstone of that language struggle and dilemma has been the *Mozaik Kréyol* album project that I led between 2002 and 2005 for Guadeloupean and KSS artist Admiral T. So many lessons on the Creole movement can be taken from that project. Much more than an album, the project boomed in 2003 in the context of making a strong declaration in favour of emphasizing Creole identity.

On the KSS label, we had achieved significant developmental work on reggae sound systems and our top artist Admiral T was enjoying some of the greatest buzz over the past decade in the French West Indies. After having produced Admiral T's first single "Gwadada", which was a big local hit, we negotiated some deals for an album. Acting as KSS's manager (with Brother Jimmy), I remember a meeting with a Paris label head who came straight to Guadeloupe. She was interested in a contract with Admiral T, but her main request was that the artist sing most of his songs in French. As we were deeply convinced that it was the right time to break away from that tradition, we finally signed with Martinique-based label Don's Music, who gave us total creative autonomy on the project. The album was dubbed *Mozaik Kréyol* to illustrate the richness and diversity of modern popular Creole culture on which the album was focused. A lot has been said and written about this album, but I will focus on the album intro, which is a statement of pride and definition of Creole culture. One significant point of information is that it was written in dedication to a well-known and old Guadeloupean poet, Guy Cornely, who decades before had released a powerful poem entitled "Guadeloupe".

From its launch this album was a big hit in Guadeloupe, Martinique and in the French Caribbean diaspora but it gained the respect of the whole French music industry the night that Admiral T mashed up the stage of the Zenith Hall in Paris and stole the show, as he was the opening act for international dancehall star Sean Paul. The rest is history. The *Mozaik Kréyol* has been signed by AZ/Universal for the French market under a licence deal, and it has expanded the career of Admiral T, who has collaborated with Wyclef Jean and French hip-hop leaders Rohff and Diam's. It was the first time that an independent artist, straight from Guadeloupe, had reached that level of success without compromising the Creole expression.

Within ten years, the message of sound systems like KSS and artists like Admiral T had moved successfully from nights in Guadeloupe to the biggest stages of France. Admiral T, through *Mozaik Kréyol*, has influenced not only generations of artists but also the public. *Mozaik Kréyol* project proved that reggae and dancehall had gained respect and credit for building an authentic, new reggae sound. From a Caribbean perspective, *Mozaik Kréyol* included collaborations with soca diva Alison Hinds and hip-hop icon Wyclef Jean. Far from being obstacles, *kréyol* elements have contributed to the authenticity and viability of a specific "Creole reggae".

Music production is another field of experimentation for the authenticity of Creole reggae. In its early days, it was natural that the Creole reggae movement would be under the influence of Jamaican trends, but it was also accused of imitation. After the emergence of local artists from sound systems, a new generation of music composers also appeared. In Martinique, Levy, leader of the RMTG backing band, was the mastermind behind most local reggae productions. Laurent Leduc was another producer. In Guadeloupe, various composers did some interesting work, but it was more underground.

A shared goal of Guadeloupe and Martinique has been the search for an authentic reggae and dancehall sound, somewhere between traditional sounds (such as the previously mentioned *gwo-ka*, *bèlè*, *beguine* and zouk) and authentic reggae groove and culture. From this point of view, DJ Exxos can be hailed as one the most innovative composers, as he is the creator of a new music genre called *kako.* An impressive compilation of *kako*, dubbed *Pass di rhum* was released in 2004. Some recordings have been done also with Jamaican artists such as Sanchez and Capleton. This confirms that new music productions from the French West Indies can gain regional and international appeal.

The Present Reggae Market in the French West Indies

After two decades of development of reggae in the French Caribbean, a new generation has emerged. But a major feature of the reggae market in this region is that it is still divided into two segments, reggae and dancehall. If reggae attracts a more adult public, the audience for the dancehall segment is the youth. The core audience is the fifteen- to twenty-five-year-old range and this fact affects other aspects of the market.

One sign of the dynamism of the Creole reggae scene may be found in the great number of artists involved. From that perspective, although reggae music is still strong, dancehall is currently playing the major role. The late 1990s and early 2000s have confirmed the explosion of present Creole reggae icon, Admiral T. As mentioned above, *Mozaik Kréyol* became a cornerstone of the movement because it sent a strong message and met with huge success. Both Admiral T albums have sold about eighty thousand copies in the French West Indies and in France. A new dancehall performer named Krys emerged in Guadeloupe in 2006 and was signed promptly to Universal France. In Martinique, the much talented singer Saël has been performing since 1996, and has released a few singles. His first album sold forty thousand units. Apart from those two major artists, the other local performers have had only local exposure, but many deejays and singers are very productive. In Martinique, we can name artists like Straika D, Easy Kenenga, Kalash, Lieutenant, Valley, Paille, Nyala and Mighty Kila. In Guadeloupe, many local acts are presently releasing new music, including Krys, Tiwony (with significant developments in Jamaica and Africa) and Saik. Regarding musicians, a few live bands perform at the underground level, but there is no major recognized reggae band.

New Production Models

For years, most reggae producers came from Martinique; I refer to artists like Admiral T (signed under Don's Music Label) and Krys (with the Kickkilla crew). So far, the major local production company remains Don's Music, which has a significant portfolio of local acts and a series of hits with various Jamaican acts. Production – and the lack of studios – has always been a constraint in the emergence of reggae in the French Caribbean, but in the past ten years major evolutions in technology have opened up new opportunities for independent productions and labels. Unfortunately, the poor quality of those new productions has lowered the level and impact of the reggae scene. Due to the profile of the audience and artists (mainly young people) and versatility, new genres such as electro seem to be emerging as competition for the reggae and dancehall movement. This has meant a return to a basic core of fans. Most of the former big labels and studios have disappeared in favour of independent and small units. The production expertise is also suffering as a result of increasing self-production and very modest labels.

Distribution Crisis

Despite an increasing number of local acts and productions, distribution has been following the same negative international trends: specifically a sharp fall of sales figures due to piracy. The biggest sellers are still overseas-based artists like Lord Kossity and Nuttea. But, apart from the two major local acts (Admiral T and Krys), most productions sell under five thousand units. All independent distributors have closed, and the major distribution networks are through megastores. When you consider that the credibility of some music genres and artists is directly related to sales figures, this is one area in which Creole reggae has to prove that it is representative.

Lack of Specialized Media

In the French West Indies, there is no media house that specializes in reggae. *Dancehall News*, a twenty-six-minute television programme produced by Don's Music, is aired weekly in Martinique and Guadeloupe. It is available to viewers by satellite. Two monthly French papers (*Ragga* and *Natty Dread*) were distributed until the closure of *Ragga Magazine* in 2007 and launch of a new edition, *Reggae*. Many websites like Reggaefrance.com or Reggae.fr are still promoting Creole reggae music, but the real buzz is increasingly created on social networks where artists can promote their music directly and at a low cost. The lack of media exposure also explains the gap in external recognition for the music.

Perspectives and Challenges

As a real fan of reggae music for over twenty years, I have developed a clear vision of both the Jamaican and French West Indian contexts and recognize that the challenges for the proper development of the music emerge from both sides – the French Caribbean and Jamaica. Creole reggae has its own characteristics. There are almost three generations of artists that support and promote the music. From an artistic level, Creole is real. It speaks for itself and about its own culture. Some developments have occurred such that Creole artists have found their audience locally and in France.

Since 1995, from the numerous direct contacts I have had with Jamaican music industry stakeholders, I have discovered a kind of misunderstanding about reggae music. As creators of reggae music, Jamaicans feel that no one in the world can compete with Jamaican productions. We have to overcome that perspective and narrow vision. I remember some discussions at King Jammy's studio as I was explaining how we had reached a stage of development where some French Caribbean acts sell more and reach a wider audience than many top Jamaican acts. Such a situation was somewhat still unbelievable for Jamaican musicians. But I am convinced that we have really reached a level where some reggae evolutions worldwide have found their own audiences beyond the initial core.

In its homeland, Creole reggae has gained full market control, and it has to get that respect and recognition from its Jamaican audience. Despite the fact that, so far, Creole reggae has not generated internationally acclaimed names, the movement still enjoys its own strength and creativity. The relatively limited impact of the francophone community, compared to the English, may be the main reason. The evolution of reggae in the French West Indies demonstrates its own characteristics and, consequently, has its own perspectives and challenges. The main one is to become independent of the Jamaican model and find its own path. Although it might be a long process, that perspective also brings a great number of opportunities.

The past years have shown an increase in collaborations between French West Indian and Jamaican artists and, once again, I will point to the example of KSS to illustrate this fact. In 2005, in the context of its tenth anniversary, KSS and Don's Music produced a concept album called *Caribbean Sessions* dedicated to the promotion of all Caribbean music genres. Even though we are devoted to the development of reggae music, the key objective, from our perspective, was to open new avenues and show how we could benefit from new experiments and fusions. In that spirit, the album mixed artists from seven Caribbean countries (Guadeloupe, Martinique, French Guyana, Jamaica, Trinidad and Tobago, Barbados, and Dominica) and experimented with different styles and genres. The album led to a live experience in Paris and a project of regional cooperation focused on music.

Even if there is a desire to keep the original flavour of reggae music, there is a wide scope for experimentation among some selected Caribbean music styles. Reggae can develop through exchanges with zouk, soca, salsa and any other genre. In Guadeloupe, new urban genres have emerged;

one of them was the *kako* music developed by DJ Exxos. That *kako* sound came out of a fusion of folk and urban influences, a mix of traditional Afro-Caribbean sounds like *gwo-ka* with so called urban genres (hip-hop and dance-hall). Major local acts from reggae and dancehall (Admiral T) and zouk (Dominik Coco) have already seized the style, and powerful Jamaican dub plates have been recorded on *kako* tracks. Collaborative projects between Jamaican and French West Indians could be supported through emerging styles like *kako*.

In that same spirit, another significant initiative emerged in 2003 with a show dubbed *Dub N Ka* which featured – for the first time – combinations of folk and *gwo-ka* icons with leaders of the new generation from dancehall, reggae and hip-hop. Two live tours were produced and also a live album and DVD were released. In Martinique, the same movement occurred with the *Bèlè Boum Bap* project led and produced by Kali (former leader of veteran band, Sixth Continent). The project combined folk *bèlè* artists and hip-hop and dancehall acts. These recent productions received a popular response, considering a central interest in the French West Indies on the gap between generations and the need to maintain local musical and cultural traditions in the face of emerging urban styles.[1]

There is a clear need for increased collaborations, particularly with Haiti and the whole Creole community (including Dominica and St Lucia) to build up a viable Creole community, not only through reggae but also other repre-sentative cultural expressions. The weaknesses remain structural, meaning a lack of technical expertise in the music business, including management, production and promotion.

Conclusion

After almost two decades of existence, Creole reggae has justified its exis-tence and its potential for creativity and development, specifically with some strategic linkages to the French market.

History has shown that it is still growing and changing from an "imported" music genre to an authentic movement. The use of Creole language to express local realities from a historical and social context is what gives the movement its own authenticity. That trend is not specific to reggae but embraces a wider "urban" movement including hip-hop, slam and other artistic expressions.

Jamaica has proved its creativity and authenticity by creating the original reggae music genre but it will have to accommodate itself to the opening up of external evolutions of that music. On our side, one of the main challenges will depend on the capacity of the new generations to develop and appropriate a real reggae music culture in the long run, on a new business model and in a new technological environment. From this perspective and with reference to the hymn to identity dubbed *In Praise of Creoleness* (Barnabé, Chamoiseau and Confiant), we can reasonably hope that Creole reggae becomes a "verticality" of our French Caribbean societies.

Note

1. A new fusion experimentation also comes from reggae singer Cali P, the son of a Swiss mother and a Rastafarian father from Guadeloupe. He fully embraces both Jamaican and Guadeloupean cultures. Blessed with a distinctive vocal talent and thought-provoking lyrical content, Cali P released his first single in early 2005, "Forward", on the Pow Pow label. The track generated international attention, paving the way for Cali P to release more than thirty other songs on seven-inch vinyl, mix tapes or compilations. In 2008 he released his debut album, *Lyrical Faya*, as well as the soundtrack for the American Freeski DVD *Idea*, the latter selling over twenty thousand copies. This was also the beginning of a new adventure: Cali P and Tanner Hall (the freeski legend) collaborated to produce the award-winning soundtrack for the Red Bull ski movie *The Massive*. Over the year 2011, Cali P has gained increased recognition from Jamaican fans and the music industry.

Reference

Barnabé, Jean, Patrick Chamoiseau and Raphaël Confiant. 1989. *In Praise of Creoleness (Éloge de la créolité)*. Paris: Gallimard.

CHAPTER 7

REGGAE MUSIC DOCUMENTARIES IN BRAZIL

LEONARDO VIDIGAL

Modalities of human expression – popular music, movies and audio-visual media – were not developed in isolation but through constant interaction. In the social circle of the cultural market, the relationship between the phonographic and the cinematographic industry is ancient, starting at least from the first talking pictures and movie soundtracks. The formula of a well-known soundtrack or the presence of a musical idol, as movie box office boost, has been many times applied, at times with great success.

Movie and Popular Music Interaction

The music industry has also benefited from this movie connection, as many films bring new bands and singers to new audiences. In most cases, such relationships represent just another component of a bigger strategy to instigate the commercial consumption of specific movies, artists and music, which are often quickly forgotten. This happens in many parts of the world, creating a gigantic audio-visual pile, now more accessible than ever due to the varied media available to the public.

In Brazil, there were a relevant number of movies which popularized musical genres nationally. The Jovem Guarda craze, for example, was a local rock 'n' roll movement from the 1960s which was popularized by movies and television programmes. But this Brazilian example did not resonate as strongly as the many musical genres which owe their spread to movies produced in the United States.[1] Some of them contributed decisively to the creation of affinity and musical memory, both conditioned to each other. These contributions were done individually as well as collectively, many times at an international level and in a broader way than what was previously planned. This strategy is present in films such as *Rock Around the Clock* (directed by Fred Sears in 1956), an important landmark in the ascension of rock 'n' roll into popular culture; *Saturday Night Fever* (directed by John Badham in 1977), which was crucial for the popularization of disco music around the world; or even *Colors* (directed by Dennis Hopper in 1988), which went far beyond the hip-hop ghetto areas of its subject matter.

Nonetheless, there was a case of movie and popular music interaction that, undoubtedly, inverted the production, distribution and exhibition routes, turning a Third World's cultural manifestation into a significant and influential cultural force in both the Northern and Southern hemispheres. This cultural manifestation is reggae music. The 1972 full-length film *The Harder They Come* directed in Jamaica by Jamaican filmmaker Perry Henzell[2] was considered by many authors as one of the main triggers of this process of cultural propagation. The compilation and commercialization of *The Harder They Come* soundtrack was done by the English-Jamaican Island Records, a fact that incited rumours about the movie being just a product of a strategy to make reggae commercially acceptable for the American and European publics (Gilroy 1991; Thelwell 1992; Barrow and Dalton 1997).[3] Certainly, Island

Records' commercial interests played a decisive part, which can also be confirmed by the recording and promotion of *Catch a Fire*, the first Bob Marley and the Wailers' album (they were not in the movie).[4] *The Harder They Come* was also a direct and indirect inspiration for other reggae-themed fictional movies, documentaries, music videos and shows, many financed by Island Records. However, the insertion of *The Harder They Come* into a specific strategy must be confronted against the precise production, distribution and exhibition circumstances, a subject that is not the topic of this chapter.

In order to establish a more precise theme, it is necessary to clarify that, far from being an isolated case, *The Harder They Come* can be studied as a vector of a wider network of transcultural communications. The transcultural aspect of this process becomes explicit through audio-visual means. Popular music, which easily goes beyond the established borders in the juridical and economical circumstances with a fluidity that has accelerated, has made this expressive network of transcultural connections even broader. It is a transcultural and complex process because this network transcends cultural limitations and even defies the usual conceptions of culture as a well-defined set of human expressions, solidly linked to a given territory. Thus, the present chapter approaches a part of this network's development and some of its elements as they articulate sounds, music and images.

However, working with movies, video and other media as primary sources for the study of reggae's network is quite complex. The complexity lies in the idea that, even when a movie is a self-defined documentary, it does not portray an objective record of a pre-existing society (Bitomsky 2001). Nonetheless, these movies create a possible audio-visual organization that can be called a "composition", which is seen as an "arrangement" of visual and musical elements. There are many variables involved, conditioned by many factors, places and people who are part of the movies, along with the available equipment, the budget and the variety of ways to look at, listen to and conceive of what is filmed. Such composition is also interpreted in many forms, according to the macro references related to the time and space of what is shown, and the micro references of each spectator, about the sonorities and the iconography presented. In order to better understand and to reveal this network of complex transcultural relations, this article will approach the works individually, searching the many audio-visual media for the echoes and the resonances that resulted from the dialogue between them (Mota 2006).

To reach this goal, this chapter will first analyse two Brazilian television programmes from the 1990s. *Jamaica: o Paraíso do Reggae* and *Documento Especial: Maranhão em Ritmo de Reggae* were chosen because of the way they create reality. After that, it will present some of the many constructions of Jamaica and popular music in the movies from the 1930s up to *The Harder They Come* in 1972. The movie *The Harder They Come* will also be analysed and reinserted in this image and sound network as it is seen today, linking language with the construction of an audio-visual composition.

Music and Iconography in the Caribbean Eden

Broadcast at the end of 1992 by Rede Bandeirantes, a private Brazilian TV channel, the programme *Jamaica: o Paraíso do Reggae* (*Jamaica: Reggae's Paradise*) was written, directed and edited on video by a team of Brazilian producers.[5] Recorded on the Caribbean island, it follows the format of the Brazilian TV journalism's special reports, with off-screen narration and a supposedly objective and impartial approach. The title *Jamaica: o Paraíso do Reggae* refers to the colonial discourse that has always associated the New World with the lost paradise, a place ready to be discovered and rescued for the joy of a privileged élite (an approach that is still often used by tourist companies). In effect, during its sixty minutes, the editing of *Jamaica: o Paraíso do Reggae* allows it to act as a cicerone showing the audience the many paradisiacal tourist attractions of the island. On the other hand, the evocation of the Genesis biblical myth suggests that reggae will be found at its own source, where it should exist in abundance. In this sense, *Jamaica: o Paraíso do Reggae* presents a history of Jamaican popular music which reflects the specialized literature on this subject. However, the music appears merely as an external element of the narrative, especially on the soundtrack associated with archival footage and the music videos shown during and at the end of each segment.

Only during the second half of the programme, when the narrative follows Bob Marley's steps through the slums of Trench Town, does the television crew finally show reggae *in loco*. This happens when the crew watches the rehearsal of the modest College Band, in a small shack where, according to the narration, "reggae's roots are still alive". The band's music continues after the crew leaves the shack, and it is used as a soundtrack for close-ups on the inhabitants of the community. The segment ends with a music video of a Black Uhuru song with a revealing title: "Solidarity". This shows that the school of reggae that the producers of the programme were looking for was what the off-screen narration calls "traditional reggae", with their "freedom and social justice themes". After these characteristics are listed by the narration, the singer and actor Jimmy Cliff shows up and comments: "you can't get justice without fighting for it, because they won't give it to you", evoking his character Ivan from *The Harder They Come*.

This concept of reggae is connected to the music videos that present successful bands and artistes such as Third World and Bob Marley (who were in three of the ten music videos shown in the programme). The first segments clearly show that Bob Marley is the main character of *Jamaica: o Paraíso do Reggae*. He is the most cited artist in the testimonies and the only one that deserved to have part of his personal history narrated. However, Marley's story is abandoned in the middle of the programme and only referred to again in the end; although this later reference lacks the intensity of the first segments.

In contrast with the reggae sought by the production crew, the dancehall genre is treated differently; it is a smaller segment of the programme, accompanied by a narration which utilizes expressions such as "commercial reggae" or "dance club reggae". The lyrics are described as having only "social and sexual themes", but their characteristics are not detailed, only suggested. However, on the few Jamaican dancehall music videos that are shown in the programme, the artists appear to be closer to their public than reggae musicians. Fab Five's video for "Jamaican Woman" is presented in this segment as dancehall and as an example of this, band members appear with local women, who are portrayed at work or having fun at bars.

However, in the images presented in the programme, there is a predominance of people, close-ups as well as long shots that do not depict an individual human figure. This, for example, isolates the Trench Town community leader or shows an empty Maroon community in the images. Presented as such, the sounds and images leave little place for the social dimension where reggae's solidarity values, established by the programme, could be practised. From the beginning, *Jamaica: O Paraíso do Reggae* establishes a distance from the natives and justifies it as coming from the Jamaicans. This message is palpable in the scenes of a Kingston market, where the narrator's voice tells us that "a tense atmosphere is present on the faces of the people, who hate being filmed". This narration is carried over an image of a market woman, caught through a camera zoom. The market woman, at first, looks towards the spectator in a suspicious way. Next, she turns away and looks to the side, a moment which is immediately frozen by the editing, emphasizing her anti-social behaviour. On the tourist dedicated segments, this distance creates emptiness and provokes a revealing incongruence between the narration and the image.

The programme discloses the effort of the television crew to present stable and recognizable visual and sound references for the Brazilian audience, using images of bands, beaches, Rastafari, marijuana plantations and the local population. However, the "postcard" aesthetics of the framing; the incongruence among text, image and music; and the social emptiness all reveal the rhetorical stratagems, the rough discursive stitches and the mercantilist intention under a thin cover of contestation. In general terms, the programme's concept of a Jamaican Eden was an incomplete official history, and not a living memory based on a daily praxis. The producers of *Jamaica: o Paraíso do Reggae* may have tried to create a Jamaica that no longer exists, but they ended up revealing that they were looking for the Jamaica created by movies and tourist folders. This audio-visual "Jamaica" will be detailed later, but first it is necessary to analyse another audio-visual composition presented by Brazilian television. This is a different programme, one which does not look for Jamaica *in loco*, but in an unexpected place: Brazil.

Maranhão: The Brazilian Jamaica

Documento Especial: Televisão Verdade (*Special Document: Television Verité*) was a special reports programme that was aired in Brazil for almost ten years, produced by a very different concept than the one that created *Jamaica: o Paraíso do Reggae*. *Documento Especial* was a reality-based programme focused on the interaction between the people interviewed in the reports and in the situations experienced by the news crew, while keeping a great part of the Brazilian television journalism format. A 1990 episode entitled "Maranhão em Ritmo de Reggae" ("Maranhão in Reggae's Rhythm") was broadcast by the now extinct Manchete TV (a national broadcast channel). The title reveals the heart of the special report: reggae in Maranhão, one of the poorest states of Brazil, whose population is essentially made up of African and native Brazilian descendants. The expression "in reggae's rhythm" suggests that the musical scene of the state will be the issue of the programme, however not in the same way as it was seen in *Jamaica: o Paraíso do Reggae*.

Within the structure of a journalistic programme, the narrator (practically the only white person to come into sight on the show) appears at the beginning of each segment in a studio. The same narrator does the voice over throughout the programme in order to provide an external perspective of the subject matter. He presents the theme of reggae in Brazil regretting that, in Maranhão, "The most popular songs were always imported from Jamaica." The narrator qualifies this situation as a "cultural distortion", because Brazil is "one of the richest countries in musical genres". The terms and expressions used let slip a concept of culture as merchandise, unattached to its creators and admirers.

The opening ends in a series of testimonies of people on the street, in short cuts, who seem to be answering a question about where Jamaica is located. They start with an old man who states surprised: "Jamaica? It is in . . . well . . ." Then, the programme moves on to a child's hunch ("I think it's in Bahia"), to a salesman's opinion ("Africa!"), to a girl at a party who wears her hair in a long plait ("I don't know, but I know it's a very crazy place"), and finally to a boy stuck on a crowded bus, who just shyly smiles and says: "Jamaica is here." The sequence ends with a performance of a fisherman, who sings a reggae song in an invented and non-intelligible language inspired by Jamaican English. This way, such editing and the previous narration seem to disqualify the practice and the discourse of the *maranhenses* (people who were born in Maranhão), suggesting that they would make the transposition of another reggae and another Jamaica to Maranhão without any meaning and cultural dimension. On the other hand, it also presents the native discourse that transposes Jamaica to Maranhão.

After this opening, the discourse of the programme is progressively contaminated by the exposition about the persons and situations captured by the camera and built by the editing, changing the depreciative tone as it emphasizes the narration of the collective experiences of the "reggae dance rooms", where the *radiolas* organize the parties. *Radiolas* are sound crews, similar to the Jamaican sound systems (referred to in Portuguese as "sistemas de som" in *Jamaica: o Paraíso do Reggae*), who are in charge of the transportation and the installation of equipment as well as bringing the DJs who select the reggae tracks, always played at maximum volume. According to the narrator, "the reggae that the maranhense likes to listen to isn't on any hit parades, not even in Jamaica", but is "a style known as 'roots', which had a lot of success in Jamaica in the '60s and '70s". However, none of the artists associated with the roots of the genre in *Jamaica: o Paraíso do Reggae* (the ones who appear on the music videos) show up on the "roots" selection of the radiolas or even on the soundtrack of this episode of *Documento Especial*. The artist's names are not even mentioned, with the exception of Bob Marley and the Tribo de Jah, the "only local reggae band".[6] Expressions such as "social justice" and "positive vibrations", or Rastafarianism in general are also not cited by the voice over or by the maranhenses interviewed in *Documento Especial* and kept by the final editing.

Documento Especial levels the reggae party goers and the "radiolas" owners, like some of the music videos exhibited on *Jamaica: o Paraíso do Reggae* which levelled the dancehall artists with their audience. As the subjective camera[7] exposes the two thousand vinyl records of a radiola's owner, he is emphatic to show his humble house, stating that he "lives in this house because [he] want[s] to follow the rhythm of Jamaica, as all their singers live in poor houses like this one." Also, the television crew sometimes interacts with the local people, always dealing with prosaic subjects related to reggae and its recreation dimension: the dating at the reggae parties, the prohibitive price of the reggae tapes and the tactics employed in order to enter the reggae festivities without paying. The specific testimonies about music by the common folk (who are not identified by subtitles) are not concerned about the names of the bands, classifications or reggae subgenres. The testimonies only disclose how people are individually or collectively affected by the music. This is exemplified by statements such as "I get very emotional with this reggae" or "reggae is a maranhense's passion", among others.

The conversion of the programme to the native discourse is transparent when the narration perceives that "reggae's musical culture" is already "rooted". This is an appropriation of the maranhenses speech and a radical transposition: "the only difference regarding Jamaica is that the maranhenses do not adopt the Rastafarian looks". In the end, the conversion process is almost completed, especially when the narration concludes that "the entire Maranhão has transformed into some kind of Brazilian Jamaica." The title of "Brazilian Jamaica" is not an invention of the programme; it was created in the 1970s and assumed by many maranhenses; this information is not cited in the narration. The adoption of the "Brazilian Jamaica" term by *Documento Especial*, without reservations, creates a fusion between the two territories that prioritizes the "Jamaican" element. Nevertheless, the sentence about the "Rastafarian looks" seems to refer to the iconographic links emphasized in *Jamaica: o Paraíso do Reggae* as territorial and cultural marks, given the absence, not only of the dreadlocks, but also of music videos, archival footage or other elements. In *Documento Especial*, the focus is on the hand camera and on dark interiors where audio is even more relevant than image. At a certain point in the programme there is even an explicit indication in the audio-visual discourse of the absence of the iconographic references among the maranhenses. This is clear when a radiola owner comments that "there are people here that have never had the opportunity to look at Bob Marley's pictures, even the reggae related people".[8] The two shows do not seem to be talking about the same "Jamaica" or sharing the same definition of "reggae".

The key to understanding this "musical fever" would be, according to *Documento Especial*, the primordial connection between Jamaica and Maranhão with Africa, from where the majority of their population's ancestors came as slaves. This is demonstrated by a scene of a percussionist executing a variety of rhythmic beats, which are danced to by another maranhense. This scene reveals the close connections between reggae and some of the local rhythms of the "bumba-meu-boi", a traditional folk street show that involves music and dance. This connection is not explored further and it is not shown in any images of bumba-meu-boi groups, the subject of other documentaries on Maranhão, such as *Música do Brasil*[9] or *São Luís Caleidoscópio* (directed by Hermano Figueiredo in 2000). The traditional culture of Maranhão appears once more in a quick shot of a "tambor-de-crioula" presentation, but the scene is so short that the viewer does not have time to learn anything about it.[10]

The Maranhão that emerges in *Documento Especial* is only unified by reggae, and was taken by a purely musical and affective "Jamaica". When the narration affirms that Maranhão "is the only place in the world where one dances very close to one another", the camera captures the couples' movement on the dance floor or at the beach, illuminating the fusion between the music and the body as a local creative appropriation. The comparison of the approaches of each television documentary to create preconceived human types leads to the conclusion that reggae seems to be more rooted within maranhenses than within the Jamaican people previously shown in *Jamaica: o Paraíso do Reggae*. In other words, the collective dimension and the physical appropriation, denied in *Jamaica: o Paraíso do Reggae*, creates, in *Documento Especial*, a "Jamaica" in Maranhão that seems to be more "alive" than the "Jamaica" created *in loco*. In this context, *Documento Especial* presents reggae in a way that removes the meaning of its historical narrative and of its explicit political direction, inserting the musical genre on the individual and collective memory of the maranhenses, where it recreates the population's daily life.

The conventional language used in *Jamaica: o Paraíso do Reggae* reflects and becomes part of a concept of reggae, that is, in the Brazilian collective mind. This is the directional focus of the audio-visual composition of the programme, but it shows empty images that paralyse the culture as a whole, symbolically. The production crew worked from a concept of "reggae" already appropriated, which was framed, narrated and edited for the Brazilian audience – a concept that does not fit well within the camera's frame. It is a territory associated with a finished musical history, something closed, locked and finalized, freezing any possibility of new influences and new directions. Alternatively, *Documento Especial: Maranhão em Ritmo de Reggae* created an audio-visual composition that still flows, because it does not get locked by the imaginary (as a collection of preconceived ideas and concepts), keeping the possibilities of appropriation open.

It was the analysis of the two audio-visual works that resulted in trans-cultural communication, which was converted in different ways while creating specific appropriations. For a better understanding of how these creative operations became possible, it is necessary to examine the collection of audio-visual productions of Jamaica and its musical genres since the end of the 1930s.

Building Jamaica as an Audio-Visual and Musical Locus

There is no space in this chapter to account for it, but it is possible to point to some movies in which many different types of audio-visual compositions about Jamaica and the popular music produced locally were explicit. One of the oldest stories captured locally on the Caribbean island is *The Devil's Daughter*, also known as *Pocomania*, an American movie shot at the end of

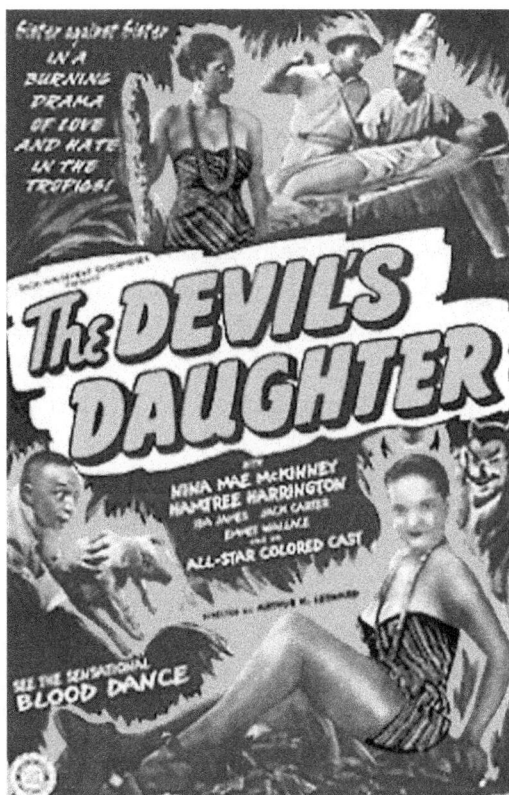

7.1 *The Devil's Daughter*, an American movie shot at the end of the 1930s, explores, in a sensationalist way, the Afro-Jamaican cult called Pocomania. Image courtesy of the Vidigal collection.

the 1930s with a cast composed almost totally of black actors.[11] It can be described as a movie that explores, in a sensationalist way, the Afro-Jamaican cult called Pocomania (establishing comparisons with the Haitian voodoo) with a soundtrack made essentially by rhythmic drumming and performed by natives in grass skirts. *Pocomania* opens with a group of natives singing "Linstead Market" and "Sweet Charlie", identified by Jamaicans as belonging to the genre called mento. Mento is considered nowadays a traditional Caribbean music, still sung by folk musicians who perform in the island's hotels and small concerts (Neely 2001, 2007). The audibility and visibility of the Jamaican music was still incipient, but the movie characterized the Caribbean as a locus of exoticism and musical expression.[12]

In the 1950s, some movies had the musical genre calypso as a theme, notably *Calypso Joe* and *Bop Girl Goes Calypso*, which featured artists like the Jamaican Lord Flea and Trinidad and Tobago's Duke of Iron. However, the most successful example of these movies was not a strictly musical movie, but the drama *Island in the Sun*, shot in 1957 in the islands of Grenada, Barbados and Jamaica. One of the reasons for its popular appeal was the presence among the protagonists of Harry Belafonte, who popularized calypso in the United States. In this movie, that also had James Mason, Joan Fontaine and Dorothy Dandridge as part of the cast, Belafonte not only sings the title-song but is a political leader in a fictitious Caribbean island. The Caribbean then fell under British rule, but, in an attempt to fit Hollywood expediency, the island portrayed in the movie *Island in the Sun* was treated as having political autonomy (Warner 2000).

A meaningful expression of this autonomy in audio-visual and musical terms was *This Is Ska,* two short films shot in 1964, one of the first attempts to register what was happening on the Jamaican musical scene by a local movie crew. They were produced by Jamaica Film Unit, a government agency that inherited the structure of the old Jamaican section of the Colonial Film Units (CFU),[13] after the island's independence from Britain in 1962. In the introduction to the movie, the disc jockey Tony Verity describes ska as a "hypnotic sound" which causes the listeners to become "caught up in a frenzy and

7.2 and 7.3 Calypso was a theme of several movies in the 1950s. One was *Island in the Sun* starring Harry Belafonte. Images courtesy of the Vidigal collection.

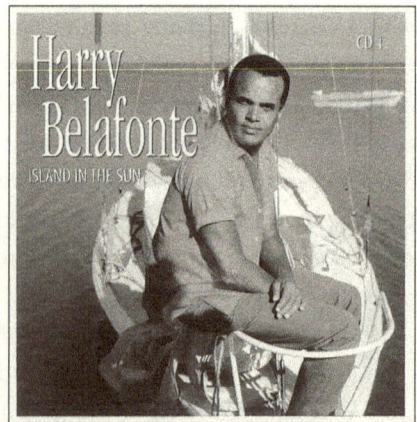

couldn't help moving to this pulsating, almost religious beat". The connection between the musical and spiritual spheres, translated in the rituals shot in *Pocomania,* seems to echo in the text, also characterizing dance as a bodily appropriation of a musical expression of a transcultural process.

The first musical number of the second part of *This Is Ska* is called "Jamaican Ska", sung by Byron Lee and his band, the Dragonaires. The lyrics of this song present ska as a new dance, inserting it along with international genres like the twist and the cha-cha-cha, and characterizing it as Jamaican. One of the segments of the movie shows the basis of the development of local milestones more easily recognizable and bound to territory, like some traditional mento songs such as "Sammy Dead". The opening is followed by simple but effective records of important Jamaican artists and groups of the time (and still important today) like Toots and the Maytals, the adolescent Jimmy Cliff and Prince Buster. The artists and their dancing audience are shown in long shots with a still camera frontally positioned, translating the concern into making them both part of a collectivity. From a contemporary and non-Jamaican point of view, there are no iconographic references that might associate the Sombrero Club and the Glass Bucket Club, where the concerts were filmed, nor its clients, with Jamaica. The images of the dancers in this movie were used in *Jamaica: Paraíso do Reggae* to narrate the passage from ska to another style, rocksteady. While the voice-over explained that there would have been "a reduction in the rhythm of *ska*", the image of the collective and frenetic dance started to slow down, while the soundtrack, composed previously with a ska, changed to a song associated with rocksteady.

Finally, another movie that can be considered a pioneer in terms of exposition of a Jamaica attached to a genre of popular music was the documentary *Reggae.* Produced in 1970 and released in the following year, it might have been the first to put the term "reggae" in the title. In it, the filmmaker Horace Ové, born in Trinidad and Tobago, attempts to capture the musical scene linked to reggae in the United Kingdom. The movie shows the Jamaican immigrants with the mods and the first skinheads, some of which had elected reggae as their favourite kind of music, exposing it in the streets and nightclubs. Dancing to popular music is presented as a factor in appropriation and overcoming of racial barriers. The documentary also includes performances of artists like Toots and the Maytals, Bob Andy and Marcia Griffiths, all performing in the Reggae Festival of 1970. This is mixed with interviews with journalists, disc jockeys, sound technicians, part of the Trojan Records and Bamboo Records crew and reports in the streets, under the London drizzle. In one of them, a citizen of approximately forty years old affirms, with a Jamaican accent, "reggae music is something from the heart, straight from the mother country Jamaica. Reggae is a sound that only black people can understand."

Jamaica and the music produced in its territory were associated chronologically, until the beginning of the 1970s, to practitioners of African cults wearing grass skirts, calypso singers wearing hats and rattles, studs in suits, big bands, dance crazes, Rastafari, hooded Jamaicans and white and bald-headed Englishmen wearing boots. The combination of these visual associations has built a complex iconography, that could not yet be comprised as a stabilized imaginary.[14] Watching these movies in a chronological sequence the progressive liberation of the expressive potential contained in the island becomes visible, as the Caribbean people try to assume part of this process and create their own audio-visual perspective.

The Harder They Come and a Musical Concept of Jamaica

The work done by the Jamaica Film Unit started the cinematographic archive on popular music made in Jamaica. After producing so many short movies, the islanders could count on qualified professionals and enough equipment so that more ambitious local productions could emerge. The favourable conditions for the productions, plus the desire to be seen on the screens and to stir up the political and cultural spheres, inspired a group to work on the concept of the first feature film done in Jamaica, *The Harder They Come*.

Perry Henzell decided that the movie would not be spoken in conventional English, but in the language of the majority of the people in Jamaica, which comprises words from many African languages and others from English, Spanish, Indian and Portuguese origin, through a grammar derived from the linguistic system of western Africa.[15] Using this language, that can be called simply Jamaican (Cooper 1995, 91), was an important decision, since film history shows a long trajectory of erasing languages, and consequently, the expression of Third World country populations (Shohat and Stam 2006). The

7.4 and 7.5 *The Harder they Come*, starring Jimmy Cliff, was Jamaica's first feature film. Images courtesy of the Vidigal collection.

rhythm of Jamaican speech can be felt in each scene and also in every song of the soundtrack, unifying the movie in a specific cadence. It is exposed by the images as part of a linguistic community and the delimitation of a territory (within a process of decolonization and construction of a new nation), making it possible for this composition to became recognizable in other places.

This "musically driven" film, as defined by Jamaican actor and producer Carl Bradshaw (Warner 2000, 162), that was created within the very audio-visual discourse according to Henzell, Trevor Rhone's vision and that of the director of photography Franklin Saint Juste, who was part of the Jamaica Film Unit team. Each turning point in the script is structured as a relation of interdependent qualification between the soundtrack and the images. One example of this interaction: when Ivan sees himself abandoned to his own luck in the dump, the soundtrack is the song "Many Rivers to Cross", whose spiritual choir qualifies and deepens what could be seen as a lack of energy in an almost despairing melancholy. The lyrics of the song, all in the first person, reflect on the "many rivers" that Ivan still needs to cross, and the very own choir forecasts the result of this reflection: the refuge of the character in a Baptist church.

The involvement of Ivan with the music scene would start the series of events that would lead to the tragic ending, which would be catalysed by the performances filmed over *The Harder They Come,* like "Sweet and Dandy" by Toots and the Maytals and the title track with Jimmy Cliff. The music, the images and the plot of the movie articulate in a way that is progressively intense. Later in the movie, when Ivan becomes disappointed with the musical scene and goes to work in the harvest and distribution of marijuana, the vibrant "You Can Get It If You Really Want", the opening song of the movie, is played one more time. The song is mixed over the images of the forbidden plants, impregnating the Jamaican countryside with the pulsating rhythm of reggae music and its lyrics, now ironic (and stressing Ivan's lack of persistence in his musical career), indicating still a new beginning for the movie and for Ivan. A little further, the song "The Harder They Come" is heard for the third time, interspersed with the reggae heard in Kingston's streets, at the point of the plot where Ivan gains great popularity as a singer, after killing a policeman and becoming a wanted outlaw. The Jamaican capital and its people dancing in the streets are exposed in travelling shots many times. These images are evoked in later movies and documentaries exploring the theme.

In this way, much more than a "musically driven" film, *The Harder They Come* was, to begin with its title, a full-length music and movie hybrid that directed musically the space and time of a territory, catalysing the operation that would, way beyond mere association, *fuse* "Jamaica" and "reggae". This movie created the iconographic and musical reference for every film, documentary and television programme made subsequently about reggae, and the Brazilian ones were no exception.

Conclusion

Not only did *Jamaica: o Paraíso do Reggae* and *Documento Especial* create different "Jamaicas" as musical concepts, but they were both transformed by the power of transcultural communication and appropriation of the movies and popular music. This movement came from the fusion between music and territory that operated through the audio-visual language of the first films done in Jamaica and epitomized in *The Harder They Come.* The analysis proposed in this chapter shows that the process of transcultural communication goes both by the audio-visual and musical products, and the individuals, groups, institutions and territories, at the same time that it changes them, something that cannot be restricted to a consumer market. This happens because movies and audio-visual works are human expressions able to affect each person deeply and, at the same time, reach the mass of spectators, intensely articulating individual and collective memories. These films, documentaries and television programmes have shown an audio-visual interpretation of the articulation among fans, producers, journalists, filmmakers, scholars, musicians, DJs and other social actors, thus creating new "acoustic territories". It is this dimension of extreme complexity that defies the centrality of the hegemonic imaginary, stimulating the production of new perspectives and new transformations.

Notes

1. Some forms of this operation and the consequences of this unequal resonance were studied in depth in Shohat and Stam (2006).
2. This article is dedicated to his memory.
3. The documentaries *Hard Road to Travel* (directed by Chris Browne in 1991) and *Midnight Movies* (directed by Stuart Samuels in 2005) deal with the reception of the film in Jamaica, and the United States and Europe respectively.
4. The way this album, released a short time after the movie, was modified in order to comply to the mixing and instrumentation standards of rock music was analysed in the documentary *Classic Albums: Catch a Fire* (directed by Jeremy Marre in 1999). An analysis of the album's repercussions and Bob Marley's representation in the British press was done by Toynbee (2006).
5. Reggae has been mentioned in songs composed in Brazil since the end of the 1960s. There are records of reggae albums arriving in Maranhão state in the 1970s. Bob Marley was in Brazil only once in March 1980, but did not do an impromptu performance there. This is discussed in my magazine article "Bob Marley in Brazil" (1997). The former minister of culture of the Brazilian government Gilberto Gil was considered the great reggae propagandist in the country, at least since 1980 when he toured the nation with Jimmy Cliff. The first local reggae bands appeared in the mid-1980s. Nowadays, there are at least a hundred bands that define themselves as exclusive reggae bands, such as Tribo de Jah or Cidade Negra, singing in English, French, Spanish and in Portuguese, sometimes with a great response from the audience. There are also many other bands that play reggae sporadically in states like São Paulo, Minas Gerais, Rio de Janeiro, Bahia, Ceará and many others (Vidigal 2006).

6. Artists on the programme included Eric Donaldson, Culture and Gregory Isaacs. They are more popular in Maranhão than in other states of Brazil.

7. Term that describes the position and movement of a camera when it takes a character's point of view.

8. Carlos Benedito Rodrigues da Silva collected several statements about the time when the was still little known in Maranhão in the mid-1970s, when the genre was called "balance" or "Jimi Clife" by the dancers, indicating the popularity of the singer Jimmy Cliff. In other testimony, Riba Macedo, one of the first to play in reggae dance of São Luís added that one of the tracks that was more successful when the genre began to dominate the dances was "You can get it if you really want" (Silva 2007, 118), establishing a link, even indirect, with *The Harder They Come*. Silva emphasized that people of Maranhão took reggae as an affirmation of black identity, in a context of poverty and social inequality in Maranhão (2007).

9. This is a 2000 documentary series about the multiplicity of musical manifestations in Brazil, directed by Belisario França and written by Brazilian anthropologist Hermano Vianna. The "Bumba-meu-boi" episode shows the "Boi da Mocidade", a "bumba-meu-boi" (a Brazilian folk dance and music that describes the death and resurrection of an ox) group from the city of Rosário (Maranhão) that sings a "toada" (a kind of northern Brazilian folk music) with reggae rhythmic elements. This "toada" lyrics states that "reggae and 'boi' have similar steps". The group presents its dance with the traditional natural-sized ox made out of fabric, with Christ's image embroidered on one side and Bob Marley's image on the other side.

10. According to the article "Jamaica's Central African Heritage" (Warner-Lewis 2004), there is a great contribution by the Bantu people (from Angola) to several culture manifestations practised in Jamaica. The Bantu was one of the most important African groups brought to Brazil as slaves, so this is a strong and unexplored link between the two countries and their people. For example, a picture of Kumina drum players in the article shows them playing their instruments in exactly the same way of "tambor-de-crioula" drummers in Brazil.

11. This movie was located in Jamaica thanks to its mention in Leah Rosenberg's abstract in the twenty-second annual West Indian literature conference on the role of religious cults in literary production in Jamaica. We have to stress its importance to the history of popular music performed on the island, because it was one of the first records of popular songs in Jamaica.

12. The traditional Caribbean music is also part of the classic 1956 movie *Moby Dick*, sang by Edric Connor, an actor and singer from Trinidad and Tobago. He played the part of the harpooner Daggoo and interpreted the song "Hill and Gully" using the rhythms of the strokes of his oar, in the first scene of whale hunting (Warner 2000).

13. These production centres were created in 1939 to produce war propaganda movies at the colonies using the structure of the General Post Office, a docu-

mentary pioneer British mail production company, managed by John Grierson. Grierson made a 1949 report for UNESCO suggesting that the Colonial Film Units supported the training of professionals within the colonies, a request that was accepted by the decadent British Empire (Diawara 1992). Citizens from Barbados, Trinidad and Tobago, British Guiana, and Jamaica went through training programmes at the University of the West Indies and were able to create their own movies. In 1955 they started making documentaries about health and family planning issues, as in *Too Late*. There were also documentaries and dramas about local workers, as the school teachers in *Builders of the Nation* (Warner 2000). In an article about the production centre (*Jamaica Observer*, 19 March 2004) Edwards wrote that the Jamaica Film Unit is also known as Jamaican Mobile Cinema Unit.

14. For an analysis about the imaginary in documentary movies, see Comolli (2006) and other works of this French filmmaker and critic.

15. Robert Stam states that the origin of the word "pickaninny", used in the south of the United States, came from the Portuguese word "pequenino" (little person, or thing), due to the colonial Portuguese monopoly of the slave market. It is reasonable to infer that "pickney", the Jamaican word for children, comes from the same root (1997).

References

Barrow, Steve, and Peter Dalton. 1997. *Reggae: The Rough Guide.* London: Rough Guides.

Bitomsky, Hartmut. 2001. "O mundo documentário". *5 Festival do Filme Documentário e Etnográfico-Catalog.* Belo Horizonte: Edições forum.doc.

Comolli, Jean-Louis. 2006. "Fim do fora-de-campo?". *10 Festival do Filme Documentário e Etnográfico-Catalog*. Belo Horizonte: Edições forum.doc.

Cooper, Carolyn. 1995. *Noises in the Blood: Orality, Gender and the "Vulgar" Body of Jamaican Popular Culture*. Durham, NC: Duke University Press

Diawara, Mantia. 1992. *African Cinema: Politics and Culture*. Bloomington: Indiana University Press.

Gilroy, Paul. 1991. *"There ain't no black in the Union Jack"*: The Cultural Politics of Race and Nation. Chicago: University of Chicago Press.

Mota, Regina. 2006. "Cinema e pensamento Brasileiro". *Revista de Economía Política de las Tecnologías de la Información y Comunicación*. Vol. 2. http://www.eptic .com.br.

Neely, Daniel. 2001. "Long Time Gal! Mento Is Back!" *Beat* 20 (6): 38–42.

——. 2007. "Calling All Singers, Musicians and Speechmakers: Mento Aesthetics and Jamaica's Early Recording Industry". *Caribbean Quarterly* 53 (4): 1–15.

Shohat, Ella, and Robert Stam. 2006. *Crítica da imagem eurocêntrica*. Trans. Marcos Soares. São Paulo: Cosac Naify. [Shohat, Ella, and Robert Stam. 1994. *Unthinking Eurocentrism*: Multiculturalism and the Media. London: Routledge.]

da Silva, Carlos Benedito Rodrigues. 2007. *Ritmos da Identidade: Mestiçagens e sincretismos na cultura do Maranhão*. São Luís: Editora da UFMA.

Stam, Robert. 1997. *Tropical Multiculturalism: A Comparative History of Race in Brazilian Cinema and Culture*. Durham, NC: Duke University Press.

Thelwell, Michael. 1992. *"The Harder They Come*: From Film to Novel". In *Ex-iles: Essays on Caribbean Cinema*, ed. Mbye Cham, 176–210. Trenton: Africa World Press.

Toynbee, Jason. 2006. "One Step Forward? Translating Jamaican Popular Music in the Core". Society of Caribbean Studies Annual Conference Papers. Vol. 7, http://www. .caribbeanstudies.org.uk/papers/2006/olvol7p9.PDF.

Vidigal, Leonardo. 1997. "Bob Marley in Brazil". *Beat* 16 (3): 51, 62.

——. 2006. "O Reggae mediado por computador: Apropriação cultural e convivência em uma lista de discussão". In *Narrativas telemáticas*, ed. Beatriz Bretas. Belo Horizonte: Autêntica.

Warner, Keith. 2000. *On Location: Cinema and Film in the Anglophone Caribbean*. London: Macmillan/Warwick University Caribbean Studies.

Warner-Lewis, Maureen. 2004. "Jamaica's Central Africa Heritage". *Jamaica Journal* 28 (2–3): 24–35.

CHAPTER 8

REGGAE
MUSIC IN THE
BLOODSTREAM

ROGER STEFFENS

I am going to do something unorthodox. Normally, when I speak of Jamaica, over the past thirty-two years, I have spoken about other people. I think it is important for me to explain my own exposure and increasing involvement in the culture of reggae because I represent a lot of people in America who have experienced the music in similar ways. And not just in America: there are folks from Brazil and from Africa, Canada and so many countries around the world who were exposed to reggae, initially, by one or two works of art that they feel changed their lives forever, as my exposure to the music in 1973 did for me.

This may be the only time in my life that I write an auto-biographical piece, so I want to try to get everything out

8.1 Roger Steffens with the very first item acquired in his extensive Bob Marley Collection. Photo: Devon Marley Steffens.

in order. I must also correct some misperceptions that I have heard about my various roles in things like the Grammys. So, I begin with the marvellous quote that I never tire of repeating: I was living in Berkeley, California, making my living by reading poetry, and I read an article by an Australian journalist named Michael Thomas in a July 1973 issue of *Rolling Stone*. He said, "Reggae music crawls into your bloodstream like some vampire amoeba from the psychic rapids of Upper Niger consciousness." It led me to rush to the store and buy *Catch a Fire*.

Moving in a New Direction

I had no idea what that meant, but I had to find out right then. I went out and, cheap as I was, I bought a used copy of *Catch a Fire* for US$2.25.

8.2 Glen DaCosta and Bob Marley kicking a soccer ball in the dressing room of the San Diego Sports Arena on 24 November 1979. Photo: Roger Steffens.

The next night, in a tiny theatre in North Berkeley with forty other people, I saw *The Harder They Come*. During the chalice scene the entire theatre became so smoky we could barely see the screen. On the way home, I bought a copy of the soundtrack and, literally, from that day forward my life went in another direction.

The next turning point was in 1976 with my wife, Mary, without whom nothing I am about to tell you would have been possible. She is the true saint in this story. My wife, Mary, and I came to Jamaica for the first time. We arrived the week Michael Manley declared the national state of emergency. We were staying in Lucea and everybody said, "Don't go to Kingston." We said "We've got to go to Kingston; we want to find some records." We got to Kingston and went to Bob Marley's record shack on the block behind Parade. There were no Bob Marley records for sale at Tuff Gong, no Peter Tosh, just a couple of Bunny's records. It turned out that Bob's single at the time was "Rat Race", and the government had told him to cool it. So he just pulled all his stuff off the market.

That experience was interesting in another way, also, because there was an extraordinary new album by Ras Michael and the Sons of Negus, a *grounation* called *Dadawah*. We heard it in a little shack on a mountainside up in Lucea and we went to twelve of the fourteen parishes looking for a copy. It was a new album at the time. We could not find it anywhere, not even in Kingston. We went back to Trench Town Records on Fillmore Street in San Francisco and found three copies in Ruel Mills's store.

Reggae in the United States: The 1970s

My experience of reggae is different from that of an expatriate Jamaican. Obviously, there were communities in Miami, in New York and other parts of the United States where the music was being exposed and utilized in a very different way. But, for me, as a white American coming new to this music, there were a lot of key points. The help of Jamaican people coming to America to expose the music was of enormous importance. I mentioned Ruel Mills in San Francisco. In Los Angeles it was Bally Barton and his wife, Yvonne. They had two stores at that time, one in the community, the other on the corner of Hollywood Boulevard and La Brea Avenue, right across the street from where Bob Marley's star sits today.

8.3 Rehanging of the Bob Marley section of the Queen Mary exhibit in 2001, now hung in Santa Barbara, California. Photo: Peter Simon.

It was in there in 1978 that I met a fellow from an American reggae band called the Untouchables and he told me about Hank Holmes. Holmes at that point had eight thousand Jamaican singles in his collection and had never left Los Angeles in his life. And for the collectors, and I know there are a lot of you, I am going to repeat a story that was contained in the discography of the Wailers – a short version. Hank worked in a one-stop – a wholesale and retail record store. The store specialized in cut-outs, over-pressings of soul albums for twenty-five cents an album. But Hank was reading the British magazines in the 1970s and took note of the little advertisements on the back that said "10 Reggae singles for £1". It turned out that these soul albums were known in England – in London, Manchester and Birmingham – as Northern Soul and they paid ten pounds or more a piece for those records. So Hank contacted some of these stores in England and said, "I'll sell these albums to you for ten pounds but I don't want money. I noticed your ad said ten singles for one pound. So why not just send me one hundred reggae singles for each of the albums I send you."

The day I met him he had just received a new supply, four huge crates of reggae singles, with four hundred records in each crate. He had a little mail order company out of his house called Reggae Beat. So he was getting one hundred records for twenty-five cents – not a bad deal. I asked him if he had ever heard of a group called Well Pleased and Satisfied and he pulled out eight mint singles by them. I was hooked, and he was a major influence on me and on reggae in America from that point forward.

Reggae Radio in the United States

Between my broadcasting background and his collection I figured we could do a great radio show because there was no reggae radio show on in Los Angeles at the time. We tried for a year to get on the air. I have found this to be a typical story of so many non-commercial radio broadcasters in the United States. An amateur, a lover of the music frustrated by not being able to hear it on the air, takes his collection to a station and says "I want to do a show." And the ripples of those events have made reggae an important force in America today.

It took us a year to get on the air. The first place we chose was the obvious one, Pacifica Radio, the great left-wing radio network in the United States. We did three shows that were very well received, but we were finally told that the station could not put us on playing reggae music because we were white. So, we went to a little public broadcasting station in Santa Monica College that had 110 watts and great promise of growth. They put us on the air and within a year we were the most popular non-commercial radio show, of any kind, in Los Angeles. And, more importantly, we were always the biggest weekly show fundraisers for the station during their annual fund drives. I have found this to be true of most of the American reggae shows. They are always among the highest earners for their non-commercial stations.

Our time was doubled after that. In the first fund drive, our show made in three hours what the entire station had made in ten days in the previous fund drive. We were then given four hours a week, commercial-free. Our first guest was Bob Marley. We'd been on the air for about six weeks and Island Records called me and Hank and said, "Would you mind going on the road for two weeks with Bob Marley?" My response: "Yeah, I think I could work that out."

We got to spend some extraordinary times with him. I would have done a lot more different things if I had known that that was going to be the only time

8.4 Steffens on L.A. Radio. Photo courtesy of the Roger Steffens Reggae Archives.

I was going to be on the road with him. But, hindsight is wonderful. It was an inspiration for me for the rest of my life watching this extraordinary performer who made some of the greatest poetry and music of the twentieth century; he was truly the artist of the millennium.

So that was a turning point as well. Also, in late 1978, a giant reggae clash was held over eight nights in San Francisco and Los Angeles. A different person hosted each evening, supplying six hours from their collections to be taped by all the participants. At one point, we had twenty-two tape recorders hooked together in sequence and everybody had to release their pause button at the same time. So at the end of that time there were forty-eight hours of material on tape.

To me, the greatest invention of the twentieth century was the cassette because it enabled all of us to share this music among ourselves. I mean, when you are talking about some Jamaican singles that had five or six hundred copies pressed, if you did not collect on tape you would have missed an enormous amount of what was produced in Jamaica. So that event led to a great many radio shows. It also led to a film by one of the participants, Jerry Stein, with the Soul Syndicate, called *Word, Sound and Power*, which he made in 1980.

L.A. Reggae Television Show

The next high point for us was in 1980 when the music broadened. A Trinidadian drummer and filmmaker named Chili Charles approached me and asked if he could come to the station and film our interviews with visiting Jamaican artists. That was the birth of the *L.A. Reggae* television show. And over the next twenty-three years Chili spent well into six figures out of his own pocket, not only to produce the show but to buy airtime. Virtually none of the things I am going to talk about have been revenue producing; they were all voluntary activities. And that is true, I think, of a great many of the people who participate in the reggae community around the world. If you are into reggae for money, you do not really understand. It would be nice if we could find ways for all of us to be compensated properly, but it is an amateur's business, primarily, which, as we all know, is a double-edged sword.

Sunsplash: Showcasing the Best of Reggae

In 1981, a man named Tom Linton, a travel agent, approached me and said, "Do you think we can get anybody from LA to come to Sunsplash, in Jamaica?" And I said, "Hey, we could fill a plane!" So we made some announcements on the *Reggae Beat* and, in fact, in 1981 we filled a plane of people. From that year forward through the 1980s at least one full plane of reggae lovers from California came specifically to Jamaica to see the Sunsplash festival. It was like an annual convention of reggae lovers from around the world that helped spread the music even more.

Another major event for those of us in the United States was in 1982 when Blue Riddim, the white American band, played at Sunsplash. And I will tell you how clever these guys were. Not only were they brilliant musicians in their own right, but they had such an impeccable instinct that when they came on at sunrise with people sleeping on their reggae beds, they decided to open with a flat out Skatalites song. It was a song that the Skatalites never recorded because it was the theme to the movie *Chariots of Fire*. The song sounded like something you knew, but you really did not know it, and it kicked in so hard that I am told the entire place was basically wide awake by the third song and hailing it as one of the greatest moments in Sunsplash history. And we

lament the loss of one of Blue Riddim's members, the trumpet player, Scott Korchak. I livicate this chapter to Scotty.

Sunsplash was a force throughout the 1980s. It is sad that we no longer have those Sunsplash festivals because they were produced by people who wanted to expose the best of Jamaica's artists: seeing artists like Mutabaruka come on stage in 1981 and just astonish people; seeing Steel Pulse doing "Ku Klux Klan" in 1981, when the guy jumped on stage in the Ku Klux Klan outfit and the whole audience went, "Woah!" I will never forget that as long as I live. People came back to America telling these stories about the tribulations and joys of experiencing reggae in its homeland. This led to reggae's growth in America even more.

Another point was the expatriate Jamaicans who came to live in the United States, in particular in my city: Ras Michael, and the father of reggae music and a dear friend, Joe Higgs. Joe Higgs's

8.5 Steffens interviewing Wailer Al Anderson at the Grammy museum in Los Angeles, May 2010. Photo: Gary Greene.

contributions have never been fully understood or acknowledged. He was one of the prime figures: without Higgs, there would have been no Bob Marley. Higgs became a father to many young musicians in America as well, and he was a coach, mentor and strict disciplinarian. Anybody who came through one of Higgs's backing bands left a much stronger person. So we have to thank the musicians from Jamaica who came to our country to teach us more about it, to teach our musicians how to play it, what it meant and what its lyrics said. Because you have to meet reggae half way in order to penetrate. It is not an easy music at first for most people, but its rewards are many.

The *Beat* Magazine

In 1981, I met a woman named C.C. Smith at Sunsplash and she said she wanted to come down and help us answer the phones at the radio station. What she discovered was fairly chaotic, so she whipped us into shape, me and Hank. Then in 1982 we finally were getting a few more reggae shows in Los Angeles – four or five artists a year would come through and that was it. We therefore decided we would not only do a little calendar of events on the radio show, but we would start a newsletter if people were interested. We said, "Send us your address and we'll send whatever we end up doing to you." The next week we had three hundred letters. So C.C. said, "Should I start a magazine?" and I said, "Sure, C.C. Start a magazine."

So she did. That was the birth of the *Beat* magazine. Originally it was a one-page mimeo playlist with a little column called "Ras Rojah's Reggae Ramblings" and "Words of Haile Selassie", two features which were still with us in our twenty-sixth year. Within a year, it evolved from the little paper issue into a real magazine called the *Reggae Beat*. Two years later we began doing a lot of work in international and world music, so it became the *Reggae and African Beat*. Then it was simply the *Beat*. It became a must read for all the serious reggae fans in America, largely because of the tireless efforts of Chuck Foster, who succeeded me when I left the *Reggae Beat* radio show in 1987. He reviewed every single reggae recording submitted to the magazine. But as the music business contracted in the new century, so too did the *Beat*. There were virtually no advertisers left and that was a problem. I do not know how people feel about the Internet. It is wonderful for many things, but when you can hold something like this magazine in your hand, it means a whole lot more. Thank you, C.C.

The Reggae Grammy

In 1984, Mike Melvoin, head of the National Academy of Recording Arts and Sciences called us and said, "It's time to start a Reggae Grammy. We would like you to be the chairman of the committee and help us put the committee together. Grammy realizes that reggae music is an important international forum and we want to honour it." Since that time, I have been the chairman of the Grammy Screening Committee. We do not choose the nominees; we do not choose the winners. We screen to make sure that only reggae music gets into the category.

In Jamaica, I have probably said the following four thousand times: "I am not responsible for you not winning your Grammy!" I have been attacked

8.6 Steffens with Al Anderson and singer Martha Veléz at the Grammy museum in Los Angeles, May 2010. Photo: Gary Greene.

on the air by Tanya Stephens. I was cornered by Eek-a-Mouse in the House of Blues; he looked like he was about to pounce on me like a panther when I walked into the dressing room.

"Youuu, why yuh nuh gimme nuh Grammy?"

"Mouse?"

"No man. Tell me why?"

"Well I'll tell you Mouse, you want to win a Grammy?"

"Yes man"

"I have the foolproof way for you to win a Grammy. If you do what I tell you to do, I guarantee you, you will win a Grammy."

"Yeah man what, what?"

"Change your name to Eek-a-Marley."

But it is true. I do not know what the Grammy is based on. We do not know how many people vote in the category. It could be two hundred people or it could be all fourteen thousand. They never tell us. It is not based on merit; it is not based on sales. I think it is probably mostly based on name recognition or a major label behind the artist. So, please, I do not have any power. To maintain my neutrality, I do not even vote. I hope that is understood now, and I have made that clear.

The "Life of Bob Marley" Show

That same year, I was invited by the National Video Festival, curated by a man with the marvellous name of Bob Wisdom. He wanted me to bring my "unofficial" videos to the festival to show the role of amateurs and non-professionals in preserving film and video culture. It went over very well and got nice reviews. I started getting requests from colleges to come and do the same thing. That was the birth of my "Life of Bob Marley" show.

For the past twenty-four years I have been presenting it all over the world: from the bottom of the Grand Canyon, where the Havasupai Indians believe that Bob Marley is the fulfilment of an ancient Indian prophecy that a black man would lead the red man to freedom; to the Smithsonian, thanks to my dear friend Dera Tomkins; and a whole heap of other strange places, most recently in the Aboriginal area of northeastern Australia and in Auckland, New Zealand, where the national holiday, as Brent Clough will tell you, is 6 February, their Treaty Day. But nobody cares about that – they celebrate "Uncle Bob Day" instead.

So it was a joy to see the Māori people, which is pronounced like Marley without the *l* (not "Mow-ree", which I have mispronounced my whole life). The Māori people regard him as one of their greatest heroes. Even non-herb-smoking, middle-of-the-road, "normal" folk in New Zealand told me that when Bob Marley played there in April 1979, the entire history of their music changed. And that is the influence that Bob Marley, and others like him, have had on the world. I have seen it first-hand.

The Emergence of Dancehall

The dancehall era began in 1985, when the music turned in a different direction. It became easier for people to make their own recordings. Our golden age in Los Angeles, and perhaps in several other places in America, was the period from 1984 to 1986. There was no week in those two years that we did not have anywhere from one to three Jamaican artists from Kingston coming to Los Angeles, and they all went home with money in their pockets.

And then the bad guys came in – the posses. It seemed like Los Angeles was ripe for the picking. And even at a show by the soulful master Alton Ellis, someone got shot in the spine, in an argument over a girl, and was paralysed for life. The audience changed. People were afraid to go out. Fewer people started to come to the shows. The whole nature of the business seemed to be affected by a malaise. The thing that has kept reggae alive from that period forward, I believe, is reggae festivals. In California we had Reggae on the River and in Miami, of course, in the 1990s, the great Bob Marley festivals on the Harbour Front. In most areas of the country there are festivals. In New England there is the Vermont Reggae festival. Those festivals have really kept reggae alive in North America. I think the artists would back me up on that, too. That is where they are finding most of their gigs.

It is getting harder to do small club shows these days. Without radio penetration, it is hard to break foreign music. The radio in America has never been terribly friendly to reggae music. Peter Tosh was always talking about how it is a conspiracy to keep black music off the radio. I think he was right then, twenty-four years ago, and I think he is still right.

I have had a lot of questions about my reggae archives. They started that day in 1973 with that gift of hindsight when I read that *Rolling Stone* article and cut it out and put it in a little manila folder. That was the birth of what now fills six rooms, floor to ceiling, of our house and a huge storage space in Pasadena. That collecting, that preserving that we have been doing, has forced us to move house three times to accommodate what we have in there.

In the process of building the archives, I have met people – scholars and students and just fans from all over the world – who sometimes knock on the door in the middle of the night and ask to come in. One night at 11:30 there was a knock at the door and there were five – it looked like – huge Samoan guys, standing at the door. They said they were a reggae band from Papua New Guinea, and they had some time between planes and could they please come in and see the archives. So, of course, they came in. I do not think I have ever closed my door to anyone coming through.

I believe that the spirit of reggae music is one of cooperation, not competition. You do not have people trying to be better Catholics than other Catholics. We are all in this together. This is the movement of Jah people and if you are a Jah person you know that we are all one. It is I and I. There is no "you" business. It is I and I. We are here to help each other and help each other grow, learn and spread that "One Love" philosophy, which is at the base of everything that we do in this business. I think that is right and righteous and just.

One of the other things that happened in the 1990s was the formation of RAW, which stood for Reggae Ambassadors Worldwide. It was founded by a man named Rastaman Nanny in Michigan and a man from Utah named Papa Pilgrim, of blessed memory. That was one of the first organizations involving the Internet that was designed to help bring fans, musicians, promoters and lovers of the music together to try, as Papa Pilgrim put it, "to forward the reggae vibe every time". It still exists. It has been a part of the lives of many of us and a very, very helpful thing to keep the music progressing. I salute all the members of RAW today.

In 1998 I was asked to go to Amsterdam to help induct Bob Marley as the initial member of the Cannabis Hall of Fame. That was fun. I met a lot of people from the European community. Though I have many stories about that event, I will tell you one thing: Rita Marley was there to accept the award, which was a twenty-four-inch flower top from a sixteen-foot ganja plant. When she saw it, she cancelled her reservation back to Jamaica immediately. I think Amsterdam is the saddest airport in the world. There are so many people crying when they leave Amsterdam because they have to leave their stash behind.

In 2001, the *Queen Mary*, the old British ship in dry dock in Los Angeles, had just completed an exhibition of artefacts from the *Titanic*. They were looking for something that would draw a younger audience and they asked me if I would mount an exhibition of my archives. We did it and a book came out from that called *The World of Reggae Featuring Bob Marley: Treasures from Roger Steffens' Reggae Archives*. The exhibition contained six thousand artefacts in frames – they are all now in storage in Pasedena. It was up for eight months and it coincided with Bob Marley being awarded the star on Hollywood Boulevard. I was on the road, but I am told that a lot of the journalists and press people from Jamaica came down to see the exhibition that day and returned with news about it. "It was very nice that this white guy up in America did that, but how come we are not doing it for ourselves down here?" That is something I have heard a lot over the years.

I do not think it has anything to do with colour. I do not think it has anything to do with how much money you have in your pocket either. If you really want to do something, if you are passionate about something, you will find a way to make it happen. If you love something, you find a way to make it happen. Anything I have ever come across in my life having to do with reggae and Rasta and the culture of the extraordinary country that is Jamaica, I try to save.

So we have run out of room again. We have this latest house and now that is full. Mary has to walk through rooms sideways to get past the boxes. There are 120 cubic feet of clippings in the house now. If you want to get your head around that, that is a square foot box, one foot high from home plate to first base and then another 30 feet beyond. That is just the clippings. It is time to make them go somewhere else, and that is what I am in the midst of.

Internationalization of Reggae

American reggae bands are very overlooked, and some of them are quite fantastic. There is a group out of Washington called SOJA (Soldiers of Jah Army). When I played the Marley show last year in Guam they had just been there. They drew five thousand people. Five thousand people came to see SOJA in Guam. This is the wave of the future, I think: the internationalization of the music. Reggae is capacious enough to accept the other influences. There are bedroom tapes, in the archives, of Bob Marley doing bossa nova reggae. All the different forms that Bob would have gotten into when he eventually would have gone to Africa and founded his studio there. That was his dearest dream. We would have had Afro-beat reggae and all the other forms. But it is still underneath – that heartbeat rhythm.

One of the best songs I have heard in recent years is by a group called Kengaru from Israel and it is a song called "Tehilim", which, I am told, is Hebrew for "soul of a man". It is Nyahbinghi drumming with a Hebrew vocal, sung in an Islamic vocal style. So they are ticking off everybody, and it is beautiful. And that music in Israel is hugely popular. The band was all Israelis and the producer, Piloni, who has a studio in Tel Aviv, produced it. I once played at a Rasta kibbutz in the middle of the Negev desert, where they have got these guys with dreadlocks and yarmulkes and a six-day a week reggae club with the latest singles from Jamaica.

I had a long talk afterwards in the kibbutz about Sylford Walker. Even Jamaicans do not know Sylford Walker. These Israeli guys with the dreadlocks and yarmulkes were having a debate about who was the best producer in Jamaica for Sylford Walker. Two weeks later, I am in an attic in Honolulu with Ooklah the Moc, a Hawaiian-Polynesian reggae band with Tongans, Samoans and Native Hawaiians. They are having a discussion about Sylford Walker, thanks to the Internet. So that is something that is offering hope for the future, too. The past is frequently catching up to the future now. If we could, someday, have something on the Internet where all the major works and the minor works of Jamaica's incredible artistic history would be available in a profit-making way to the rest of the world, that would be the answer, I think, to all our prayers.

Postscript

I would be remiss in not mentioning *Reggae Beat International*, a weekly one-hour syndicated show that Hank and I collaborated on. It was heard on 130 stations worldwide, including continent-wide on the Voice of America Africa Service, from 1983 to 1987.

CHAPTER 9

THE JOURNEY OF REGGAE IN CANADA

KLIVE WALKER

I f reggae is taken as an overarching umbrella term for all forms of Jamaican popular music, then reference to reggae in Canada could mean the touring exploits of Byron Lee and the Dragonaires who began performing their version of ska in Canada in the mid-1960s (Jay Douglas, interview by the author, February 2008). That broad interpretation of reggae would also apply to the music of bands like the Sheiks with lead singer Eddie Spencer, the Cougars featuring the lead voice of Jay Douglas, Wayne McGhie and the Sounds of Joy, and the Hitch-Hikers showcasing the Mighty Pope. During the late 1960s, they treated Toronto audiences to quality doses of ska, rock-steady, soul, rhythm and blues, and funk at venues such as the West Indian Federation at College and Brunswick

streets and two establishments in the heart of downtown Toronto on Yonge Street – Fitz Riley's Club Jamaica and the Blue Note. Many of the Jamaican musicians in those bands began their relationship with Toronto as touring musicians and eventually decided to make that city home. Keyboard player Jackie Mittoo, a vital contributor to the creativity of Jamaica's ska and rock-steady periods, and trumpet player Jo Jo Bennett were both important to that period of Toronto's soul scene which continued through the first half of the 1970s. Those early Jamaican-Canadian bands issued recordings at the time but they soon vanished into obscurity. More than thirty years later in 2006, the company Light in the Attic released *Jamaica to Toronto: Soul, Funk and Reggae 1967–1974* and *Wayne McGhie and the Sounds of Joy*, two albums that pulled together many of those obscure tracks. Those reissues ensured a place in music history for several seminal Jamaican-Canadian reggae artistes.[1]

Bob Marley and Jamaican Roots Reggae in Canada

No overview of reggae in Canada can ignore the enormous impact of Bob Marley and the Wailers, particularly when that band was at the height of its worldwide, mainstream popularity in the late 1970s. At first Marley restricted his Canadian tour dates to Toronto. His first performance was at Massey Hall in June 1975 and a year later in May 1976, he brought his exhilarating reggae showcase to the University of Toronto's Convocation Hall. When Marley went back to Canada in 1978, buoyed by advancement in his international profile, he returned to Toronto to play Maple Leaf Gardens but went on to appear at the Forum Concert Bowl in Montreal and the Queen Elizabeth Theatre in Vancouver. By 1979, when his superstar status was assured, he travelled to Canada in the fall, returning to Maple Leaf Gardens and Montreal's Forum but this time decided to perform at Kinsmen Fieldhouse in Edmonton, Alberta.[2]

Marley's Canadian tours produced more than simply very satisfied audiences. He was able to establish reggae as music with mainstream appeal. He cemented an imprint of influence for rock and folk musicians who may have already been hip to reggae-flavoured rock through Eric Clapton or by punk bands like the Clash. On his tour dates, if he was able to spend time in a particular city, Marley always connected with Jamaican-Canadian friends and acquaintances as well as people with heritage in the English-speaking Caribbean. This meant that he was very conscious about maintaining close ties with what can be termed his "natural" or "core" audience despite his ever growing mainstream popularity. Marley also had a direct connection to the incipient Canadian reggae scene. Olivia "Babsy" Grange, then a booking agent and Canadian resident, introduced Marley to Toronto-based Truths and Rights, a band with which she did business. Marley was supportive in his comments to the group, insisting that the cause of reggae required their efforts.

Marley was not the only Jamaican reggae performer and recording artiste with the international credibility to popularize reggae in Canada; Peter Tosh, Burning Spear, Third World, Dennis Brown and Black Uhuru were also influential. Black Uhuru is the only Jamaican reggae group from the roots era that recorded a song whose title and lyrics reference Canada, specifically Toronto. The 1981 track "Youth of Eglinton", written by the group's lead singer Michael Rose, is a commentary on youth gun violence. It discusses youth who could be considered part of the Jamaican diaspora. The song, though, did not attempt to glamorize these actions, as the following lines of the lyrics suggest:

> Stop and listen
> They want you to fight the good fight
> But save you strength
> For strength of life.

The song displays its social conscience with these lines that accurately depict the complexity of youth crime and its possible causes:

> They are responsible
> for a lot of children
> And they need food
> And they want to go to school . . .
> A very thin line to start the crime.

It is unfortunate that, thirty years after the song was written, the social conditions for this type of youth crime in Toronto still persist. The song mentions, in addition to the youth of Eglinton, the youth of Brixton in London, United Kingdom, and the youth of Utica Avenue in Brooklyn, New York, but its title is reserved for the Toronto avenue whose west end accommodates the area that has been described as "Little Jamaica". The significance of the song, for this assessment, is that it discusses the problems of prominent Jamaican diaspora communities in major metropolitan centres. These are problems that the vast majority of Canadians, Americans and British people of Jamaican descent, who are law-abiding, would rather not tackle in such a public way. The song's inclusion of Toronto is surprising in some ways because for a very long time it has been overlooked or seen as a minor contender with regards to reggae culture. Michael Rose's brother "Rap" lived in Toronto and was involved in the music business as a record producer, so Michael would have been very aware of Toronto's hidden potential as an important reggae location.

Canadian Rock Stars and Reggae

Reggae in Canada can also mean Canadian rock stars adopting reggae. Bruce Cockburn, a gifted folk-rock musician and Canadian music icon, is a good example. Cockburn's 1979 album *Dancing in the Dragon's Jaws* became popular in Canada and the United States partially as a result of its hit single "Wondering Where the Lions Are", a reggae track displaying the skills of Jamaican-Canadian band Ishan People. Cockburn's follow-up album, *Humans*, contained the hot reggae track "Rumours of Glory". On that recording Cockburn was joined in studio by Bernie Pitters, Benbow and Leroy Sibbles, another group of musicians who were Jamaican residents of Toronto.

Jamaican Icons Nurture Canadian Reggae

Before Marley's Canadian tours and before Cockburn's adoption of reggae, Jamaican musicians and singers migrated to Canada and continued to grow their careers in their new home. Jackie Mittoo and Jo Jo Bennett were joined by other important reggae personalities including the above mentioned Leroy Sibbles, Stranger Cole, Nana McLean, Willie Williams, Carlene Davis and Ernie Smith, who all moved to Toronto during the 1970s and became pioneers of the reggae scene. It is worth taking a closer look at Mittoo and Sibbles and the role they played in the development of reggae in Canada.

Jackie Mittoo

Mittoo was a member of the Skatalites, a band of gifted jazz musicians that included the great trombonist Don Drummond. The Skatalites defined the ska era. When the band split up, Mittoo became a leading member of Coxsone Dodd's studio session band. As a solo recording artiste he was responsible for various popular instrumentals including "Ram Jam" and "Who Done It". "Who Done It" was a tune that became one of the most popular songs in Jamaica in 1969, the year he migrated to Canada. While in his new country of residence, Mittoo frequently travelled back to the nation of his birth to maintain his connection with the Jamaican music industry, but he also began an association with the growing scene in Toronto. One of Mittoo's important contributions to Canadian reggae was as a mentor to up-and-coming artistes throughout the 1970s and 1980s. His mentorship assisted R. Zee Jackson, the Sattalites and Jason Wilson, to name three examples. Wilson, a Euro-Canadian reggae singer, keyboard player and recording artiste with no Caribbean heritage, spoke in the 2006 documentary *Reggae Roots Run Deep* about his huge musical debt to Mittoo. Mittoo died in Canada in 1990 at the young age of forty-two.

Leroy Sibbles

Leroy Sibbles started his musical career as lead singer and chief songwriter for the Heptones, one of the most revered harmony trios of rocksteady and early reggae. Three of the Heptones' classic hits of that period were "Fatty-Fatty", "Equal Rights" and a superb interpretation of Bob Dylan's "I Shall Be Released". Apart from having one of the best voices in reggae, Sibbles was a groundbreaking bass player. Like Mittoo, he was an important member of Coxsone Dodd's 1960s studio session band. He provided arrangements and laid down bass lines for several popular recordings, one of them, "Satta Massa Gana" by the Abyssinians, became a pervasive roots reggae anthem. When Sibbles arrived in Canada in 1973, he was already a pivotal force in reggae. He too assumed the role of mentor to participants in the ascendant reggae scene. Sibbles was not narrow or parochial about whom he encouraged and promoted as reggae artists. He was not one of those mentors that thought aspiring reggae musicians he nurtured had to be Jamaican. Quammie Williams, a percussionist of Trinidadian heritage with Truths and Rights, has gone on record discussing Sibbles's generosity in encouraging and supporting the efforts of a band whose members were Caribbean but non-Jamaican (Quammie Williams, interview by the author, January 2001).

One night in 1991 at a Leroy Sibbles concert in downtown Toronto, I witnessed a special performance in which two Euro-Canadians – Richard "I-Sax" Howse, a saxophone player, and trumpeter Sarah McElcheran – were part of a mainly Jamaican-Canadian backing band. I was surprised when Sibbles, in the middle of performing his classic "Party Time", brought I-Sax and McElcheran centre-stage to perform their solos and to trade notes with him as part of a great extended version of the song. But Sibbles was not just a nurturer. He had his share of a mainstream profile in Canada. In 1985 he was selected as one of the few black artistes to participate in a recording by mainly Canadian superstars to assist famine relief in Ethiopia. That recording, "Tears Are Not Enough", was the Canadian equivalent of the United Kingdom's *Live Aid* and America's "We Are the World". In 1987, he received the Juno award (the Canadian version of a Grammy) when his album *Meanwhile* won in the reggae category. Sibbles's exceptional talent was widely respected in the Canadian music industry.

Facilitators

Managers, booking agents, concert promoters and other kinds of facilitators in the music industry can sometimes play a significant role in assisting a genre to develop and grow. Karl Mullings and Olivia Grange were two of the many facilitators whose involvement with reggae in Canada during the early years was crucial. Mullings, who died in 2005, was a pioneer. He managed the original Sheiks when they toured Canada in the early 1960s and later the Cougars, after he decided to make Toronto his home. Mullings was instrumental in opening Club Jamaica, the West Indian Federation Club and the Caribana Club, where Jamaican musicians could showcase their talent. Mullings's most cherished achievement was promoting the career of his daughter Tanya, a Toronto reggae singer (Dunphy 2005).

Grange, appointed as the minister of culture in the Jamaican government that was elected to power in 2007, has had a celebrated connection to the reggae industry crowned by her involvement with Shabba Ranks's huge international success during the 1990s. Her contributions to the Canadian scene were made in the late 1970s when she lived in Toronto and had a hand in advancing the careers of Carlene Davis, Truths and Rights, and Leroy Sibbles, among others.

9.1 Former minister of culture Olivia "Babsy" Grange with Chris Blackwell at the 2008 Reggae Awards. Grange made an invaluable contribution to the Canadian scene in the late 1970s. Photo by Colin Hamilton; courtesy of the Gleaner Company.

Reggae in the Caribbean Diaspora

One aspect of reggae in Canada is particularly intriguing – I have coined the term "reggae of the Caribbean diaspora" to describe it. What does that concept mean? For me, it is music by those reggae artists of Caribbean heritage living in the United Kingdom, the United States and Canada, who were not interested in merely attempting to imitate Jamaican reggae. I am referring to musicians, singers or poets whose reggae is deeply influenced by a Jamaican frame of reference but whose lyrics reflect the social conditions of Caribbean people in the diaspora. I am talking about creative reggae artists in the diaspora who are confident enough that their reggae is able to absorb from the musical environment of the country in which they live, without losing its identity (Walker 2006, 159–60).

My use of the term is designed to describe specific types of reggae or reggae-inspired music that originated in Toronto and Montreal in Canada; New York and Miami in the United States; and London and Birmingham in the United Kingdom. That, of course, does not mean that reggae in the Caribbean diaspora is limited to those cities, but they represent some of the major centres of the English-speaking Caribbean diaspora. Why the Caribbean diaspora? Why not just the Jamaican diaspora? A brief history of this kind of reggae will reveal the distinction.

"Reggae in the Caribbean diaspora" has existed for over thirty-five years. For example, during the 1970s and 1980s, diasporic reggae in the United Kingdom produced the triple threat of Steel Pulse, Aswad and Linton Kwesi Johnson. It produced Maxi Priest, whose star shone in the late 1980s and through the 1990s. It also gave us reggae pioneer Dennis Bovell, an innovative bass player, whose band provided poet Linton Kwesi Johnson with a unique reggae and dub sound in studio and in concert.

Caribbean Rather Than Jamaican Diaspora

Now, here is where the promise to explain what is meant by a Caribbean as opposed to Jamaican diaspora is fulfilled. Dennis Bovell is in fact British of Barbadian heritage. Steve "Grizzly" Nesbitt, the original trap-drummer of Steel Pulse, is actually from St Kitts–Nevis. At least one of the three major forces in Aswad, Brinsley Forde, possesses Guyanese heritage, and the other two members of the most famous line-up of the group – Angus "Drummie Zeb" Gaye and Tony "Gad" Robinson – could have backgrounds originating from Guyana, Trinidad or elsewhere in the Caribbean. So it would be very restricting and exclusionary to talk in terms of simply a Jamaican diaspora.

This characteristic of reggae in the diaspora is very important because one of the things it signifies is that reggae culture became the youth culture of successive generations of teenagers and twenty-somethings in the diaspora regardless of where in the English-speaking Caribbean they drew their heritage. This phenomenon began in the early 1970s at a time when Jamaican reggae was just breaking internationally. Some of these young people living in the diaspora, and immersed in reggae culture, became the artists who led the charge of a new reggae initiative – not just in the United Kingdom, but in Canada and the United States as well. Here are three more examples from the United Kingdom to illustrate that this phenomenon still persists today. In the first decade of the new millennium, performers like Bitty McLean, reggae-influenced R&B singer Ms Dynamite and the heavily dub-seasoned hip-hop of Roots Manuva have continued the tradition.

America: Sound System Culture, the Deejay's Art and Hip-Hop

In America, the development of diasporic reggae travelled a different path. The influence of the sound system culture and the art of the deejay had a much more prominent role in terms of how reggae became a "Trojan Horse" inside America's popular music culture. In the early 1970s, Clive Campbell, a young Jamaican living in the Bronx, New York became one of the founding fathers of hip-hop. Campbell, whose DJ alter-ego was Kool Herc, accomplished that by creatively deploying two turntables and a sound mixer to sample and cross-pollinate funk and Latin records and by drawing on the aesthetics of Jamaican sound system culture. The DJ in hip-hop is equivalent to the selector in reggae, the deejay in reggae is the mike MC in hip-hop. The birth of modern hip-hop as it relates to Kool Herc's skills on the turntable has its origins in the sonic sensibility of the Jamaican sound system and the art of the selector in creating something different from an existing recorded tune.

New York during the early 1980s was the breeding ground for reggae in the Caribbean diaspora in the United States. Shinehead, Sister Carol and Shelley Thunder were three of the most talented Jamaican-American deejays to achieve success as products of the diaspora. In response to an environment in which sound system culture and hip-hop had a symbiotic relationship, Sister Carol and, particularly, Shinehead had great skill in blending Jamaican deejaying with New York rap style. By the mid-1980s, the second wave of hip-hop MCs included Heavy D and Boogie Down Productions which featured MC KRS-One and the late DJ Scott La Rock. In addition to having Jamaican or Caribbean heritage they all worked an emphatic reggae influence into their beats and rap flow (Walker 2006, 244–45). In more recent times, the work of dancehall star Shaggy, hip-hop MC Busta Rhymes and the reggae-spiced pop of Sean Kingston fits comfortably within that American diasporic framework.

Diasporic Reggae in Canada

The history of reggae in the Caribbean diaspora as it relates to Canada is just as interesting. Similar to the rise of diasporic reggae in the United Kingdom, the Canadian equivalent initially offered primarily roots reggae bands and dub poets. Ishan People, a roots band that emerged in Toronto during the early 1970s, is a good starting point for a discussion about diasporic reggae in Canada. The majority of the band members, though from Jamaica, were not recognized reggae artists there. In fact, some were not even professional musicians when they lived in Jamaica. So, in that sense, they were very different from Sibbles or Mittoo, who both came to Canada as major figures in the Jamaican music industry. Ishan People, whose members included bass player Larry Silvera, the late Michael Murray on guitar, drummer Karl Parris, percussionist Glen Daley and keyboardists Scott James and William Smith, was attempting to make its mark in a Canadian context. A difficult task, at the time, because the audience for reggae was mainly the so-called ethnic Caribbean market who were interested in reggae from Jamaica or artists living in Canada who brought with them a recognizable Jamaican reputation. In some ways, Ishan People reflected the pressure of attempting to satisfy the needs of the audience in their home market. By 1976, the band was signed to major label GRT, which released their first album, entitled *Roots*. On that

9.2 Ishan People, a Canadian band whose members possessed Jamaican heritage. Photo on the cover of the album *Ishan People* courtesy of Klive Walker.

recording, guitarist Michael Murray provided lead vocals. The band's second GRT release *Ishan People* came out in 1977 and featured Johnny Osbourne as lead vocalist.

Osbourne, though not as well known as Mittoo or Sibbles, had created a name for himself in Jamaica before arriving in Canada. Osbourne's Jamaican career began with the 1969 release of the Winston Riley produced single "Warrior" and the launch of his debut album *Come Back Darling* that same year. So, when Osbourne migrated to Canada a few years later he was already on the radar of fans having more than a passing familiarity with the Jamaican scene. Osbourne provided Ishan People with a certain Jamaican pedigree. Ishan People was a band attempting to grow a career as reggae artistes from the diaspora but not necessarily as a band rooted in the Caribbean-Canadian experience. The band's brand of reggae was more in the vein of the Jamaican group Third World. Ishan People was a very talented, pioneering band, but they represented Canadian diasporic reggae in search of an identity. That identity began to take shape as the 1970s gave way to the 1980s through the work of Jamaican-Canadian dub poet Lillian Allen and the band Truths and Rights.

Lillian Allen's first explorations in writing reggae poetry during the early 1970s coincided with the initial efforts of Mutabaruka, Oku Onuora, Linton Kwesi Johnson, Brian Meeks and others. This contradicts the idea that dub poetry had one initiator. Even though it is true that Johnson was the first dub poet to record his verse, others were writing, reading and in some cases publishing their work during dub poetry's gestation phase throughout much of the

1970s. Needless to say, Allen, originally from Spanish Town, was a pioneer of the overall dub poetry scene and a seminal figure of the dub poetry landscape when she migrated to Canada in the early 1970s.

Allen's contribution goes beyond just being an early practitioner. Her work with reggae bands, either in concert or in studio, offered a mature idea of what reggae by a diasporic Canadian artist could represent. Allen's frank lyrics discussed racism in Canada through recordings such as "Riddim and Hard Times", a track that deals with an extreme example of police brutality in which Albert Johnson, a Jamaican-Canadian was shot to death in 1978. It meant that her lyrics would examine issues of women's rights in "I Fight Back", a poem looking at the plight of Caribbean women working as nannies and domestics in Canada. There is also "Nelly Belly Swelly" about the rape and child abuse of a teenage girl living in Jamaica. In one of her classic poems, "Rub-a-Dub Style inna Regent Park", she vividly describes a harrowing scene that takes place in an inner-city community of Toronto heavily populated with individuals of African-Caribbean descent, which involved a mother watching her son being shoved into a paddy wagon by police. In many ways, Allen's lyrics reflect the concerns of the black activist movements attempting to address those problems. Allen's art evolved, in part, out of her own involvement as a community activist. Above and beyond Allen's accomplishments as a pioneer and as a key representative for Canadian reggae as an art form that discussed issues facing Caribbean-Canadians, Allen gained recognition for her work. She won Juno awards in 1986 and 1989 for her albums *Revolutionary Tea Party* and *Conditions Critical*.

One of the bands that provided musical support for Toronto dub poets during those early days was Truths and Rights. A distinctive feature of the band is that it was not Jamaican. The core musicians of Truth and Rights – guitarist and vocalist Mohjah, conga drummer Quammie Williams, bass player Xola, trap drummer Abnadengel, keyboardist Iauwata, percussionist Ahmid and vocalist Ovid were from Trinidad, Guyana and nations of the Eastern Caribbean, while lead guitarist Vance Tynes was originally from Nova Scotia. Like the United Kingdom's Aswad or Dennis Bovell, Truths and Rights is a fine example of a roots band reflecting the reggae ethos of the Caribbean diaspora. They present a fine example because they were a truly talented and creative band that opened for Steel Pulse and Third World in major Toronto concerts. In 1983, the *Toronto Star*'s December 28 edition contained an article by mainstream music critic Peter Goddard describing Truths and Rights as Toronto's "Band of the

Year": not reggae band of the year but best overall band. Truths and Rights were a hard-working club and concert band. They only issued one single and an EP (a record that is more than a single but less than a full-blown album). The lead tune on the single was "Acid Rain", representing what has to be one of the earliest reggae songs to tackle environmental concerns of industrial pollution. These pollution problems caused by the burning of fossil fuels are of particular concern to Canada and Canadians of all nationalities regardless of race or ethnicity. "Metro's Number One Problem", the lead recording on their EP, deals with the issue of racial violence perpetrated against various racial minorities in Toronto. Truths and Rights and Lillian Allen both represent an approach to reggae in Canada that privileges the struggles for equal rights and justice as it applies to all Canadians and all visible minorities in Canada, but in particular Canadians of African and Caribbean descent.

The Roots Reggae Era in Canada

The roots reggae era in Canada lasted throughout the 1980s and into the initial years of the 1990s, particularly in terms of live reggae shows. In addition to Allen and Truths and Rights there were a whole host of talented singers, dub poets and bands that emerged. Some of the more notable singers were Errol Blackwood, Chester Miller, Lazo and Adrian "Sherriff" Miller. The poets included Devon Haughton, Clifton Joseph, I-Shaka, ahdri zhina mandiela, Anita Stewart, Afua Cooper and, from Montreal, Kali and Dub. Some of the important bands were Earth, Roots and Water, Twentieth Century Rebels, Culture Shock, Messenjah and Sattalites. Messenjah and Sattalites were among the more successful bands.

Messenjah was formed in 1981 in Kitchener, Ontario, a city fifty-six miles west of Toronto. The band was the brainchild of two Jamaican-Canadians, bassist Errol Blackwood, an ex-member of a rock band, and guitar player Rupert "Ojiji" Harvey, a musician who had played in the high-profile rhythm and blues unit Crack of Dawn. The integration of rock and R&B influences into their brand of roots reggae gave the band a distinct sound. Messenjah's music was always characterized by a high level of musicianship and they subsequently attracted the attention of WEA, who signed the band and reissued their independently released debut album *Rock You High* in 1983. After their follow-up WEA album *Jam Session* came out in 1984, they were dropped by the label. Blackwood soon departed the group to embark on what turned out to be a lucrative solo career with his own band. This new group favoured an edgy, blues-rock-influenced reggae. Messenjah, then led by Harvey, moved more in the direction of crisp, R&B-style harmonies and smooth lead vocals but maintained a rugged roots reggae rhythmic sensibility largely as a result of extraordinary bass player Charles "Tower" Sinclair, who joined the band in 1987. Sinclair possesses a distinct, creative sound that is melodic, resonant and bold. He is simply one of the most outstanding reggae bassists working today. Despite the band's personnel changes (such as going through three trap drummers, including the influential Crash Morgan) Messenjah always maintained a commendable quality in their music. In terms of their recorded output, some of their most successful tunes were covers of popular R&B standards such as their version of the Spinners' "Could It Be I Am Falling in Love" from their 1990 album *Rock and Sway* (Caudeiron and Prior 2012).

Like Messenjah, the Sattalites was formed by two musicians: Jo Jo Bennett and Euro-Canadian saxophonist Fergus Hambleton. They had both previously worked together in the horn section of Leroy Sibbles's band. It was Bennett, however, who brought an impressive reggae resume to their partnership. Bennett acquired his music education at Alpha Boys School, the same institution that produced the exceptional talents of saxophonists Joe Harriott, Wilton Gaynair, Tommy McCook and Cedric Brooks, as well as trumpet players Dizzy Moore and Eddie "Tan Tan" Thornton. After graduating from Alpha, Bennett became lead trumpet with the Jamaica Military Band before leaving to perform in Montego Bay. Eventually, he was recruited by Byron Lee and the Dragonaires and was a member of that band when it arrived in Canada for a concert at Expo '67 in Montreal. Bennett decided to stay in Canada after that gig. Like many of the early reggae pioneers, Jo Jo travelled back to Jamaica to participate in a music industry whose stars were on the verge of international acceptance. In 1970, on one of those trips back home, he was freelancing as a studio session musician and working with a variety of bands in live performance. At the same time, Jo Jo recorded the album *Groovy Joe* which included the Jamaican hit single "Leaving Rome" and "The Lecture", a track regularly sampled by the first generation of dancehall producers (Barrow and Dalton 1997, 246).[3] The first reggae band that Jo Jo initiated in Canada was the Fugitives, which began making its contribution in the early 1970s.

9.3 Messenjah was established by bassist Errol Blackwood and guitar player Rupert "Ojiji" Harvey. Photo on the cover of the album *Messenjah* courtesy of Rupert Harvey.

Bennett and Hambleton formed the Sattalites in the early 1980s. The easiest way to describe the band is to say that, as a two-tone or racially diverse group of musicians who play a horns-driven, pop influenced style of reggae, they are like a Canadian UB40. Sattalites were briefly signed to WEA and experienced success with their singles that covered the pop hits "Gimme Some Kind of Sign" and "Too Late to Turn Back Now".

Major Label Blues

For some reggae artistes, there is often a struggle to maintain a balance between producing reggae with integrity that advances the art form and the ability to earn a comfortable living as a recording artiste. Reggae with integrity does not dilute itself in a non-creative way for the sole purpose of finding success in the mainstream. Bob Marley is an example of someone who was able to beautifully balance the task masters of art and commerce in his work. Burning Spear was also quite successful at maintaining the integrity of his music. When you add the crucial factor of dealing with major record labels, the balance can be upset or in some cases destroyed on the altar of the label's objectives that may contradict the goals of the recording artists. In the Canadian reggae landscape the major label has been less positive than in other regions of the diaspora. Ishan People, Messenjah and Sattalites, all Canadian bands who managed to sign with major labels, were not necessarily marketed as bands with a Canadian reggae sensibility. In contrast, Steel Pulse, Aswad and Linton Kwesi Johnson signed to Island Records early in their careers and were able to produce work that gave them a presence as bands that offered a particular UK reggae sound, reflecting lyrics specific to the black experience in the United Kingdom. Lillian Allen and Truths and Rights were not afraid to identify themselves as Canadian in their lyrics. They realized that signing with a major label would probably restrict them to an amorphous identity and would mean a dilution of their lyrical content. They adopted that position because in Canada there was no Island Records or Trojan Records who had a sense of how to manage, package and promote reggae. That might explain why so many quality Canadian reggae acts have flown below the radar of international recognition. It is important to note that Truths and Rights, Messenjah and Sattalites all performed at Reggae Sunsplash in Jamaica, at different times, during that festival's "golden age" of the 1980s. The appearance at Reggae Sunsplash gave those bands Jamaican and international exposure in one event.

Canadian Reggae: Conservative, Radical or Both

There is a particular perception of Canadian reggae that deserves mentioning. Daniel Caudeiron and Corinna Prior have suggested that "One hallmark of Canadian reggae is the . . . relative absence of confrontation, a legacy of the country's conservatism and placid social ambience" (2012). Lillian Allen, Truths and Rights, dub poets Clifton Joseph, Michael St George and d'bi. young anitafrika as well as reggae hip-hop artistes Devon Martin, Kardinal Offishall, MC Collizhun and Motion would take serious exception to that comment. All of them have used reggae to accompany lyrics that confront racism and, in some instances, sexism. Those artistes represent Canadian reggae over a range of thirty-plus years and prove that there is a tradition of confrontation in Canadian reggae.

9.4 Truths and Rights were not afraid to identify themselves as Canadian in their lyrics. Here pictured on the cover of Toronto's *NOW* magazine, July 1982.

Dancehall in Canada

From the late 1980s to the early 1990s, dancehall completed its conquest of the reggae world. In many ways, it displaced roots reggae as the music's dominant form in Jamaica and most of the diaspora. In the United Kingdom, deejays Smiley Culture and Tippa Irie had already experienced mainstream chart success in their homeland, while another deejay named Papa Levi had a number one hit in Jamaica. In America, Shinehead signed with major label Elektra, and Island Records issued an album by Shelley Thunder. In Canada, Carla Marshall and Kid Fareigna were two of the deejays that emerged. Marshall, in particular, earned a reasonably high profile with her brand of mainly slackness lyrics.

Diasporic Reggae Fuels Canadian Hip-Hop

In Canada, however, many of the best talents of the new generation of diasporic artistes used hip-hop rather than dancehall as a vehicle to express their reggae. The work of the vast majority of successful Canadian hip-hop acts, particularly those from Toronto, is fuelled by reggae. Michie Mee, Maestro and Dream Warriors were three of the seminal hip-hop artistes who began their rise to prominence during the late 1980s.

Michie Mee, a Canadian of Jamaican heritage, released her debut album *Jamaican Funk, Canadian Style* in 1991. The title of that album announced that her particular mix of hip-hop and reggae was distinctly Canadian. Some tracks from that album were recorded in Jamaica. *The Black Tie Affair*, the second album of Maestro, a Guyanese-Canadian, also hit the streets in 1991 featuring the hit "Conductin' Thangs", a track which boasted an energetic ska beat complete with the appropriate horn riffs that gave his diasporic connection an added level of distinction by using ska rather than reggae. King Lou and Capital Q, two Caribbean-Canadian MCs combined to form the Dream Warriors, a group that was a pioneer of hip-hop-jazz fusion. Island Records released their debut album *And Now, the Legacy Begins* in 1991. That recording not only included their massive international hit "My Definition of a Boombastic Jazz Style" but also another hit single called "Ludi". It was a cool reggae track that sampled the rhythm of Slim Smith's "My Conversation". On the group's 1996 album *The Master Plan*, their tune "Sound Clash" featured a collaboration with Beenie Man, while another track, "Dem No Ready", included guest vocals by General Degree.

Dub Poetry Tradition

As the first wave of Canadian hip-hop established a presence, the dub poetry scene in Toronto, always a strong component of the city's reggae environment, continued to renew itself. One of the most important dub poets to emerge during the 1990s was Michael St George. The interesting thing about St George is that even though he was influenced by Oku Onuora, he has worked hard to develop his own distinct voice as a performer and recording artiste. St George, who migrated to Canada from Jamaica in 1989, has always been open to creatively advancing the musical and stylistic aesthetic of dub poetry. Like some of the best dub poets, St George possesses a voice that chants his verse with a dramatic power that is not one note or monotone. In performance he has used either a full reggae band or just hand drums and possibly an acoustic guitar. This has meant that St George has kept his particular style of dub poetry fresh and interesting. To date, St George has three albums: 1995's *Self Assession*, 1998's *Root 2 Fruit*, 2004's *Dubbin de Vibes* and a new album titled

9.5 Michael St George is one of the most important dub poets to have emerged during the 1990s. Photo: Katherine Fleitas.

The Ital Suite is in progress. In terms of the themes of his lyrics, St George has distinguished himself by discussing the plight of senior citizens in his poetry. Root 2 Fruit is a concept album containing several poems that highlight the importance of seniors, in particular seniors of Caribbean heritage.

The Reggae and Hip-Hop Connection

During the initial years of the new millennium, the expression of reggae as an integral element of a certain kind of hip-hop blossomed into a full-fledged phenomenon. It is not merely another crossover mechanism, though it certainly has, on occasion, followed that path. It is more than a fusion experiment, though it can be considered in that way. Shabba's celebrated collaboration with rap icon KRS-One on "The Jam" and Shinehead's ground-breaking merger of Jamaican deejaying and New York rap style on tracks like "Unity" set the tone for this development.[4] At least since the careers of Shabba and Shinehead peaked in the early 1990s, reggae culture has been on the rise as part of hip-hop culture and by extension as part of youth culture generally. This is true in the United States, the United Kingdom and Canada, and in many other areas of the world where hip-hop and dancehall go hand in hand.

It is generally known that the origins of hip-hop are related to reggae. What has been overlooked by scholars of both hip-hop and dancehall is that the interconnection of these art forms has not subsided over the thirty-five years of hip-hop's existence. We can see a clear thread of this interconnection from Kool Herc and Afrika Bambaataa through to Shinehead, Sister Carol and Boogie Down Productions to Heavy D, Michie Mee, Dream Warriors and Busta Rhymes to the United Kingdom's London Posse and Roots Manuva. Of course, the crucial reggae hip-hop artistes of Canada are a significant aspect of this thread.

By the late 1990s, a second wave of hip-hop performers entered Canada's music scene. They continued the tradition of distinguishing their work through the creative use of reggae rhythms by collaborating with dancehall deejays and through the use of Jamaican language. A good example of a reggae hip-hop artiste from Toronto who has made his mark in the first years of the new millennium is Kardinal Offishall. He has placed his Jamaican heritage front and centre and has advanced the merger of hip-hop and reggae in creative ways. Kardinal is one of the premier rap artistes in Canada. His reputation has been generated by the following he has gained in America with fans and with well-known American rappers who love his work. That is directly related to the fact that he is not trying to imitate an African-American style but instead grounds himself in the reggae that reflects his Jamaican heritage. His debut album *Quest for Fire: Firestarter, Volume 1*, released by MCA in 2001, still stands as a tour de force collection of landmark recordings. Five of the more popular recordings on the album are heavily reggae-influenced. Those tracks are "BaKardi Slang", "Ol' Time Killin", "Husslin'", "Money Jane" and "Maxine". "BaKardi Slang" is like a hip-hop anthem for youths of the Caribbean diaspora, describing how they embraced the aesthetics of reggae culture specifically as it relates to language. "BaKardi Slang" is essentially a translation of hip-hop speak into the language of dancehall. Check out a few of the translations from the song:

> We don't say "youknowwhatumsaying"
> T-dot says "You dun know"
> We don't say "Hey that's the breaks"
> We say "Yo, ah so it go"
> You cats steady sayin "Word"
> My cats steady sayin "Zeen"
> You're talkin' about "Yo, that girl's hype"
> We like "She's the bundown"
> Y'all say "A DJ battle"
> We say "A clash between two sound"
> When you talkin "Thug nigga"
> We talkin about "A shotta"
> When you think you got it locked
> T-dot comin' much hotta

Those lyrics may look simply like a translation into the language of Kardinal's Jamaican heritage. But there is a verse in the song that places this translation squarely in the context of reggae in the Caribbean diaspora when Kardinal raps: "You think we all Jamaican when nuff man a Trinis, Bajans, Grenadians and a whole heap of Haitians, Guyanese and all of the West Indies combined to make the T-dot O-dot one of a kind." Those lines suggest that dancehall-talk is one cultural element that unites Toronto youth with their Caribbean heritage despite the specific nation in that region with which they are affiliated.

Kardinal has also engaged in some truly outstanding collaborations. He worked with Sean Paul on "Money Jane", with Bounty Killer on the remix of "BaKardi Slang" and with Busta Rhymes on the remix of "Ol' Time Killin'". The importance of the collaboration with Busta Rhymes is that both he and Kardinal are diasporic artists: one from New York, the other from Toronto. Each of them privilege their Jamaican heritage through dancehall-talk. The "Ol' Time Killin'" remix offers a duet in which edgy – and sometimes politically incorrect – lyrics are dispatched with a flow that carries a satisfying level of skill. Busta Rhymes opens the track with a blistering attack of raw Jamaican language spoken with the rhythmic timing of rap rather than dancehall. Kardinal highlights the theme of this collaboration by throwing out the line: "reppin' the T-dot from BK back to Yard" ("representing Toronto from Brooklyn back to Jamaica"). With that statement – Busta injects a similar phrase – both artistes link each of their diasporic communities to Jamaica, the birthplace of the rude bashment language they invoke.

Kardinal is just one example of a host of new millennium reggae and hip-hop artistes in Canada. The Rascalz, a hip-hop group from Vancouver, is also known for using reggae beats and dancehall language and they were the first hip-hop artistes to collaborate with Barrington Levy on the track "Top of the World" released in 1999. Other reggae-influenced hip-hop artistes include Motion, MC Collizhun, K-OS and R&B singer Jully Black.

New Millennium Reggae

That discussion about the hip-hop and reggae connection is not designed to leave the impression that there are no contemporary reggae artists in Canada or that the reggae scene is not vibrant. On the contrary, there are lots of roots reggae bands and singers operating across Canada. The bands include Tabaruk, Ibadan, Leejahn (now Chinatown), Lazo, Dub Trinity and a reconstituted Truths and Rights. Some notable reggae singers are Jah Beng, Len Hammond, Humble, Sonia Collymore, Belinda Brady, Tanya Mullings, Toni Anderson, L JX, Steele and Korexion. Though dancehall activity in Canada continues to search for a bigger profile, there are some quality deejays, among them are Lindo P and Jah Brilliance. Canada has produced some very creative dub artistes (not to be confused with dub poets) who have crafted some very interesting reggae soundscapes over the years. In the 1980s Patrick Andrade emerged as the engaging sound artiste the Fire this Time, the late 1990s gave us Jeff Holdip as the innovative Bobby O'Luge. The first years of the new millennium has produced Jesse King as Dubmatix, whose satisfying creations have pushed Canadian dub closer to the spotlight of popular recognition.

There is a tendency to associate all things reggae in Canada with Toronto or more broadly Ontario. That thinking is rooted in two facts. The first is that the history of Jamaican music in Canada has had much of its genesis in Toronto; the second is that a large number of artists are based in that city. The idea that Toronto is the reggae headquarters of Canada is being challenged. Certainly, the Calgary Reggae Festival is a significant example of that challenge. The festival, a very well organized quality event, which began in 2004, has deliberately ensured that Canadian reggae talent from across the nation is properly showcased and promoted. That kind of approach should be automatic for Canadian concert and festival promoters. Sadly, some Canadian reggae promoters are not in the business of appropriately nurturing Canadian reggae artists. Other challenges to Toronto's centrality are also being mounted by some engaging artists. Mikey Dangerous is based in Montreal. Ibo and KinDread band are from Calgary. Jahranimo is a resident of Vancouver. Edmonton is the base for the band Souljah Fyah. Those are just examples of the kind of talent that exists outside of Ontario.

9.6 Souljah Fyah is a good example of the talent on the contemporary Canadian reggae scene. Publicity photo courtesy of Janaya Ellis.

The Contemporary Canadian Reggae Scene

In terms of current talent, singer Treson, singjay Blessed, dub poet d'bi.young anitafrika, deejay Mikey Dangerous and Souljah Fyah band are five good examples. They represent five very diverse acts that reflect the broad spectrum of Canadian reggae found in cities that are some of the major reggae nerve centres of the country.

Treson was born in Montreal and raised in a Jamaican foster home from the age of five. He returned to Canada at seventeen and embarked on a career as a reggae and soul singer. In 2005, his first single "Treson Meets VX" was released. In 2006, he issued recordings "Jen-Ee-Rocka" and "Dirt, Dust and Sand" from the album *Atomic Subsonic* by Dubmatix. In terms of live performances, Treson has been in the company of reggae greats. In early 2007, he opened for Marcia Griffiths and Beres Hammond on the Toronto date of their North American tour and later in the year he was opening act for a Sly and Robbie showcase in the same city. Treson's distinction is his rich, mellifluous voice that is clearly in the tradition of soulful reggae singers such as Delroy Wilson or Ken Boothe.

Blessed, who was born in St Thomas, Jamaica, and moved to Canada at age twelve, has been fortunate to have his recordings get heavy rotation on Flow, Toronto's mainstream black radio station. His first hit was 2002's "Love (African Woman)", which earned him a Juno award for best reggae recording. His single "Empty Barrel" (featuring Kardinal) kept his profile high in 2005. The ska-fuelled "Reggae Time" secured a second Juno for him in 2006. In 2007, a mixtape collection of recordings surfaced under the title *Shelved: Red X Presents Blessed* which featured some hard-edged and more politically volatile tracks than the more commercial fare of his popular hits. Blessed is one of the most prominent reggae artists in Canada in terms of overall profile. He has a unique singjay style and offers social commentary with hardcore rhythms as well as material aimed at commercial radio.

young was born in Jamaica and grew up in Kingston's Maxfield Avenue community. She migrated to Toronto when she was eighteen. As an artiste, young is inspired by the pioneers of dub poetry which include her mother Anita Stewart, Jean Binta Breeze, Mikey Smith, Linton Kwesi Johnson and, the mother of them all, the late Louise Bennett. However, she is not held hostage by their styles and methods. She is driven by a creativity which has allowed her to find her own poetic voice and her own vision. That creativity has allowed her to journey beyond the perceived limits of dub poetry. While we hear in her work echoes of the pioneers, we also recognize the future of dub poetry as she incorporates elements of dancehall, hip-hop, Latin and punk. For example, on the tracks of her 2003 album *Blood*, recorded in Cuba, we can hear all those elements conform to the objectives of the reggae aesthetic, an aesthetic which is reflected in the way her voice uses rhythm, enunciation and drama to express her poetry regardless of whether that aesthetic is supported by beats that are Latin, beatbox or militant roots reggae. Through her art she is also able to convey a sincere sense of community, a sense of activism and social justice that are at the core of the more progressive aspects of reggae culture. young has performed in concerts and festivals across Canada, in Jamaica, Cuba and on Broadway in New York. That Broadway performance was featured on HBO's *Def Poetry Jam*.

It is important to understand that music is only one aspect of reggae culture. That culture also includes but is not limited to literature, visual art, film, dance and theatre. young has utilized her poetic and dub sensibilities as an aesthetic that powers her persona as a skilled playwright and gifted actor. In 2006, young was the recipient of two Dora awards. Dora awards are

9.7 d'bi.young anitafrika uses reggae to accompany lyrics that confront racism and sexism. Photo: Che Kothari.

the pre-eminent mainstream theatre awards in Canada. She won a writing award and an award for acting, both for her play *blood.claat*. young has to be seen in the context of reggae culture, not just music, not just dub poetry but also performance art, playwriting and acting. What is interesting is that she could easily market herself as a dancehall poet or just simply go with the generic spoken word label but she proudly identifies as a dub poet. young is an innovator who represents a new era for dub poetry.

Jamaican-born, Montreal-based deejay Mikey Dangerous conveys the classic vocal timbre of contemporary reggae dancehall. Recently, his skills have gained him the ultimate recognition from Canada's music industry when he won the 2008 Juno Award for Reggae Recording of the Year for his single "Don't Go Pretending". He has performed at a variety of high-profile concerts including the Montreal International Reggae Festival in his hometown, the Barbados Reggae Splash in the Caribbean and the Calgary Reggae Festival. He has also appeared on the same stage as a host of hip-hop artistes including Ciara and Lil Jon as part of the Summer Sizzle concert series in Montreal. Time will tell whether Mikey Dangerous sustains his current successes and breaks through to the next level.

Souljah Fyah is an integrated reggae band featuring lead singer Janaya "Sister J" Ellis; percussionist and hand drummer Bongbiemi Nfor, known as the Original Tribesman; lead guitarist Deanne Michelle, also known as Lady Blaze; Dorant "Saint" Ricketts on trap drums; Stormin' Norm Frizzell on keyboards; and 2Tall Paul on bass and various instruments. Ellis is a Trinidadian-Canadian; Nfor is originally from Cameroon; Ricketts has Jamaican heritage; Michelle, Frizzell and 2 Tall Paul are Euro-Canadians. Those diverse ethnic backgrounds mould Souljah Fyah into a potent multicultural force placed in the service of a creative roots reggae groove. Another distinct aspect of the band is that the lead singer is a woman, something that is, unfortunately, still rare in reggae. Souljah Fyah, however, is not simply a band that meets some random politically correct gender and "multi-culti" criteria, their music is their most important contribution. Their 2008 album *Truth Will Reveal* hit the Top Ten of the national campus and community radio chart for several weeks during the summer of 2008.

Conclusion

This overview of reggae in Canada has considered the pioneers and introduced the notion of reggae in the diaspora of the English-speaking Caribbean. It has discussed the strong legacy of dub poetry and briefly referenced the notion of reggae culture. It has assessed the expression of reggae through hip-hop as it relates to Canada. And, finally, it has provided some examples of the promising talent in Canada's contemporary reggae scene.

Notes

1. Jay Douglas (interview by the author, February 2008); Kevin Plummer, "Toronto's Lost Soul and Reggae Stars Revisited", *Torontoist*, 12 December 2007, http://torontoist.com/2007/12/torontos_lost_s/; Mathew McKinnon, "Bring the Beat Back: Jamaica to Toronto Revisits the City's Soul, Funk and Reggae Roots", 30 June 2006, originally published on CBC.ca, but now only available online at http://groups.yahoo.com/group/Caribbean_Today/message/707
2. Detailed breakdown of Bob Marley's tour dates on the ThirdField.com website at http://www.thirdfield.com/new/tours.html.
3. See biography of Jo Jo Bennett at http://bunjo.technodread.net/jojo.htm.
4. "The Jam" appears on Shabba Ranks, *As Raw as Ever*, Sony, 1991; "Unity" appears on Shinehead, *Unity*, Elektra/ WEA, 1988.

References

Barrow, Steve, and Peter Dalton. 1997. *Reggae: The Rough Guide*. London: Rough Guides.

Caudeiron, Daniel, and Corinna Prior. 2012. "Reggae". In *Encyclopedia of Music in Canada*. http://www.thecanadianencyclopedia.com/articles/emc/reggae.

Dunphy, Catherine. 2005. "Karl Mullings, 63: Toronto's Reggae", *Toronto Star*. 4 October.

Walker, Klive. 2006 *Dubwise: Reasoning from the Reggae Underground*. Toronto: Insomniac Press.

CHAPTER 10

REGGAE GRIOTS
IN FRANCOPHONE
AFRICA

CHEIKH AHMADOU DIENG

O nce upon a time . . ." – that is how many stories
begin. This is often relevant because life is a story,
in a way. The keepers of the stories in some communities are the griots, the keepers of records
and memories of their societies; that is to say they were the
historians before the word was created by any academy. In
Africa, authorized academic voices have worked on their
role. A role and position of ambivalence, of ambiguity as
related to our traditional way of life, which was and still is
strongly deranged (in the Western psychological sense of
the word) by colonization and foreign interventions.

The Role of the Griot

What we have to keep in mind is a many fold problem as far as the griot is concerned. He is a panegyrist extolling the merit of the ruler and his social function. As such he participates, in his way and on the basis of the social code as a convention, in the stability of the society. There is a happy confusion (I should say intermingling) of roles that partake in social harmony which has been destroyed by external and malevolent socio-economic approaches, all foreign to the black and to his realities. In our West African context, the griot needs and is needed as an intrinsic part of a harmonious social fabric. He exploits (I should say that he uses) the whole community with the power of his words. Remember that creation began with the word or verb in Islam and Christianity (I limit my references to these two religions as a Muslim speaking in a country where there are many Christians).

I have to make it clear here that the social and political function of the musician fits into a clearly organized social structure. It is not a choice as it is in the modern Western world, even though it is changing today and, in a way, conforming to the universalized Western norms. Not everybody can be a musician. In Africa (maybe I should restrict the statement to Senegal) the great singers and musicians are still members of the griot families – take the cases of Youssou N'dour, Baba Maal, Thione Seck and so on.

The Baye Fall

Now, let us consider what the situation is in the specific context of Senegalese socio-historical structure as related to the art, and more specifically to music – and by that I mean reggae. To begin with, we have the group of people we call the Baye Fall – the name comes from Cheikh Ibra Fall, a follower of Ahmadou Bamba. We have to make it clear that Senegal, a former French colony where the colonizer destroyed the traditional social fabric, or I should say tried to do so, had many dignified and socially organized communities before the colonial factor disrupted Africa. There was resistance, there were bloody wars, and only the technological advance and power of the Europeans of the time could change the course of history.

Senegal is about 95 per cent Muslim. Our Islam is organized around Tariga or brotherhoods, the equivalents of your church denominations, which all come from abroad (Tijanya, khadiya and so on) except the Mouridya which is a local brand founded by a man called Cheikh Ahmadou Bamba. It all happened in a context (geographically and socially) of what we can call illiteracy (not for Senegal, but for the dominion of Mouridya) which will follow us as a community. Even though, at the beginning, many followers of Bamba were illiterate, we still have to recognize the erudition of many great relatives and admirers whose sons and descendants become great minds.

The Baye Fall, the colourful person dressed up like a modern Jamaican Rasta or, to be closer to chronological and historical truth, like whom the modern Jamaican Rasta dresses, is a man whose apprehension of life and spirituality is based on the teachings and examples of Ahmadou Bamba: "pray as if you were going to die today and work as if you were immortal". This teaching, used as a viaticum in the Latin sense of the word and a creed, will have many dimensions in the existence of the Baye Fall. The first is the dimension of physical appearance with dreadlocks, symbolizing here closeness to nature. Not the "natura naturata", but the "natura naturans", that is instead of the way things are as they are, the way they are as a result of some volition based on awareness, consciousness and a force and will to power, guide and change. This is obviously very different from ignorance.

The second and most noticeable thing is the sartorial aspect. The Baye Fall usually dresses up in patchwork, that is, in the colours of the rainbow and much more. That is inclusive. The Baye Fall is not a megalomaniac; patchwork is the "thing itself" (see Shakespeare's *King Lear*) even though this means something totally different "in the play".

The third aspect, and I must say that these aspects are not classified in order of importance, is psychological. The Baye Fall is the one who, in a context of total hostility to Islam resulting from the Judeo-Christian colonial power, and the traditional pagan beliefs of local chiefdoms and power structure, taunts all, goads all. He is not afraid. He believes in himself and remains self-reliant, knowing that he can provide for his needs and solve his problems without external interventions. This means that he is not covetous, that he can manage with what is available and still be happy and clean.

The fourth dimension has to do with spirituality and race. Bamba is the messiah as far as black people are concerned. This spiritual acumen is stronger than symbolism and it goes, as far as the Baye Fall is concerned, beyond what Haile Selassie means to the Rasta – we see here that symbolism has its limits, which are somehow short of the dedication of the Baye Fall.

The above leads us to the existence of grounds for comparison when we look at the perception of the Rasta as a physical and physiological image and phenomena as nothing new in Senegal; it has nothing shocking, either, because the older counterpart in our culture is an intrinsic part of our social fabric. In Senegal, the marginalized Baye Fall – not all – has always been tolerated as a smoker and a user of alcoholic beverages by many (even though the trend is changing). In the cultural psyche, the parallel perception or psychomental identification process is here: a negative perception of the Baye Fall leads inevitably to a negative perception of the Rasta.

Here resemblance is identification; a positive perception of the Baye Fall leads to a positive perception of the Rasta. We have the natural result that in the Mourid community, by and large, the Rasta is tolerated and accepted as a symbolic member of the brotherhood. The Baye Fall paved the way for the arrival, physical presence and acceptance of the physical Rasta.

This is the background set for two important phenomena: May 1968 with the so-called revolution in western Europe and other parts of the world on the one hand, and on the other, the advent of reggae in francophone Africa. May 1968 saw a world ablaze. There was protest everywhere against a world seen as sclerosed or stiffened by outdated ways that must be replaced. It was a time for a youth revolution, generous in ideas and, to a point, unflinching and uncompromising in principle. The prevailing order was attacked and questioned with unprecedented vigour. Myths were destroyed and authority, under its secular guise, was vilified. Taboos were shaken and the whole story leads to a reconsideration of world order and human values:

- in politics, the foundations of habits and certainties were questioned;
- in literature, new areas were explored;
- in economics social and human relationships were attacked;
- in culture, shackles were broken and the youth of the world seemed to fly with new wings; and
- in the arts, new domains were explored, opening new perspectives along the way.

Reggae: A Phenomenon Whose Time Had Come

It was in this context that reggae reached out beyond the shores of Jamaica as a weapon in the hands of protesters who would not be stopped – not stopped by language, not stopped by geography, not stopped by politics, not stopped by colour, not by race or religious creed. It took root since the youth of the world grabbed it as "an idea whose time has come". It even became more than that, since it turned into a "phenomenon". The popularity of reggae is not a matter of chance. It is an intrinsic part of a world dialectics corresponding to socio-political needs. I remember, in my youth, the popularity of Jimmy Cliff, before we discovered Bob Marley.

If I parody the famous Ibo wisdom that "proverbs are the palm oil with which words are eaten" (Achebe 1958, 5), I can say, literally, that "reggae is the palm oil with which life is eaten" in this specific context. It all happened at a moment of historical unrest. Coups are daily occurrences in Africa and on other continents. Urbanization is a serious problem with its uncontrolled congestion and contiguity; poverty breeds prostitution and violence in despondent and hopeless slums and tenements. Injustice and exploitation reign, not as exceptions, but as the rule.

When reggae stepped in and addressed these issues, it became popular in Africa in the mid- and late 1960s. It has held its ground ever since, sticking to people's lives and concerns as a protest art form and a protesting movement quite at odds with the griot's traditional music. With an anti-conformist posture and messages carried through quite palatable rhythms (or a certain definition of music as "a combination of sounds agreeable to the ear"), reggae is hailed and appropriated by the youths of West Africa who keep their eyes on Jamaica, always.

Alpha Blondy

If we travel in the imagination, we will certainly find the little dot where wisdom and madness intersect, where the self-declared fool jerks and spits out the truth from his guts. That is the stand of reggae and the realm of "foolosophy" with its undeniable impact on the collective psyche. I will take just one example here. Alpha Blondy, the most outstanding representative of francophone reggae artiste out of West Africa, is, as Shakespeare would say, "an honourable man" (*Julius Caesar,* act 3, sc. 2, ln. 100) – not like Brutus, but in the non-derisive sense of the word. This shows us his recognition of reggae and the leading role of Bob Marley as a locomotive. Humbling himself, Blondy declares:

> I am just a disciple. . . . I was seduced by Marley's message and fight . . . and I realized that this fight was also the Africans' own fight. We had to translate the message into African languages and French so that the African brothers could understand that it is not a problem of smoking. . . . We have to defend our identity, to give the floor to the dispossessed, to people who have been stifled by the colonial systems.[1]

Blondy is aware that expressing the truth is a form of madness. Say the truth and you transport yourself to the outskirts of a regular society, of convention, and of the socially and politically correct. It is, for sure, a gamble and a challenge. His rejection of the "one-party system" aims at building "a politically stable Africa before we can talk about an economically stable Africa. . . . Those who shout 'Hail the president' are the same who will say 'Down with the president'." Blondy speaks out as a committed African reggae artist: "I was a member of the Black Panthers Party – African section, when I was at high school. . . . And I was also a member of PUSH (People United to Save Humanity), the very political version of the Black Panthers."

The self-dubbed "rastafoolosopher" does not shy away from political action and commitment. His personal relationship with the then president of Cote d'Ivoire is one of mutual respect, where the son or grandson conforms to the African tradition of respect and consideration for the elders. There is, here, no contradiction between the will to change and the wisdom to nurture and protect. Blondy's attitude towards the perpetrators of crimes who cut Cote d'Ivoire in twain during a long protracted war he called "interminable" turned into "inter-minable" is a vivid criticism of politicians who are more concerned with personal profit than with communal welfare. The common good has no place in the programme of civil war, looting and egotistical self-aggrandizement. Blondy is, in his way, a messiah who tries to reunite his nation, or at least to play a part in the reunification process, not as a remote onlooker, but as an actor. His attitude during the Cote d'Ivoire civil war can be, in this respect, paralleled to that of Bob Marley during the conflict between Edward Seaga and Michael Manley in Jamaica. His conviction is that you have "the innocent people who kill each other on behalf of people who know each other and who don't kill each other. The mean ones are not those who go to the frontline,

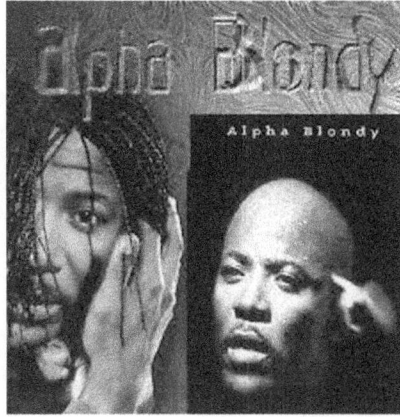

10.1 and 10.2 Alpha Blondy album covers.

but rather those sitting in offices and sending other people's children to be butchered."

His message has strong sociocultural tones, and he goes back to his mentor, Bob Marley, who: "took the ghetto out of indifference . . . Bob gave the floor to all the children from the ghetto, from all ghettos, whether they be the African, from the West Indies, from America or Europe. Take Bernard Lavilliers, he is a ghetto guy and he quickly identified with this music. Not to name Serge Gainsbourg."[2] Blondy is the messenger. He has no specific plans, but his contribution remains the landmark in francophone Africa. "When *Operation Coup de Poing* was released in Cote d'Ivoire, that was the accidental birth of African reggae and Francophone reggae." And again: "My reggae has given birth to many babies, among them Tikken Jah Fakoly. . . . Somehow, I am a happy father. When I went there (to Jamaica) and decided to bring back this music, I didn't want to be the only one to play it. It would have been stupid. . . . My goal was to create this African Reggae in the image of Jamaican Reggae." The word and the rhythm spread to Senegal, Guinea, Congo Brazzaville, Gabon, you name the countries.

Lyrics are used by Blondy to fight against poverty and illiteracy, but also to find solutions to the endemic problems of his African communities. He proposes to send children to university and school instead of the army and on to the streets. To get his message home, Blondy takes a firm cultural stand: "In 1976, my Jamaican friend Clive Hunt told me that to carry our message through, you should sing in your language. He was right." [3]

Notes

1. Unless otherwise indicated the quotes have been translated from an interview with Alpha Blondy from the Ivorian publication *L'Inter*. This interview was available online, but is now no longer accessible.
2. Translated from the website *Africahit.com*. The article is no longer available online. All quotations from this paragraph are from this web article. A copy of the interview can be located here: http://www.waxx-music.com/artistes/interview/Alpha-Blondy_149.html.
3. Translated from Réjane Ereau, "Alpha Blondy: 'Tant qu'il y aura de l'injustice, il y aura du reggae'", 1 March 2007. http://www.respectmag.com/alpha-blondy-tant-qu%E2%80%99il-y-aura-de-l%E2%80%99injustice-il-y-aura-du-reggae.

References

Achebe, Chinua. 1958. *Things Fall Apart*. Johannesburg: Heinemann.
Shakespeare, William. 2001. *Julius Caesar*. Ed. Richard Proudfoot, Ann Thompson and David Scott Kastan. Arden Shakespeare Complete Works, 3rd ser. London: Thompson Learning.

CHAPTER 11

ROOTS, DIASPORA AND POSSIBLE AFRICAS

LOUIS CHUDE-SOKEI

Reggae is mine, reggae is mine

yeah yeah . . .

Reggae is mine

yeah yeah yeah yeah yeah . . .

– Lucky Dube, "Back to My Roots"

t is all too often the case that certain black popular music charts history and signals stylistic and social transformations through the index of time and judgment that is murder: murder as topic, metaphor and symbol, murder as the raw product of the sharply divided social and embattled historical locations from which black musical forms invariably sound. Reggae is no stranger to this mode of historical awareness. It has, arguably, been the most prominent of the forms of the African diaspora to narrate a post-/ neo-/omni-colonial world as it shifted from the rhetoric of revolutionary violence to the *boombastic* language of street-level sectarianism, where narco-terrorists and all manner of *badmanism* would emerge in the vacuum between political "independence" and socio-economic and cultural freedom. From ska to roots to dancehall and hip-hop; from symbolic and ritualistic *sound-boy burials* dependent on lyrical gunfire, to the actual threats of *boom bye bye* where rhetoric becomes a gauzy fabric separating cultural poetics from social and individual will. From revolution to murder, one could say, as the politics of pan-African solidarity fragmented into increasingly narrowed commitments for generations far too late for organized resistance but suddenly armed in ways their elders could never have imagined.

The Dark Side of Reggae

Though well known for its optimism in struggle, its revelation of the celebratory nature of resistance, Jamaican reggae also harbours a not-so-secret history of intra-racial terror, violence and murder. Though the list of songs that memorialize the victims of gunfire is long and noteworthy, this dark side of reggae is actually captured best in dub, the swirling echoes also of metaphors of loss and alienation, the disembodied voices in the mix truly the sound of ghosts, the sudden dead. It is this dark, violent vision of the African diaspora that reggae has bequeathed to its two primary progenies: dancehall and hip-hop. These are genres that often feature elegiac celebrations of the recent dead while simultaneously drawing from the omnipresence of murder an unassailable sense of racial authority and the tinge of melodrama essential to the market-based dissemination of black musical forms beyond their own cultural and national borders. Because it has all too often been disengaged due to a legitimate fear of racial stereotyping, this vision has been explored via the genteel spaces of representation, accompanied by a willy-nilly fetishizing of "resistance" or "rebellion". Indeed, too much criticism has ignored just how much blood flows in the name of black dissidence and with the sanction of cultural forms which often exploit racial justice, colonial

11.1 Lucky Dube, like many African reggae artistes, manifested the tendency of mimicking either Bob Marley or Peter Tosh. Here pictured at a 2006 concert in Falmouth, Jamaica. Photo by Noel Thompson; courtesy of the Gleaner Company.

oppression or economic exploitation as justification for seemingly masculine incommensurabilities.

Lucky Dube

But now that an *African* performer of a Jamaican idiom has been so canonized, one wonders less about the fate of African reggae than about that process by which the diaspora concept is appropriated, popularized and indigenized in Africa. That Lucky Dube was a victim of the kind of gun violence that has come to represent notions of black ghetto authenticity and manhood along-side still incomplete notions of national "independence", his murder reveals a great deal about the legacies of black on black, transnational, cross-cultural politics in sound which, in turn, reveal a great deal about the legacies of pan-Africanism and the distinctly modern and populist space of metaphor called "the black diaspora". In this particular case one wonders about the curious process by which pan-African *roots* gets rooted in the place that it had long mythified as its un-problematically historical origin and its source of all manner of wild authenticities. Curious, because despite Lucky Dube's adoption of Rastafarianism and its "Back to Africa" mythos, the sporting of dreadlocks and the deployment of the icons, terms and images of an imported utopia, he and other continental reggae artists struggled for legitimacy largely due to being merely *literal* Africans. Regardless of their talent and the depth of their commitments, their primary handicap would come from not being directly produced by the symbolic gestures and romantic themes of exile and racial trauma that emerged in and after the Atlantic slave trade.

The Black Diaspora and Alternative Africas

It is too well known to have to restate here the fact that the very notion of Africa, of a possible singularity, is indebted primarily to two things: first, the colonial envisioning of a conceptually containable and politically controllable whole and second, due to black diaspora resistance movements like Ethiopianism, pan-Africanism, Négritude, Black Power, civil rights and Negrismo, which erected themselves on that primary colonial symbolic architecture.

These traditions would all feed into roots reggae sound, ideology and politics. What has not been explored enough is how so many of the central tenets, assumptions and sensibilities of these movements were technologized, popularized and globalized by black musical forms from gospel to jazz to calypso to funk and hip-hop. However, it is reggae which has had a dominant purchase on not only advocating Africa before, during and since decolonization, but on replacing the Africas of colonialism and independence with a panoply of possible Africas drawn from quite diffuse global black radical traditions. More so even than earlier sounds, roots reggae seemed always to directly invite itself to Africa. In song it demanded blood-citizenship and its right to have a say in continental governance and its processes of postcolonial identity formation. In sound it claimed a remedy for exile, absolution for the sin of distance. In keeping with its roots in colonialism, poverty and a fundamentalist sense of manhood, this millenarian and nakedly utopian music also sublimated its fantasies of power and vengeance in its language of justice and liberation (there is always, after all, an echo of revenge in revolution and of murder in freedom).

These alternative Africas produced in black diasporic sound may have been shaped by desire, nostalgia and trauma, but were primarily produced and configured by the local politics of America and the Caribbean. And so, they have been fraught with ambivalence and fear, and have been riven with class and sexual tensions. They have also been shaped by the radical sociocultural and ontological tensions at work among the illiterate, the preliterate, the non-literate and the post-literate. These contradictory factors feed as much into pan-Africanism, the "black Atlantic" and the black diaspora as do the much-feted and often exaggerated notions of resistance, subversion and revolution. When expressed in musical terms, these possible Africas have all been grounded in and by the authority of the metaphor of roots – perhaps the most potent, dangerous and unstable metaphor known to humanity. But since a sense of black *roots* was never a given assumption for continental Africans, perhaps in death it can grant the kind of authenticity granted those whose artifice outlives crude, simple flesh. Lacking the geographical distance that gives gravity to longing and authority to metaphor, perhaps murder will ultimately guarantee Lucky Dube's authenticity in a diaspora that often renders Africa secondary to its imaginings of it, its soundings of it and its representations of itself in relation to it.

In his brief but remarkably productive life he was more than a little aware of this curious position of being a merely literal African in a relentlessly poeticized diaspora, one which required the symbolic and moral charge of the continent but which would often silence it by subsuming its differential concerns into universalized or transnational metonyms of racial identity. Lucky Dube's awareness of the curiosity of his position is reflected in the fact that it was with roots reggae that he chose to make his claims on racial justice in an apartheid-ridden South Africa and simultaneously on a diaspora that had long announced its politics, intentions and differential cultural sensibilities in print, on radio, on vinyl, on screen and, eventually, on the Internet. This issue of choice will return since it is important to note that his performing this particular music was a strategic choice, not the eruption of a global sense of shared African *gnosis* as most within the reggae and Rastafari continuum had it. For him and a generation of musicians from West and South Africa, reggae may have found itself back "home" but did so as the preeminent form of black popular art to define itself in diasporic terms while rooting itself explicitly in the rhetoric and assumptions of generations of black radical thought. It would be *chosen* for its global pedigree and for what it could offer to an Africa suffering from the legacies of colonialism and apartheid but also inter-ethnic tensions exacerbated by both colonial domination and by "independence". It would be chosen also by this native of a nation that had erected itself on fantasies of white African authenticity, an indigeneity dependent on a political and historical displacement of blacks that did *not* require their total physical displacement. It was an Africa comprised of *homelands*, black centres made diasporic by institutionalized, racist fantasy in a nation that long imagined itself in but not of Africa.

But how a music that begins as a statement of Jamaica becomes globalized and translated as the sound of the very world itself, and then is appropriated due to its relentless symbols of Africa by Africans themselves, is very much the context if not topic of this tribute. Beyond reggae, this is a largely underexplored and undertheorized facet of modern African and African diaspora histories and politics. It is at times, ironically, marginal to much "black Atlantic" thought. To state this more forcefully, it is the case that modern and contemporary Africa is often left out of or marginalized by the "black Atlantic" framework, celebrated for its anteriority yet seconded to the echoes of its cultural influence. This, despite the fact that the refractive homing of cross-cultural diasporic influence has signalled more than one transformative moment or movement on the continent: from the arrival of blackface minstrelsy, jazz and rumba, through the influence of Edward Blyden, Garvey, Négritude and decolonization, to the contemporary global hip-hop, sports and media complex. In this final context of today's media, the seemingly limitless freedom of hyper-visible black American icons is consumed by a continent so destabilized by promises that it has begun to choke back its expectations. In the face of these ludic images and sounds of black possibility – which emphasize the distance between Africa and its diaspora – the more liberal legacies of transnational racial solidarity have diminished throughout the continent. After all, they may provide much to a diaspora always hungry for orientation and definition, but often offer little to the continent itself.

Lucky Dube's Music

Lucky Dube's music, produced by his claim on externally produced notions of African origins, should be heard in this context of a prismatic and refractive homing of *roots*. Now it might seem obvious to some that an Africa-obsessed music would find a welcome home in Africa, more even than many other black popular musical and cultural forms. Yet the micro-politics of how this happened and the philosophical implications of why go far beyond the obvious to tell a broader story of not just Africa's place in the global black imagination, but, more importantly, of how various peoples on the continent find their way into global conversations being held in their name but largely without their participation. It tells a story, ultimately, of how Africans so often have to find their way into the conversations and assumptions of the "black Atlantic" or the black diaspora by ironically mimicking and performing the questions and assertions of African authenticity or racial utopia produced by those very conversations and assumptions. For a non-Jamaican to proclaim and appropriate that Africa of roots was in fact no mean feat. For an African to do so was not an expression of the overwhelmingly obvious, since for those not produced by the poetics and politics of exilic longing and Western racial taxonomies, this appropriation was counterintuitive.

It is true that throughout Africa the appropriation and/or imitation of African-American and Afro-Caribbean styles, attitudes, ideas and identities have often been seen as much less than the glorious statements of the pan-African or transnational solidarity that many claim. They are more often seen as curious, subversive and dangerously inauthentic by those for whom "tradition" is being assaulted on too many fronts to count and for whom "race" is no guarantor of community or shared origins. For example, to some ears Lucky Dube's Rasta-roots performance was a gesture of colonial submission. In some contexts it signalled the weakening of indigenous tradition with Western blackness merely a mask for imperial intentions masquerading as liberationist possibilities. And, it is the case that Lucky Dube's quasi-orthodox stress on the authenticity of roots reggae was often deployed against local tastes and the new digital authenticities being produced in township musical culture. Take, for example, a song like "Back to My Roots", which was a hit in both South Africa and Nigeria. "Back to My Roots" is clearly paradigmatic of the context and issues being explored here largely due to the irony of its claim on racial authenticity and cultural orthodoxy. This song – as many Jamaican roots tunes have done – lambasted "crackadoo" and "shoobee doobee" music, forms that, though popular, were "not good for a Rasta man". In this particular narrative, it is the presence of these sounds that impels a return to a notion of roots wired in from Jamaica and its overdeterminations of the African continent.

This more general scenario faced by Lucky Dube and his generation of musicians on the African continent was not in itself unique, though the formal and political displacements of the South African state did render the concept of "Africa" perhaps more problematic there due to the explicit and formal white claim on it. However, it is not unusual for this crisis of legitimacy or confusion of authenticity to manifest wherever and whenever groups and cultural forms migrate, transform and then dare to operate within the same terms or categories of classification. But the continent of Africa has had perhaps the hardest and most uniquely ironic struggle for full recognition and inclusion of its appropriation and deployment of contemporary black diaspora forms such as reggae and hip-hop. It also still struggles with black New World notions of racial solidarity which have reached most on the continent through these musical forms despite the long and rich legacies of African anti-colonial nationalisms and the cross-currents of multiple generations and definitions of pan-Africanism. Though not the first to employ and appropriate reggae music on the continent, Lucky Dube's was arguably the most successful indigenizing of it up to that point; he was certainly the one who had most loudly captured the ears of Jamaican reggae musicians, promoters and international fans. However, beyond the crisis of authenticity, he never fully escaped the sense that his participation in this music was merely "exotic" to Jamaican listeners or to the global market for Jamaican sounds. Few African reggae artists of his generation could escape this, though they were ironically sheltered from it by a white international audience that evaluated their authenticity by quite a different standard. The fact that his fan-base, outside of Africa, was less West Indian or African American than it was white – the primary fan base for roots reggae from Bob Marley's generation to the present – was telling. His global popularity had emerged not only during the death-throes of apartheid, but also during that moment when roots reggae seemed on the decline in Jamaica, and the global audiences for reggae were quite hostile to the digitized dancehall that emerged in the wake of Bob Marley's death.

Central to Lucky Dube's significance was his internationalization of roots *as an African* during that period when dancehall was being heard by many as the sound of an island abandoning its universalizing mythologies and collapsing into its own hermetically sealed, fully digitized sound-world, locked into the rhythms of an accelerated and increasingly violent capitalism. Although dancehall has today found itself integrated into contemporary African sound-worlds, at the moment of its ascendance it was in fact heard by the growing continental *massive* as well as its global white audience as dangerously inauthentic in its machine poetics and too fiercely protective of its aesthetic and dialectal "borders" to provide a vision of either shared cultural origins or utopian possibilities. As the music's dependence on those techniques of echo so dear to the generation of dub-roots began to diminish in its production, what was heard was not a shared and open space, but something hard, sharp, crisp and closed. An African *roots* seemed then the perfectly hyperbolic, double-dose of the black organic necessary to counter that synthetic eruption of sound-scaping that began to redefine how Jamaica was heard globally. With Trinidad soca and calypso also going digital more or less soon after this, Caribbean sound began at this time to append itself to the techniques and referents of electronic music rather than to the anti-modern idylls expected of post-hippie touristic spectatorship.

Many still say that Lucky Dube's indigenizing never quite made the transformation from a heartfelt and impassioned mimicry to the full flowering of something utterly distinct in the way that, say, Jamaican rhythm and blues would transcend its complex cross-cultural origins in the birthing of authenticity called ska. In much the same way that the pre-ska, pre-independence generation of Bob Marley, Peter Tosh and Bunny Wailer studied and mimicked the voices, styles and universalizing gestures of their African-American civil rights–era heroes (Sam Cooke, Otis Redding, Smokey Robinson and, most certainly, Curtis Mayfield), Lucky Dube did manifest the primary tendency of African reggae artists to model their voices via a stringent mimicry of either Bob Marley or Peter Tosh. Prominent examples of this include Nigeria's Majek Fashek and Victor Essiet, and Ghana's Rocky Dawuni, though there were, and are, countless others. In Lucky Dube's case the sound-mask he opted for was Peter Tosh, whose murder strangely prefigured his own and which his death profoundly echoes. It would not be until Ivorian Alpha Blondy that a distinctly non-Jamaican voice would emerge in African reggae. However, Alpha Blondy would only play John the Baptist to the magnificent indigenization of Jamaican *roots* manifest in the contemporary work of his fellow Ivorian Tiken Jah Fakoly, an artist who has attained a level of political controversy that no African roots artist has ever had and which no Jamaican artist has had since Bob Marley himself. It is worth noting that in this black African micro-political context the indigenization of roots reggae radicalism and confrontation was as much a factor of *translation* as it was one of appropriation, an equal product of anglo-phone and francophone colonial differences in which both Christianity and Islam engage each other in the sound culture of the black diaspora.

Those critical of Lucky Dube's inability to fully indigenize roots reggae in the way that Jamaican crooners and musicians had themselves done remain unaware of the complexity of his very choice of mimicry and the depth of his ability to hold steady to an uninflected performance. For example, very few outside of South Africa knew that he was recognized for and successful in a variety of local indigenous musical styles and idioms, all of which had long been fusing and percolating in the crucible of apartheid's intensely creative, competitive and often violent township culture. He was, in fact, quite famous as a *Zulu* musician years before reggae or Rasta. Lucky Dube recorded six or so traditional *mbaqanga* albums *and* a Zulu and Africaans rap album under the name Oom Hansie before his first reggae album *Rastas Never Die* in 1984 – banned by the South African censors. This was also before his international breakthrough record *Slave* in 1987. Even at the height of his popularity as a reggae artist, his local fans continued to complain that this "world" or "Jamai-can" music was too far afield for them and that they were eager to hear him return to *mbaqanga*, which was at the time much more popular and marketable in South Africa than roots reggae. In his words, "The change was brought about by the fact that I wanted to reach the world. With mbaqanga I would have been seen as a tourist musician."

Though many outside of South Africa consider that multiplatinum selling Oom Hansie project as a novelty (titled *Help My Krap*), it did emerge in the transition from *mbaqanga* and other township styles to roots reggae. The very fact that roots and hip-hop had come to share cultural space and were both seen as possible options in his quest for a global and trans-ethnic language reminds us that despite the attention, excitement and growing panic concerning hip-hop in Africa today, reggae remains the most popular of the forms on the continent. It is reggae that is crucial to the very notion of a trans-ethnic – that is, "black" – popular culture. Hip-hop has merely been grafted onto the structures of feeling and expanded sensibilities made possible by reggae from before even Bob Marley's concert for Zimbabwe's independence in Harare, 1980, a date many mistakenly take to be the moment of reggae's arrival or popularization on the continent. Reggae had in fact been trickling onto the continent from the "blue-beat" and ska era, arriving with West African students and migrants from London where it was a significant sound in the climate of both black European immigrant culture as well as the provider of the sonic re-mapping of a more expansive black dispersal before, during and after decolonization. Hip-hop borrows explicitly from the fragile networks of consumption and production that were established by reggae on the continent and which were key to its indigenizing through the construction of local markets and local media, particularly in West and South Africa.

Reggae and Black Consciousness

To return to a choice expressed in black on black masquerade, in his own words, Lucky Dube's switch to reggae was due to the acknowledgement that reggae was not simply a Caribbean or specifically Jamaican music. It had attained the status of a global or world cultural form and had carved out a trans-cultural and international space of popular dialogue, something that seemed to *invite* pan-African participation and continental echoing precisely due to its relentless references to and imaginings of Africa. These were things that, say, *mbaqanga* could not do, so rooted as it was in Zulu culture, history and language and in a society that, despite the clear-cut binaries of black and white during apartheid, it never managed to supplant earlier and older, and possibly stronger, inter-ethnic divisions and differences. What must be understood is that for Lucky Dube and the myriad musicians and fans on the continent, despite its fundamentalism and deep essentialism, reggae offered not an authentic or a true Africa but a series of possible Africas that could stand above and beyond the ethnic particularities of the continent and could enable the intrusion of merely literal Africans into the black diaspora's conversations and into its creation of foundational assumptions. At its most generously utopian, roots offered a vision of possibility that, because it framed itself in the language of African ancestry, functioned in contemporary Africa as a possible future and an enlarged, cross-cultural sense of tradition that masquerades and therefore authorizes itself via the mask of the past. It may have arrived as a music of racial and economic dissidence in a post-/neo-/omni-colonial world, inspired by an oftentimes singularized and static cultural whole called Africa; but when translated, mimicked and appropriated it presented a *praxis* of cross-cultural unity and visionary possibility not rooted in specific ancestral tribal traditions or prejudiced by local identities or hierarchies based on age. In short, the Africa of roots is one that could only have emerged from *outside*, where black identities and meanings had to be carefully borrowed and invented and could never be taken for granted since they were relentlessly embattled.

It must be made clear that, in many ways, roots reggae – particularly the Rastafarian reggae that would inspire Lucky Dube and so many others on the continent – was deliberately structured as a "universal" form in its construction of Africa. This was not only due to its roots in pan-Africanism, Ethiopianism and civil rights soul and rhythm and blues, but also to the deliberate efforts of influential Rastafarian ideologues in the 1960s. In fact, a generation after ska had evolved into a deep roots style, dominated by Rastafarian ideology, there was an intense debate among some of the grass-roots theologians and organic intellectuals of the movement about the use and meaning of that Africa which had long seeped into the popular music and culture and which had been taken for granted as a known quantity or knowable object. Rather than accepting the semantic promiscuity of the term, and the fact that from slave Christianity and Ethiopianism it had spread throughout the poor and working-class cults, sects, churches and communities and into pre-reggae musical forms like mento and calypso, there was a clear attempt in that period to formalize and cohere an image of Africa. Was it to be maintained as a literal space, a target for black migration or should it function primarily as a motivating symbol, imagined origin and discursive centre? Though the rhetorical traces of the former would continue to motivate roots reggae, it was the latter opinion that prevailed and guided the work of everyone from Burning Spear to Bob Marley to Lee Perry and their multitudinous legacies. However, because this deliberately non-literal view did prevail, it remains arguably the most fragile ideological tenet of the movement since this construction of Africa would forever be threatened by not only the messy presence of an actual Africa, but even more so by literal Africans.

Despite, or perhaps because of, this ideological flexibility and political fragility, roots reggae did propose a strategic way for continental Africans to speak above the sound of their ethnicities and engage a global and transnational conversation that was denied them due to the legacies of apartheid, racism and colonialism. It must be remembered that they were simultaneously being framed and at times obscured by the overwhelmingly universal presence of the black diaspora itself and its dominance in the very redefining of Africa by way of sounds, symbols, texts and technology. This is, after all, a diaspora not simply defined by geographical sprawl and the epic legacies of racial suffering; as mentioned before, it had actually defined itself and its ambience by its deep historical implication and involvement in the technologies of sound recording and through the global dispersal of black New World music during and after colonialism. So to speak as an African, to the world at home and abroad, required Lucky Dube to adopt the language of Africa spoken by Caribbean blacks whose Africa was radically distinct from his struggles on the streets of a Johannesburg where he confronted pass laws and the infamous Group Areas act. This Africa was distinct, also, from that of his Zulu people, who still struggled against the legacy of apartheid as well as against the sometimes-imperial tendencies of many of Africa's ethnic groups, themselves included.

Now it is no secret that the global currency in the popular symbols of racial slavery is in no small part due to roots reggae, which accomplishes in sound what Edward Blyden, Marcus Garvey, W.E.B. Du Bois and generations of pan-Africanist literature and politics struggled for but could only dream of. Indeed, as diaspora pan-Africanism began to fade as an active political movement in the wake of independence, civil rights and then apartheid, and as global racial politics began to engage their own micro-politics, roots reggae maintained the dream of a common context if not a shared politics through its relentless remembering of slavery. As if to stress this point, Lucky Dube's international breakthrough album was called *Slave*, and it was a success due, in part, to his appropriation of a particular Africa and that powerful and internationally recognized symbol of racial holocaust which he would superimpose upon the then crumbling apartheid system, a system which had itself become a metaphor for colonialism's enduring legacy. He also consistently named his touring band, the Slaves. But, it must not be forgotten that though slavery may have become a symbol of the African diaspora, it is not a universal *racial* symbol on a continent where ethnic affiliations differ radically from those of the West and are shaped via distinct and still underexplored processes.

Black Consciousness in South Africa

Lest it be suggested here that roots reggae was the first or singular form of black diaspora consciousness available or present in South Africa, it is true that like other places on the continent it had long been appropriating the black diaspora's notions of race in limited but influential ways. This occurred from before the presence of Lucky Dube (one here remembers the work of the legendary Steve Biko and his "Black Consciousness Movement" which was largely influenced by the work of both Aimé Césaire and Frantz Fanon and which was seen as a potent threat by Mandela's ANC) and even before the presence of Marcus Garvey and *The Negro World*. Also, South Africa had been producing its own indigenous notions of difference and historical dispersal primarily due to the system of apartheid itself. Apartheid, in its naked system of racial hierarchy, managed to foment distinct types of cultural and political identification. Still, Lucky Dube's appropriation of the Africa of roots reggae and all of its meanings would, in this climate, find itself struggling with and against local listeners for whom it was at best exotic or at worst an imposition. Because apartheid was a structure of binary racial conflict (and because binary racial conflicts are much privileged in the black diaspora, so much so that for many the end of apartheid was the end of pan-Africanism), this superimposition of an appropriated Africa on a quite specific Africa was eventually sanctioned. The power of this gesture was, and is, clearly obvious, being that it claimed an authenticity broader and more flexible than specific African ethnic traditions. Its acceptance in South Africa was likely due to two more practical factors: first, these imported metaphors and images of Africa were seen by the white power structure as non-indigenous signs of "outside", therefore were ultimately non-threatening. There were, in fact, many whites who found it odd but amusing that he was singing Jamaican songs about Jamaican issues. Second, because it was so extremely metaphoric and non-specific, it was thought that few blacks would directly connect it to the social arrangements of apartheid. Indeed, roots reggae's global popularity as a music of rebellion is due precisely to the flexibility of much of its referents and the sometimes hazy "universality" of its politics. It was due to these factors that *Slave* and other albums by Lucky Dube were able to pass by the extremely rigid and intensely paranoid South African censors despite their oppositional and confrontational sounds and lyrics.

It is very important to note that in South Africa, as in other parts of the continent, popular song forms exist which are critical of authority, but very few of them are rooted *as forms* in explicit political protest or outright confrontation – certainly not in racial confrontation. As is well known (a topic much too rich and complex to do justice to here), much of the music of the continent ranges widely from the ritual to the historical to the incantatory and features many "praise song" forms that are geared primarily towards "bigging up" or celebrating and legitimizing the status quo. Those forms that turn their tongues to criticism are not themselves oppositional or protest *forms*, though the public chiding or critiquing of authority has always been a part of their social function. Nor is the singer or poet seen as the kind of radical social outsider that is part and parcel of the roots reggae singer's persona, one who is as inassimilable as their vision, and who could not be integrated unless the system were reformed and restructured around utterly different moral, political and spiritual principles. For this persona to function in African traditional cultural structures which are overwhelmingly organized by consensus, convention and which generally frown on rebellion, a reorientation in the social fabric was precipitated in order to make sense of both this new kind of being and of this quite novel space from which this new kind of critique was sounding. The presence of roots reggae as an explicitly protest form of popular song has thus helped legitimize and strengthen the oppositional gesture in popular African music and culture, particularly for those generations born after decolonization. It has also helped legitimize new forms of social identity and political affiliation, particularly in a context where youth must always defer to age and where the future must always be silent before the past.

Reggae in Nigeria

During the period of Lucky Dube's ascendance, Nigeria had established itself as a roots reggae stronghold on the continent with artists like African China (also known as Chinagoro), Ras Kimono, Victor Essiet and the Mandators, Daddy Showkey and Majek Fashek (also known as "the rainmaker"), to name a few. Here roots did not need to function in relationship to an explicitly racist power structure coded in black and white. The long era of dictators throughout the 1980s and 1990s – from General Ibrahim Babangida to General Sani Abacha – was perhaps the "golden age" of reggae in Nigeria. With the latter being a sworn enemy of a free press who ruthlessly arrested, tortured and executed dissenters while establishing one of the most feared police states in postcolonial Africa, the deployment of reggae's "outside" mythologies and often abstract metaphors of race and freedom no doubt spared many of Nigeria's reggae artists the kind of treatment faced by the confrontational work of the legendary Fela Kuti. Yet, because its listeners were quite attuned to its symbols and icons (whereas the military elite seemed so myopic as to forget or deny the presence of a world outside), reggae in Nigeria, during this long dictatorship, helped provide less a global sense of African belonging than it did the sense of being a community under siege, colonized from within. And for a nation for whom genocide is still a living memory, reggae became the music of a singular tribe adrift in Babylon while still technically imprisoned in the Zion of reggae mythology.

During this long and still scarring period very few non-Western artists of any sort of music toured Nigeria. This lack of external cultural interaction, coupled with the danger of public protest, forced many Nigerian musicians to reassess and redefine their roots through the already popular form of reggae and its language of exile and protest as well as its celebration of a much different Africa than that ground beneath their feet. Again, since this period was also the period of dancehall's ascendance, the indigenizing of roots was a response to or rejection of that new form of reggae that for many Nigerians at the time was heard as a sound which no longer privileged their presence through its echoic language of Africa and no longer insisted on a common context or shared origins. Though roots reggae and dancehall still remain popular in Nigeria, two things were detrimental to roots reggae's growth there, suggesting that the impact of the music was largely due to its symbols, its mythology and its oppositional stance: the freeing of Nelson Mandela in 1990, and then the death of General Sani Abacha in 1997, while in office. It was in the space between these two drastic changes that hip-hop, dancehall and contemporary rhythm and blues began to emerge as the dominant forms of new popular music in Nigeria, complete with new mythologies, new political sensibilities and new orientations to what was beginning to seem yet again like a different Africa.

Preceding this, the most important Nigerian musician to help establish and indigenize reggae in the 1970s was the beloved Sonny Okosun, who passed away much more recently than Lucky Dube and to whom this essay is also dedicated. Okosun blended it with many Nigerian and Ghanaian popular forms and used it as one of many musical vehicles of social and political criticism. Despite the fact that his music was much more light-hearted than that of Fela and much less *dread* than that of those who would become reggae artists in his wake, Okosun would do more to Nigerianize reggae than any of the singers to come after him. The target of his critique was always twofold: first, that local post-independence elite and its status quo founded on the corruption of the "petro-naira"; second, at apartheid. But clearly the major precedent for popular and trans-ethnic protest music in Nigeria and therefore Africa is Fela Anikulapo Kuti, whose music, though in no way describable as reggae, shared its pan-Africanism and its "Third World"-centrism. Fela, in his long extended instrumental grooves, evoked the subversive psychedelia of dub reggae in an era when the twelve-inch remix and the extended "discomix" were ascendant in global dance music. Though Fela notably despised reggae (feeling deeply threatened by its claim on Africa, its "third-worldism" and no doubt its rapid success), after Bob Marley's death he self-consciously embraced the mantle of "Third World" music superstar and popular voice of Africa if not the African diaspora.

As is well known, Fela's Afro-centrism and panAfricanism were primarily – though not exclusively – instigated and informed by his experience with members of the Black Panthers (primarily one Sandra Isidore) in Los Angeles while living and working there in 1969. Some will erroneously claim that it was this experience that encouraged him and his band to begin to incorporate the influences of James Brown, the JBs and the Meters into his nascent "Afro-beat". In truth, these sounds had already been growing steadily in their music largely due to the impact of and competition with the successful Sierra Leonean bandleader Gerald Pino, "the Nigerian James Brown", who had been introducing the militant funk styles of black America into West Africa on the eve of the Biafra war and the genocide of the Igbos and before Fela's direct experience of James Brown and the JBs, who toured Nigeria in 1970. His experience with a militant African-American pan-Africanism (particularly after reading *The Autobiography of Malcolm X*), when coupled with the harder new funk styles of the time and their increasing reliance on racial pride and references to the "motherland", would give his "Afro-beat" a musical and symbolic charge that was paralleled only by the work of Bob Marley and others of that generation. What is generally less acknowledged in accounts of these crosscurrents, however, is the significance of Fela and his "Afro-beat" before and after the impact of African-American radical politics and before and after the influence of James Brown and the techniques, styles and cultural politics of black American funk. What is in fact *neglected*, largely due to the obsessive reduction of the black world to its reactions to colonialism and racism is his impact on black on black cross-culturality in a Nigeria still haemorrhaging from the genocide of Biafra and then throughout a continent riven with inter-ethnic strife. With his appropriation of an African-American invention of Africa, Fela and the innumerable groups that sprang up in a post-Biafra Lagos fomented a pan-ethnic sense of Nigerian community based on what was a new notion of race and solidarity. It was, quite frankly, the sound of an Africa that had never existed but which could be made: one that was not Yoruba or Igbo or Hausa or Ibibio or Ijaw or Edo or Fulani or Tiv or any of the multitude of ethnic groups in Nigeria, all of whom suffered due to the war.

Conclusion

This new, possible Africa created a climate that welcomed and fed roots reggae and its globalizing of all currents of pan-Africanism and black radicalism in a music of popular protest. This was something that the continent would forever have to contend with because however alien it might have seemed as a concept or value, it ultimately authorized and authenticated itself in sound via the shared image, symbol and sign of Africa. It is this authentication of the various cultures, politics and identities of postcolonial Africa with the myth of a possible Africa that roots reggae sound must also be credited for. No, it did not initiate this process, nor is it solely responsible for it (indeed, that process is the diaspora itself, structured as it is by sound and the black engagement with technologies of sound modulation). Considering reggae's often blithe indifference to contemporary continental realities, it should not necessarily be praised for it either. For example, due to a blind commitment to an unchanging *anciency* and a suspicion of modernity so complete as to erase their indebtedness to it, Rastafarianism has yet to be taken to task for its support for some of the continent's most reactionary regimes – most notably in Ethiopia.

Yet, despite, or perhaps due to its contradictory and sometimes fanciful notions of black diasporic *anciency*, *roots* did take root on the continent in such a way as to help signal a transformation in how that continent both sees and hears itself across a global landscape. It is not an overstatement to say that this landscape continues to prove itself to be more attuned to speaking *about* Africa than actually listening to Africa speak. So it is not just sound and music here to be memorialized, nor is it simply the life of a remarkable musician like Lucky Dube, in whose wake new singers, producers, deejays and rappers emerge to continue redefining Africa in the language of the black diaspora. In Lucky Dube's murder what is revealed to be at stake is how the black world hears the sounds of the continent beyond the overwhelming echoes of its own desires, fantasies, wounds and its own dreaming. Herein lies not just centuries of the West's complex and varied representations and imaginings of Africa, but also the black diaspora's implication in this history of projection and construction, particularly since what we call the black diaspora is in fact an intimate component of Western modernity – not so much a "counterculture", but a constituent element, as collusive as it is resistant. However, despite its language of primal authenticity, those Africans seeking entry into the echo chamber of black modernity found in roots a language that, unlike most other languages, privileged them. In reggae these performers found not their roots or even their past. Instead they found a future, which ultimately means the ability to transform roots via the authorizing symbol of an Africa that they have grown to accept as inevitable.

References

Lucky Dube. 1984. *Rastas Never Die*. Gallo Record Company.

——. 1986. *Help My Krap* (As Oom Hansie). Plum/Gallo GRC.

——. 1989. *Slave*. Shanachie Records.

——. 1996. "Back to My Roots". *Serious Reggae Business*. Shanachie Records.

——. 2007. Interview quoted in *Mail and Guardian* (South Africa). 18 October 2007. http://mg.co.za/article/2007-10-18-lucky-dube-shot-dead-in-joburg.

CHAPTER 12

GENDER, CLASS AND
RACE IN
JAPANESE
DANCEHALL CULTURE

MARVIN D. STERLING

Already around four decades old, the scholarship on contemporary globalization has documented and analysed many empirically, as well as theoretically, compelling instances of the flows of culture, people, commodity and ideology around the world (Ong 1999; Appadurai 1996; Basch, Schiller and Blanc 1994). To such instances might be added the case of Japanese engagement over the past several years with dancehall, roots reggae and Rastafari. What makes this engagement so intriguing is the way in which it unsettles some deep assumptions about aspects of social power in Japanese society such as gender, class and race. It is using the adoption of Jamaican popular culture as insight into contemporary Japanese society, understood particularly in these three terms, with which I am concerned in this essay.

The 2000s witnessed a remarkable surge in the popularity of reggae music in Japan. While primarily a subcultural phenomenon, this popularity has extended its reach into the mainstream media in the form of several chart-topping hits by Japanese reggae acts and dancehall-inspired fashion. This surge has centred primarily on dancehall music, but also incorporates an earlier Japanese fascination with roots reggae and, primarily by extension, Rastafari. Roots reggae arrived in Japan in the mid-1970s, much as it did elsewhere in the world outside of Jamaica. In Japan, it began taking off as an underground movement in 1979 when Bob Marley performed in the country, subsequently taking shape throughout the 1980s under the influence of several independent magazines, concerts, small record labels and other modest entrepreneurial efforts. With Reggae Japansplash as its premier event, roots reggae and early dancehall achieved boom status from the late 1980s to the mid-1990s, particularly in the summer. Reggae bars and clubs proliferated all throughout urban Japan, and even in some rural towns.

Two developments have helped to galvanize the most recent Japanese interest in reggae music. The first was the sound system Mighty Crown's surprising victory against an all-Jamaican field of competitors at Brooklyn, New York's World Clash in 1999. The second was the perhaps even more surprising victory by "reggae dancer" (as dancehall dancers are called in Japan) Junko "Bashment" Kudo in an all-Jamaican field of competitors in Jamaica's 2002 National Dancehall Queen Contest. Largely inspired by these two victories, there are hundreds of sound systems all across Japan today, more than in Jamaica itself, and about 250 women have registered as dancers with One and G, a company that has taken the lead in branding the reggae dance phenomenon in Japan. The number of active dancers nationwide not registered with One and G is difficult to come by, but without doubt it elevates the number well above 250. In 2007, forty thousand fans reportedly filled Yokohama Stadium at an annual event organized by Mighty Crown, making it one of the largest (and probably the most lucrative) one-day reggae events in the world. In addition to Mighty Crown, among the most well-known Japanese reggae performers today are Moomin, Ryo

12.1 The sound system Mighty Crown. Publicity photo.

the Skywalker, Fire Ball, Hibikilla, Pang, Chehon, Papa B, Pushim, Minmi, Munehiro and Mighty Jam Rock.

Given its status as a popular cultural phenomenon, much of the socio-political significance underlying the adoption of reggae music in Japan is evidenced on the level of representation. In this essay I will explore such representations – primarily visual and textual material such as magazine photography, DVD covers, album art, song lyrics and fiction writing – that have appeared out of deeply underground as well as broader mass-mediated Japanese dancehall reggae. I will explore these representations for the way they disclose mutually informed dynamics of gender, class and race in contemporary Japan. My discussion will be significantly (though not primarily) comparative, since these representations – reflecting as they do an effort to shape reggae culture so it fits with the Japanese context – often invoke the image of the Jamaican.

Class, Gender and Race in Japanese Society

Many scholars, Japanese and Western alike, have characterized Japan as a hierarchical, group-oriented society whose individual members – in families, in professional, educational and other social contexts – depend upon and submit to the authority of the collective (Doi 1981). They view Japan as a homogenous society (Dale 1986), an orientation which, the argument goes, has helped to facilitate Japan's stunning ascent from a war-ravaged society to an economic juggernaut in the second half of the last century. The single-mindedness of the Japanese people, it is claimed, has helped create a fierce sense of purpose that has powered Japan's economic rise in the world today. Part of this perceived homogeneity registers on the level of class: Japan is supposedly a classless society in which the gap between rich and poor is less pronounced than in other industrialized countries. In such a society, men and women have clearly assigned roles within the socio-economic order: men work in the public sphere; women are conventionally expected to quit their jobs and be married by age twenty-five, have children and rule the household. In addition to the class-based terms of a Japanese society supposedly unified by equal economic opportunity (for men), in addition to a supposed gendered consensus about male and female roles within this economic order, this image of Japan as a homogenous society is further inflected in ethno-racial and nationalist terms (Dikötter 1997). Many Japanese imagine themselves to be one people, whose kinship as such reaches deeply into the haze of mythological time, to the Emperor Jimmu, whose blood runs through the veins of every Yamato (the dominant ethnic group) Japanese. With Japan, then, one has a case of the (mythological) ethnonation, in which the nation is seen as constituted of a single ethnic group.

Japanese success in international reggae can in some ways be incorporated within the ideological terrain just described. This success accords, for instance, with the old idea of Japan as a powerful ethnonation whose citizens, by working very hard (*"gambaru"*), are able to accomplish much in the world beyond its borders. But reggae in Japan might also be understood as informed by the historically specific context of its emergence (which is not to say that this context has been *necessary for* this emergence). Japan has been experiencing an ongoing recession dating back to the early 1990s (Yoda and Harootunian 2006). Many Japanese companies have struggled as they never had before: the lifetime security that they have, famously, been able to afford their workers is no longer guaranteed. More and more Japanese youth leave universities only to become *furiitaa*, so-called free-timers who are hired only part-time and/ or temporarily. These developments increasingly problematize ideas about Japanese society as comprised of a single middle class. Not coincidentally, *jibun sagashi* (the search for self) emerged as a prominent keyword in the Japanese public sphere beginning in the 1990s, unsettling easy assumptions of Japanese as a group-oriented people. With this term as their nominal banner, documentaries, books and newspaper articles, for example, feature the stories of male corporate workers who have forsaken the pressures of the business world in search of self-actualization by spending more time with their families.

In ways such as these, the clear-cut social roles prescribed to Japanese men and women have come to be in some degree of flux. Many female workers do not so readily quit their jobs at twenty-five, but rather work and play further and further beyond this age. Some of these women have been unkindly characterized as "parasite singles": women who live at home rent-free and who use their increased purchasing power to pursue their various interests domestically and overseas.

These developments are critical for understanding the demographic to which many Japanese reggae artists belong. They are often men and women who are marginalized by or have chosen to distance themselves from the mainstream Japanese socio-economy. Nearly every male reggae artiste I met, at least before the dancehall boom, was indeed *furiitaa*, working part-time to support his interest in reggae music. Not atypically, one member of Mighty Crown, in the late 1990s, was doing manual labour for a cable company in the day and working on his music at night. Many Japanese dancehall divas do not particularly or immediately aspire to the role of housewife and mother. Instead, they work as assistants in restaurants, boutiques, hair salons, hostess clubs and other such professions to which young women have been conventionally restricted.

I would not want to overstate how much Japanese women "benefit" today as a result of their professional marginalization in many Japanese workplaces (Ogasawara 1998). But, in a sense, the recessionary environment, one which includes rhetorical calls for self-searching and self-discovery, is one in which women are especially able to flourish. This is compared with men who have, by gendered convention, been locked into working long hours, five or more days a week, so they can provide for their families. Women as the "beneficiaries" of their husbands' labour have not been unaccustomed, as one sign of their middle-class privilege, to exploring the meaning and value of life beyond the grind of the workplace, such as through hobbies and travel. In this way, it is an easier transition for young Japanese women, a little more certainly deprived now of the full-time employment opportunities they have never really collectively had, to spend the full range of their twenties and even thirties travelling the world, pursuing their artistic interests (including subcultural musical interests), searching for themselves.

Among the Japanese women and men who are part of Japan's reggae scene, the search for artistic self-actualization unsurprisingly tends to be more felt for artists than for most fans. Erotic dancehall music and dance for these artists are not only means by which they pleasurably assert their desirability as men and women, but also as skilled musicians and dancers who wish to test their artistic mettle with the best in the world outside of Japan. Self-exploration through art and international travel are not particular to this current era. *Jibun sagashi* (the search for self) furthermore does not necessarily exist as a concrete idea in the minds of given Japanese reggae artists, one that they seek to self-consciously realize by travelling to Jamaica, New York, London and other parts of the international Jamaican community. I treat this concept, rather, as a public discursive manifestation of the socio-economic developments of the 1990s, one which facilitates the idea of travel to countries like Jamaica in search of artistic self-fulfilment.

Gender in the Japanese Dancehall

Having briefly discussed what I see as some key socio-economic aspects of reggae's contemporary situation in Japan, I want to discuss how the intersected issues of social power – gender, class and race (circumstantially inflected in terms of ethnicity and nation) – emerge in embodied, visual, textual and other forms of representation in Japanese dancehall culture. I begin with gender. Dress today, among many male dancehall practitioners and fans, as much in Japan as in Jamaica, is strongly influenced by the hip-hop look of athletic apparel, do-rags, jewellery and other accessories. In Jamaica, the "blinged-out" artist is not merely evidence of a crass materialism that has been cited as a sign of dancehall's ideological distance from older, nobler roots reggae. These materialist displays *are* ideological in ideology's aspect as social wish-fulfilment: in a country struggling economically, young Jamaican men are meant to identify with the blinged-out artist on the basis of a (self-evidenced) material success that so many of these young men have been brutally denied.

In comparing gendered self-representation in Jamaican and Japanese dancehall, Japan, as a far wealthier country, is enamoured of consumption as much as any place in the world. (This, however, is not to miss the fact that there is also poverty, homelessness and unemployment all across the country.) An ironic consequence is that materialist self-display is generally *less* foregrounded in the Japanese dancehall: there are not as many Japanese dancehall music videos, for instance, in which the artiste is seen swathed in luxury items in the way that Jamaican reggae artistes often are. Materialism is, perhaps, so much more a given in Japan so as to recede into the background. When I first began this research in the late 1990s, dancehall and roots reggae subcultures were quite discrete (practitioners and fans steeped in one Japanese scene often sharply distinguished themselves from those in the other). Things may have changed a bit with dancehall's popularity in recent years, with articles, for instance, about roots reggae being published in dancehall magazines to expand the range of genre coverage in these magazines and hence their marketability. However, the less strenuous focus on materialism in Japanese dancehall is perhaps in keeping with a sensitivity found more clearly in roots reggae music and, by extension, dancehall. As both are viewed as "Third World" Jamaican music, they generally are seen as the antitheses (even as they are in many ways actually expressions) of the consumerism of modern Japanese society.

What are some recurring features (visual, verbal) of Japanese dancehall style (and referenced ideology), in the way, for example, that Buju Banton's urbane roots look moves to reconcile the ongoing appeal of roots spiritualism with more recent dancehall secularism? This particular example is not arbitrary, reflecting as it does one of the most noticeable aspects of contemporary Japanese reggae. That is, the Jamaican reggae call for a return to Afrocentred tradition is articulated in Japanese reggae as a return to the Japanese premodern. This call is often constructed in the lyrics of male dancehall artistes through the figure of the samurai. The samurai is represented as an ancient icon of honour, discipline and loyalty, a return to which would right the course of a contemporary Japan whose unprincipled ways have led it astray. Striking in the use of the samurai figure is the way in which this use occurs simultaneously with references to the modern world beyond Japan. For instance, in his song, "Born Japanese", Nanjaman – if there can be a Jamaican "Ninjaman", why not a Japanese "Nanjaman"? – describes samurai as bearing *yamato damashii*. This is a nationalistic term in which Japan's national soul is seen to reside with the dominant Yamato ethnic group. In "Born Japanese", Nanjaman muses about how those Japanese today bearing this spirit leap into the world in search of something truly important ("*hontō ni daiji mono o sagashi ni*"), something beyond Japan's dishonest politicians and narrow pursuit of yen. In other songs, the sword and topknot (a hairstyle associated with samurai) are specifically invoked as the masculinist signs of Japanese agency in the world outside Japan. Such representations partly function to permit the male Japanese artist to essay into the international, confident in the knowledge that he is heir to an icon of masculinity recognized and respected around the world.

Songs like these link the recently ascendant discourses of the search for self and *kokusaika* (internationalization), a link in which deeper, truer selves are forged in the fires of the danger of the outside world. Both discourses, however, are themselves linked to that of *nihonjinron*, or theories of the

Japanese people, especially popular in the 1970s–1980s. Here, arguments for Japanese uniqueness are made not so much through comparison between Japan and any given country or group of countries in the world at large, but between Japan and a West that has long figured as a source of anxiety and menace for Japan. Indeed, in Nanjaman's song is a stinging condemnation of an America that robbed and killed Indians; made black people slaves; bombed Japan and, more recently, Iraq; and allows marriage between men (an assertion that reflects efforts toward parity between Japanese and Jamaican dancehall masculinities, even as this comparison does not absolve Japanese artistes of what must ultimately be seen as their *own* homophobia). While Japanese dancehall artists' use of the samurai metaphor is complex, it partly reflects an auto-Orientalism (Said 1979) that has defined so much of *nihonjinron*. Western power is made weaker as the male Japanese artiste enamours himself with the austere, particularly Japanese discipline of the samurai. The samurai, then, represents a way into an "authentic" Japanese reggae music vis-à-vis his resemblances to the masculinist, pre-modernist Rastafari. He shares with the Rastafarians, at least by imputation, scepticism about the morally ambiguous modernities associated with the West, both at home and overseas.

The predominantly male sound system crew and DJ culture is accompanied by an also vital female "reggae dance" scene. In some ways, Japanese dancehall as a commoditized phenomenon is felt most intensely in this aspect of the subculture. In addition to dub plates, CDs, DVDs, and other products directed toward male and female practitioners and fans alike, are fashion products directed specifically toward female dancers and fans. Even though dancehall remains, for the most part, an underground phenomenon, the subculture has generated a veritable avalanche of mass-consumed commodity. In 2006, dancehall fashion constituted something of a style boom, with a number of reggae as well as non-reggae magazines running specials on dancehall fashion and dance. In these magazines are advertised skirts, blouses, T-shirts, halter tops, purses, handbags, shoes, belts, perfume, earrings, hats, dolls and other products. All of this is in the service of providing stylistically inclined Japanese a broad range of merchandizing through which to articulate their chosen identifications, deep and not so deep, with Jamaican popular culture.

Among the commodities and services associated with the dancehall style boom are instructional videos and studio dance classes by some of the more accomplished Japanese dancers like Junko Kudo and Kiyo. In these studios, reggae dance is not so much that organic pleasure emerging from and shared casually, relatively without status, among small groups of (Jamaican or Japanese) women. It is not the pleasure which, at its most minute, is derived from the execution of particular, self-contained moves. Rather, reggae dance is deconstructed under the watchful eye of an authoritative instructor into everything from calisthenics to strength training. Like male Japanese MCs' and deejays' efforts to learn patois or to acquire even some of the most obscure records produced by Jamaica's very prolific musical industry, these women's efforts reflect the seriousness and respect with which they regard reggae dance. Despite the profoundly negative judgment that parents, boyfriends and potential boyfriends express towards this highly erotic dance, these women, often ruefully, and at great expense to their personal lives, insist on dancing. They do so mostly because they love it, and because they see in reggae dance a subculturally rich, gender-exclusive code through which they can spend their late teens, twenties or even their thirties, for dancehall's performative focus on creativity in fashion and dance affords an "ideal" way of being a young woman. While these women do perform against each other in competition, reggae dance is also, importantly, a way for them to commune *with* their subcultural peers. Unlike in Jamaica, it is very common in Japan for women to compete as duos or in small groups.

Some veteran dancers, witnessing the scene's growth in the 2000s and the hundreds of young women drawn to it, have commented on the increasing separation between reggae dance and the Jamaican culture it came from. (A related process has taken place with the musical productive side of the subculture, in which there is now a category of music known as "J-regee" or "japaregee" that has been made distinct from its Jamaican counterpart.) The veteran dancers object to the way in which the younger women, without any deep appreciation of Jamaican dancehall dancing, have allegedly reduced the dance to just vulgar bump and grind. Part of the concern of these veteran dancers comes from mainstream representations of the dance in precisely these terms. It is an anxiety, I imagine, that has been heightened with the introduction, by several Japanese pornography companies, of videos featuring "real reggae dancers". Seen in deep subcultural context, there is subversive potential to this dance in which large groups of women forgo gendered propriety to engage in a highly erotic dance that celebrates a woman's performance and control of her sexuality. However, as subcultural performance reaches broader and broader audiences, this potential often comes to submit to and reinforce the hegemonies of the mainstream. Reggae dance in this environment is stripped of its subcultural complexity, becoming just another opportunity for Japan's corporate patriarchy to commoditize and profit from the bodies of Japanese women.

Classist Hegemony in Japan and Overseas

In my discussion so far I have invoked class in a number of ways. Male and female dancehall practitioners find themselves in a struggling economy that undermines the middle-classist dimensions of the myth of homogeneity. The marginalized labour of *furiitaa* and the free time that this marginalization affords facilitates new visions – including those that come into view under the aegis of the search for self and of internationalization – of how they want to live their lives; some of these young people, with such a vision of their lives already in mind, *choose* to become *furiitaa* for the freedom it affords them to pursue their artistic and other interests.

This is not to say that the old socio-economic order and the middle-class values underlying it are gone. If only on the level of aspiration, they very much continue to exist. Even as this myth of middle-class homogeneity has been undermined by the growing numbers of people unable to realistically aspire to it, the ability to consume and hence "domesticate" the foreign remains an important part of Japan's sense of itself in the world. In the era of internationalization, the foreign includes not just the West – Johnny Walker whiskey, Hollywood actors paid great sums to appear in silly commercials, McDonald's, Kentucky Fried Chicken, French pastries and so on (Tobin 1992; Watson 1997) – but also the fashion, craft, music and cuisine of Third World countries like Jamaica. Japan's intense consumption of dub plates and vintage records is only one part of what is an almost encyclopaedic rigour with which Jamaica and its must-visit spots have been mapped, its people, vistas, flora and fauna photographed, the minutiae of its politics and cultural history documented in a long stream of books, articles and television programmes. The consumption of reggae music and ethnically othered "things Jamaican" represents one among many means by which "homogenous" Japanese, even in these hard times, remain part of a national community of consumers.

Still, when I questioned artists specifically (and, to be sure, some fans) about what motivated their interest in reggae music, what emerged was a powerful sense that reggae music provided a way to speak to their sense of disaffection with the world they saw around them, both within and outside of Japan. Nanjaman's song is but one in which the Japanese reggae artiste voices his contempt towards exploitative politicians, whose posters – familiar fixtures on Japan's semiotic landscape come election time – "reek of lies". "Babylon" is seized upon as a powerful metaphor through which to critique the darker side of life in urban Japan. Explicitly invoking the rude-boy image, the artiste Sawa describes himself, in a song entitled "Raggamuffin inna Tokyo City", as a disaffected urbanite adrift – much like Nanjaman's transoceanic gaze – in search of something plainly lacking in this city.

This sense that Tokyo is part of a Babylonian capitalist order taken to dehumanizing extremes recurs not only in Japanese reggae music but also in fiction writing on Japanese travel to Jamaica. Jah Hirō's *Rastaman Vibration* is one such work. The first section of the novel, entitled, "Babylon", is set in Tokyo. Gorō, the protagonist, is a construction worker who feels intensely disaffected with life in this vampirish city. Furuta, a friend of Gorō's, feels much the same way: "Three years after leaving college, two years after starting to drive taxis, the grime of living was soaking into every crevice of his body" (Hirō 1991, 20). While in Jamaica, Gorō similarly marvels at the divide between rich and poor evidenced upon the physical landscape in the form of hilltop mansions and the lower sprawl of urban slums. Like many of my research participants, Gorō gives the name "Babylon" to the colonialism-cum-capitalist system that has engendered the suffering he witnesses in Japan, New York and Jamaica.

In Jamaica, many observers assume that such political sensitivities are borne more by those in tune with roots reggae and Rastafari – of which there is a small but significant following in Japan – than those drawn more to the materialism and erotica of dancehall reggae. The spiritualist message is indeed more explicit in roots reggae and the secular message of consumerism and heterosexual bravado more clearly heard in dancehall reggae. However, both roots reggae and dancehall emerged from the urban Afro-Jamaican poor. As such, one continuity between the two genres of music is a fluid relationship between the sacred and the secular, a fluidity readily found throughout much of African diasporic musical culture (hence, for instance, the musicological kinships between "sacred" African-American gospel and "secular" blues). Some Jamaican Rastafarians have taken issue with how secular roots reggae music has, in their view, clouded the message of Rastafarian faith. Another example of how "subcultural" values often become compromised when brought into the mainstream, this is no doubt true to a significant degree. But this should not be reason to lose sight of the fact that much of the complexity and appeal of the Rastafarian message lies in how it addresses both the spiritual and worldly needs of its followers. Despite the differences between Rasta and roots, and between roots/Rasta and dancehall, given all their interconnections, including their shared origins among the Afro-Jamaican poor, dancehall too is ideologically invested (albeit, sometimes, with calculated, artistic repertoire-building in mind) both in secular (critique of poverty, murder and other crimes, political tribalism, governmental apathy) and in spiritual terms (such as seen in dancehall's turn to Rasta in the early 1990s).

The divide in Jamaica between roots and Rasta on the one hand and dancehall on the other feels generally more pronounced in Japan. Roots reggae and Rasta people (who tend to be in their thirties and older, products of the older interest in reggae music going as far back as the mid-1970s) often deride dancehall people as noisy and vulgar. Dancehall people (who tend to be in their teens and twenties, products of the boom in dancehall beginning in the early 2000s) sometimes ridicule roots people for their inappropriate adoption of Jamaican ways (including marijuana consumption). But, despite this divide, dancehall in Japan is not without concern for deeper political issues. Even as they relish the erotica and materialism of the dancehall, Japanese artists do sometimes speak – directly and discreetly, in onstage performance and in interviews – to issues of social power such as those related to class.

One way of thinking about this is by considering the case of the statement by sound system Mighty Crown's Masta Simon. He declared during Yokohama Reggae Sai (meaning "festival") in 2006 that Mighty Crown was unlike mainstream J-pop (Japanese pop music) acts, given how the sound system has risen to prominence outside of the industry's easy manufacturing of juvenile, palatable acts. There is a discreet critique of class here: the same anonymous corporate forces that dictate what music is to be played on the radio, on television and in record shops, that dismiss true talent and creativity for the formulaic pursuit of profits, are, loosely speaking, the same responsible for the reduced economic circumstances of much of contemporary Japan. Perhaps as part of this class-outsider imaging, Simon's onstage Japanese is pointedly rough, declining to address his audiences in conventionally polite Japanese. This crudeness, in addition to fitting with the independent self-imaging, represents an act of subcultural translation or adoption in which the boisterous spirit of the underclass Jamaican rude boy is made to fit the ethos of Japanese youth who feel they have never belonged to or who have abandoned, in whatever degree of permanence, middle-class aspiration and decorum. An example of this Jamaican-referential braggadocio is the photo of Mighty Crown in Yokohama (figure 12.1). Sammy T, third from the left, wears a shirt declaring in rude-boy manner his expertise in sexual matters: "Punany Specialist" ("punany" is a vernacular Jamaican expression for "vagina"). In these ways, young men like Sammy T and those who admire him perform the entirety of their remove – again, in whatever degree of permanence – from the middle-class world of corporate and civil service. Despite the patriarchal nature of this world, such attire would be unimaginably "low class".

Hybrid Cool: Ethnicity and Race

Of course, the social "riskiness" of wearing this shirt is undercut by the fact that most Japanese do not know the meaning of the word "punany". "Punany Specialist" approaches the status of a pure sign, one whose (initial) meanings are precisely about its lack of immediate meaning beyond the sign system itself. But while not all Japanese readers might appreciate the "punany" reference, there are other elements of "the meaning" of the overall image that are more readily available to this readership. One such element might be the decor of the gate and architecture behind the three men. This photograph was taken in Yokohama's Chinatown area, where two of the members of Mighty Crown, Masta Simon and his brother Sammy T, who are Japanese of Chinese descent, are from. The image belongs to a familiar visual (as well as, of course, lyrical) tendency found in urban black music in which the artist celebrates the street, the neighbourhood, the city where he is from (Forman 2002). Often this is a place that is marginalized in the mainstream imaginary, from Trench Town to the South Bronx to "the Dirty South". While Yokohama's Chinatown may not be impoverished in the way that many African diasporic cities are, Yokohama, in the historical Japanese imaginary, is a place of foreign and thus potentially dangerous difference, a port city that has been the residence for Western, Chinese and other foreigners arriving in Japan since the late nineteenth century.

Rather than keeping their Chinese heritage out of view, however, the brothers celebrate it. They mobilize it as a sign of a domestic ethnic difference that bridges the gap between "homogenous" Japan and distant, different and (as object of knowledge) desirable Jamaica. One practical way in which this might be appreciated is in the fact that Sammy T and Simon, growing up in this international area, have spoken English for most of their lives, making the leap from Japanese to patois more manageable for them than for most Japanese. Other Japanese reggae artistes have used reggae music to speak to their personal sense of ethnic difference in Japan. Even though she does not particularly sing about her Korean heritage, the singer Pushim has said that she feels reggae music has given her a voice through which to "be" in Japan. One research participant who is *burakumin*, a member of Japan's outcaste group, described how he felt connected to Rasta and roots reggae music because of the similarities he saw between the oppression experienced by black people and by *burakumin*.

These are, properly, examples of ethnicity, the sense a people have of themselves *as* a people based on such factors (imaginary or real) as shared history, language, religion and so on; the boundaries of the ethnic group are clarified when framed against (oppressive or dangerous) ethnic others. However, race as a pseudo-scientific, globally circulated regime emerging originally from the West during the Enlightenment, one in which intellectuals and scientists sought to place all human diversity into a handful of discrete groups (black, white, yellow, red and so on), is also relevant for an appreciation of reggae in Japan. As Japan ended about two centuries of seclusion from the outside world in the mid-1800s, it adopted more and more the thinking of a powerful West, including racially chauvinistic attitudes towards people of African descent. Black people, who have subsequently been visually represented throughout Japanese modernity as uncivilized, buffoons, brainless studs and athletes, were to be looked down upon in Japan's aspirations to become a respected power in the order of modern nations. Many Japanese intellectuals adopted Social Darwinist thinking according to which Japan's upper classes were presumed to be, as a product of "social evolution", morally, intellectually and otherwise "fitter" than the lower classes; Europeans more so than non-Europeans (including Japanese); and Japanese more so than non-Japanese Asians. The third view was used to help justify Japanese colonialism throughout Asia. To the extent that Japanese used race to explain their supposed superiority over other Asians, Japanese attitudes in these terms about Koreans and Chinese in Japan are not only about domestic ethnicity but also global race.

Western-received ideas of blackness continue to be posited in Japan, today, as the antithesis of an idealized racial whiteness, a whiteness with which Japan has historically identified (even while fearing its foreign difference). This is evidenced in nearly routine representations in contemporary Japanese media of blacks as dirty, dangerous, aggressive and promiscuous and of whites as kind, romantic and sophisticated (Russell 1998). However, there is also a history in which Japanese have seized upon blackness as a figure of protest and resistance against imperial, capitalist, and other forms of hegemony (Koshiro 2003). As Japan first embarked on its journey into modernization, it looked to African-Americans as a non-white people who had risen to the ranks of politicians, entrepreneurs and scholars despite their continued struggles with racism in the United States. Japanese Marxists and *burakumin* scholars have looked to black people as international allies in class-based and ethno-racial terms. This positive reading of blackness as politically empowering might be linked to readings of blackness as cool: while offensively stereotyped, black people are viewed with admiration for the athletic, sexual and artistic gifts with which they are imagined to be endowed.

How is race, and blackness particularly, reflected within the Japanese dancehall? Again, it is difficult to separate a discussion of race from that of class and gender. With regard to race as linked to class, I will only briefly reprise a couple of points that I made earlier. Among the many commodities associated with reggae music are dolls that caricature the physical features of black people. These products are very reminiscent of Western figurines, comic book characters and similar images from the late nineteenth century onward in which black people are represented with black skin and white lips or, as with one item called "Jamaica Guitar", with brown skin and luridly red lips. The ability to racially objectify and consume blackness in the form of commodities like these indexes a common identification as Japanese. This is Japaneseness understood specifically as middle-class ability to consume the world, to "take the best and leave the rest" (and to make "the best" into "the rest" in the taking). Even at its cutest (such as another collection of dolls featuring Rastas wearing tams and dashikis), Jamaican blackness here is essentially something to be commoditized.

Race in Japanese dancehall can also be seen through the prism of gender: as noted above, male dancehall artistes transpose the sartorial, gestural and other subcultural encodings of black Jamaican masculinity onto their own faces and bodies. A fan told me once that there was just something about Japanese reggae legend Nahki that other Japanese reggae artistes did not have. While this remark could have meant anything, I want to suggest, based on several images of Nahki that I have seen, that part of this mystique has to do with a certain self-referential gesture toward racial blackness. Nahki's rounded forehead, full lips, dark skin and flat top hair cut – popular throughout the African diaspora in the 1980s and 1990s when Nahki's fame was at its height – are meant to signify a coolness located somewhere between the Afro-Jamaican and the Japanese. To name this location "black" or "Jamaican" misses the point: rather, what is aspired to is a creative, artistic self-styling with blackness, intensely unnamed, as just one resource. Accordingly, the caption of one magazine cover, in which what appears to be Nahki's monochromatic, photographically darkened, face fills the page, queries the hip reader – significantly not in familiar Japanese but in foreign English – "Are you domestic alien?"

Also, as in Jamaica, women's bodies in Japan are offered up to the male gaze but also bear their own iconic agency, one which, in the Japanese case, can inhere in its ability to claim and manage both the identity of Japaneseness and the difference of the Afro-Jamaican. There are the many images – the covers of CDs and event flyers that feature photographs of Afro-Jamaican dancers, for instance – that suggest that Afro-Jamaica remains a primary referent through which Japanese appreciate reggae dance. Many Japanese dancers perceive Jamaican donnettes as more muscular and athletic than they are and seek to develop this aspect of their dancing. However, compared with other societies, such as those of the African diaspora and the West, in Japan, the blackness with which this athleticism is associated is less fully assumed to be the absolute phenotypic property of black people. Given the relative absence of black people in Japan, blackness is more readily seen as, and is more uncontestedly reduced to, manipulable symbolization. The cover of one

12.2 CD cover by Japanese artist Ryoono

reggae dance DVD, for instance, features two Japanese, bikini-clad dancers whose bodies, including their bared backs, are tanned a deep bronze. Their "blackness" is metonymically linked to the word "muscles": the video is aimed at developing the physical strength of Japanese reggae dancers. In this image, the cover of a CD painted by the artist Ryoono, there is a similar blending of the Jamaican and the Japanese, the racial and the ethnic, on the erotic, exotic canvas of the woman's body. The woman is marked as racially black by her darkened skin, but also racially Asian, potentially, by her ambiguous face, by the tan line running across her hips. In ethnic terms, the geisha references – the distinctive hairstyle and ornamental hair pins, the strategically placed fan – mark her as Japanese. The flowers resemble the hibiscus, a popular Jamaican flower, ethnically marking her as Jamaican; the flowers, which seem to emerge from her body, are in various stages of bloom, strongly evoking the sense of a young woman, Jamaican or Japanese, coming into sexual maturity. And yet, "the flower", as one metaphor of the natural, supplements that of the woman's (apparent Afro-Jamaican) blackness as another metaphor of this natural.

The overall impression is of a dense interlinking of the multicultural, multiracial, and subcultural elements identified with the Japanese geisha and the Jamaican donnette (figure 12.2; note the bra and heels). Any reckoning of what she singularly is, given how emphatically the evidence points both one way *and* the next, would be pointless. But, perhaps, in the end, the woman is Japanese, to the extent that she is a product of Japanese creative agency, of a Japanese pleasuring in the Afro-Jamaican global in a way that is (il)legibly local.

Conclusion

There is a tendency to judge Japanese adoption of world culture, from reggae and Rasta to hip-hop, as poor imitations of the original. Japanese have been seen as not quite getting jazz music, for instance, because rather than embracing the music's improvisational spirit, many early Japanese artistes sought to imitate the African-American masters. An opposite accusation today has been that Japanese do not quite get urban black music, because they do not experience the poverty and suffering that this music comes from.

Both accusations miss the fact that Japanese adoption of global cultural forms like reggae music will ultimately proceed not according to Jamaican, but ultimately Japanese socio-political prerogatives. With regard to the first accusation, that of Japanese imitativeness: rather than being seen as some sort of failure of the creative mind, such an imitation might be more productively seen as rooted in Japanese traditional approaches to cultural learning (Atkins 2001). This approach is one in which novices pursue an art or a craft as part of a master's "house" in precisely the way this master (as opposed to another master in this same art form) does. It is possibly for this reason that so many Japanese have travelled to Jamaica seeking out specific elders (like Mortimo Planno and herbalist Dr Bagga), musicians (such as Augustus Pablo) and dancers (like former national dancehall queen Stacey) from whom to learn Rastafari, reggae and dancehall dance respectively. The second, "opposite" accusation, again, is of the superficial adoption of the art form; "superficial" here not so much in the sense of "mere" imitation, but in the sense of adopting only some elements but not others, or incorporating Japanese elements that apparently do not belong. However, such an adoption can never be seen as superficial given the complex, gendered, class-based and ethno-racial (among other) terms in which they are received in Japan. The gap between the Jamaican and the Japanese becomes not so much a sign of Japanese failure to understand the Jamaican, but rather signals a transition in which Japanese try to root what they have learned from their Jamaican masters in terms that can be most meaningful in Japan.

This process, of course, is not politically innocent. In this essay I have discussed gender, class and race as dimensions of social power, in the context of twenty years of recession, that give meaning to Japanese adoptions of Jamaican culture *in Japan*. But, as Jamaicans become aware of Japanese interest in Jamaican music, and as Japanese travel to and even reside on the island, an important future concern will be not only how the Jamaican as encoded in dancehall is worked through in Japan, but also how this Japanese presence in Jamaica is received according to *Jamaican* issues of social power. While I have hinted at these issues as they emerged in the original development of the cultural forms in question, I was not able to more fully address these complex issues in this chapter. Further pursuit of these issues, however, will provide important perspectives on the scholarship of global cultural and demographic movement, postcolonial studies, and the Afro-Asian, among others. In Japan, Japanese may encounter little resistance to the commoditization of the bodies of Jamaican people, in which, for example, Jamaicans are reduced to cute or grotesque caricature, physical musculature, and the iconicity of dark skin divorced from fuller humanity. In Jamaica, however, Japanese confront Jamaicans as human beings, including the stark realities of poverty and vice on the island, Jamaican suspicions about Japanese appropriation of and profit from Jamaican music (the issue of "cultural theft"), and a postcolonial Jamaican landscape in which there are Chinese and East Indians but in which Japanese (despite their recent successes in international reggae) do not, in some ways, for many Jamaicans, fully exist. The above bodies of literature represent important perspectives on these issues, and, in turn, may be importantly informed by the case of Japanese pursuit of Jamaican culture at its Caribbean source.

References

Appadurai, Arjun. 1996. *Modernity at Large: Cultural Dimensions of Globalization.* Minneapolis: University of Minnesota Press.

Atkins, E. Taylor. 2001. *Blue Nippon: Authenticating Jazz in Japan.* Durham, NC: Duke University Press.

Basch, Linda G., Nina Glick Schiller, and Cristina Szanton Blanc. 1994. *Nations Unbound: Transnational Projects, Postcolonial Predicaments, and Deterritorialized Nation-States.* Langhorne, PA: Gordon and Breach.

Dale, Peter N. 1986. *The Myth of Japanese Uniqueness.* New York: St Martin's.

Dikötter, Frank, ed. 1997. *The Construction of Racial Identities in China and Japan: Historical and Contemporary Perspectives.* Honolulu: University of Hawaii Press.

Doi, Takeo. 1981. *The Anatomy of Dependence.* Tokyo and New York: Kodansha International.

Forman, Murray. 2002. *The 'Hood Comes First: Race, Space, and Place in Rap and Hip-Hop.* Middletown, CT: Wesleyan University Press.

Hirō, Jah. 1991. *Rastaman Vibration.* Tokyo: Jahplan Press.

Koshiro, Yukiko. 2003. "Beyond an Alliance of Color: The African American Impact on Modern Japan". *Positions: East Asia Cultures Critique* 11 (1): 83–215.

Ogasawara, Yuko. 1998. *Office Ladies and Salaried Men: Power, Gender, and Work in Japanese Companies.* Berkeley: University of California Press.

Ong, Aihwa. 1999. *Flexible Citizenship: The Cultural Logics of Transnationality.* Durham, NC: Duke University Press.

Russell, John. 1998. "Consuming Passions: Spectacle, Self-Transformation, and the Commodification of Blackness in Japan". *Positions: East Asia Cultures Critique* 6: 113–77.

Said, Edward W. 1979. *Orientalism.* New York: Vintage Books.

Tobin, Joseph, ed. 1992. *Re-Made in Japan: Everyday Life and Consumer Taste in a Changing Society.* New Haven: Yale University Press.

Watson, James. 1997. *Golden Arches East: McDonald's in East Asia.* Stanford, CA: Stanford University Press.

Yoda, Tomiko, and Harry D. Harootunian, eds. 2006. *Japan after Japan: Social and Cultural Life from the Recessionary 1990s to the Present.* Durham, NC: Duke University Press.

CHAPTER 13

OCEANIC REGGAE

BRENT CLOUGH

To anyone plying reggae routes nowadays it is obvious that Jamaican music has an untiring need to be outward bound, to move energetically through circuits of international and extra-national exchange. In the long echo of music from Jamaica heard in the Oceania region (Australia, Aotearoa/New Zealand and the Pacific), it is also possible to detect a longing for an intimate sense of the local, for the construction of a home-place, even an imagined nation. In 1995, at the University of the West Indies in Kingston, the keynote address at the Marley's Music conference was given by UK scholar Dick Hebdidge. Hebdidge noted that Marley invoked a particular sort of belonging: "the Marley nation isn't tied to a particular ground or territory and its boundaries will

never be mapped. . . . Its roots are plastic in the original sense of being vital and in flux, ever-changing. Those roots are always spreading outwards, seeking new connections along the lattice-work of fault-lines that underlies and undermines the old colonial structures" (2003, 9).

Reggae roots in the twenty-first century are certainly vital, mutating and rhizomatic in Oceania, but when Bob Marley brought his *Babylon by Bus Tour* to New Zealand, Australia and Hawai'i in April and May of 1979, the colonial structures in the region were still largely intact. Numerous island states and populations in the Oceania region were "governed in association with", "cared for" or directly controlled by France, the United States, Indonesia, Australia and New Zealand, a situation which continues, to some extent, to the present day. In that neocolonial context, people on small islands in the Pacific Ocean as well as in urban centres like Port Moresby, Sydney, Auckland, Suva and Honolulu registered the Marley wave, feeling the sudden rush of his depth-charge metaphors and the resurfacing of subaltern histories. In villages deep in jungles, to apartment blocks by freeways, Marley's potent song-texts of the "sufferers" – the marginalized, the dispossessed – brought a familiar fragrance of far-off Jamaica – a blend of ganja, burning garbage and the bush after rain. In recent years, Marley's music and image have become ubiquitous in Oceania, even if still mostly restricted to the repertoire of his "international" years, most commonly represented by the compilation *Legend* (2002).

The anniversary of Marley's birthday, on 6 February, now has considerable significance as a day of celebration in New Zealand (or Aotearoa – its Māori name) because it falls on the modern state's contentious birthday, Waitangi Day. It has become a day when deeper questions attend notions of "One People" and "One Love" (*Aroha Tahi*) for those citizens of the Marley nation, indigenous or non-indigenous, who flock to reggae concerts around the country.[1] Across Oceania, hundreds, if not thousands, of amateur and professional musicians are interpreters of Marley's songs or play Marley-style reggae. Cassettes, CDs or sound files of his songs are staples in many private collections. Marley's songs are part of folk memory and can be called up in spontaneous performance at parties and social gatherings. The title of a popular 2006 Hawaiian reggae compilation asserts it plainly: *Everybody Loves Bob Marley*.

Marley's continued presence as the unchanging model for reggae in Oceania underscores the myth of a singular, originating figure for the music and although he's often referred to respectfully as "Brother Bob", or by a younger

generation as "Uncle Bob", Marley also serves a symbolic paternal role for some. Marley historian Roger Steffens relates an incident on a lecture tour of Aotearoa in 2007. After a well-attended talk in Auckland, the following occurred:

> [A] thin man with two little children at his side stood up and made a minute-long speech in the Māori language. Then, as he began to translate what he had said into English, his voice broke with emotion and, fighting back tears he said, "We welcome you to our land. This is a place that loves Bob Marley and the message he carries, which you have brought to us today, and we thank you for that. When I was young, I had no father, no mother, no sister, no brother – and Bob became my father, as he is like a father to our people too. (Roger Steffens, Australia and New Zealand travel journal, November 2007, e-mail correspondence, October 2008)

13.1 Pioneering Australian Aboriginal reggae band No Fixed Address in 1981. *(From left)* Billy Gorham, Joe Geia, Bart Willoughby, Peter O'Rourke and Chris Jones. Photo: Carol Ruff.

Although his music arrived on vectors of global pop dissemination, Marley also shadowed old trade routes to the Oceanic realm – where family was waiting. In this sense reggae was not imported, it was *expected*. Indigenous people and settler descendants alike were reminded by Marley and other Jamaican roots artists of "the half that's never been told" – lingering stories of dispossession, displacement and colonial exploitation. And, as a partial antidote to mission-supplied moralism there was the unexpected and welcome combination of earthy carnality and earthly redemption.

Dean Hapeta, otherwise known as Te Kupu, pioneer of hip-hop in Aotearoa with his crew, Upper Hutt Posse, says of Marley's music and the reggae he heard in the late 1970s: "I was strongly influenced by the defiant nature of reggae protest songs, but at the same time much enthused by the love content in songs. Bob Marley is still the most listened to reggae artist in Aotearoa and every new generation internalises his musical and lyrical prowess. . . . Māori can connect with the words and rhythm of liberation. Uncle Bob's music and message will stay strong for us always" (e-mail to the author, November 2008).

Tigilau Ness: Aotearoa's Grandfather of Reggae

Tigilau Ness, the man dubbed Aotearoa's "Grandfather of Reggae", was born in Auckland after his parents moved there from the small Pacific island of Niue. After years of racist scapegoating, dawn raids by police on so-called Pacific over-stayers, and ongoing street violence in the 1970s, Ness and other young Pacific islanders formed a self-defence and civil rights organization affiliated to the Black Panthers in the United States – the Polynesian Panthers, for which he became minister of culture. By 1978 he had formed one of the first reggae bands in the country called Unity.

Ness first heard Marley's music in the mid-1970s when friends brought an album back from the United States – *Natty Dread* – and told stories of this man who, allegedly, smoked a pound of marijuana a day, and was inciting revolution and rebellion against the "Babylon system". As well as the mystique of Marley, there was something familiar about the sound of the music, the rhythmic *skank* of it. Ness explains the appeal: "I immediately took it all in and related to the music which, to me, had a Pacific Island flavour to it, and the lyrics were powerfully Biblical. It re-awakened in me my love of the Bible and gave me a new sense of purpose. To me it was a mystic revelation. Rasta-fari!" (e-mail to the author, December 2007).

Bart Willoughby: Australia's Bob Marley

Around the same time Tigilau Ness was forging an identity via music, in Australia an indigenous Pitjantjatjara youth who had been born on a Christian mission station near the vast Nullabor Plain and had made his way as a teenager to Adelaide was also listening intently to Marley's music. Drummer, singer and composer Bart Willoughby saw "Get Up, Stand Up" on television and his life changed. He says: "I just freaked out.

13.2 Henry Gibson "Seaman" Dan from the Torres Strait Islands, Australia. Photo Kerry Trapnell.

It was powerful. I was thrashing the albums when I was about eighteen. I practised all the words, all the rhythms. It was a time of waking up and when Bob came he woke us up – quick. He taught us what no-one else could have. We had to find out really, which would have taken fifty years. . . . He made sense, he popped out of nowhere and he made a whole lot of sense" (interview by the author, October 1997).

George Lipsitz in the book, *Dangerous Crossroads*, suggests that Marley's "pan-African vision" helped Indigenous Australians transform themselves from a tiny national minority into part of the global majority of "non white" people: "Like the Maoris [*sic*] . . . Indigenous people in Australia found the Jamaican's genius for situating 'blackness' in the Caribbean, African, European and North American contexts helped them understand what it meant to be 'Black' in former British colonies in the South Pacific" (1994, 142).

In *Wrong Side of the Road*, a 1981 semi-documentary feature film, directed by white Australian Ned Lander, Bart Willoughby (by then already being called "Australia's Bob Marley") and his band No Fixed Address are seen enduring police harassment and rocking Aboriginal audiences with a sound that has since defined popular indigenous music in the country – an assemblage of roots reggae, ska, country, rock 'n' roll and now hip-hop – allied to the proclamation of contemporary black identity, a style which remains potent for youth in Aboriginal communities.[2]

Māori Reggae Bands

Throughout the Pacific, but most fervently in Aotearoa/New Zealand, roots reggae (in ways rarely evident in the context of earlier imported musics like rock and soul) was appropriated in the late 1970s and 1980s as a vehicle for seething social and political views. Formed around the nucleus of an earlier band called Back Yard, Herbs was an Auckland-based reggae group with members from Tongan, Māori, Samoan, Cook Island and English backgrounds. They coalesced in 1980, the year after Bob Marley's visit to Aotearoa. *What's Be Happen?*, Herbs' 1981 debut album featured songs about violently suppressed local protests against the racist Springbok rugby tour of New Zealand during the same year. Other hot topics which received commentary by the band included Māori land rights struggles, the displacement of Polynesian migrants, run-ins with the police and a moving tribute to the recently passed Bob Marley, with the promise to him that his legacy in Aotearoa was assured: "Reggae's Doing Fine". Eventually Herbs carried their pan-Polynesian take on reggae to a global audience, and, importantly, back to neighbouring islands in the Pacific, where their songs opposing French nuclear testing at Mururoa and Fangataufa atolls in French Polynesia received widespread support. Other largely urban-based Māori reggae bands followed Herbs' lead. Chaos, Aotearoa, Sticks and Shanty, Mana, Dread Beat and Blood, David Grace, and Injustice, among others, established the music as a highly politicized new style.[3] At one point in the mid-1980s, Wellington, the epicentre of reggae in Aotearoa, was identified as the Southern Hemisphere's largest market for reggae record sales – a claim still made by local record companies and artists (e-mail correspondence with James Moss, director of Jayrem Records, November 2007).

In the years following the first wave of Māori reggae bands, the Wellington-based group Upper Hutt Posse (UHP) developed their own fusion of reggae and hip-hop, fuelled by revolutionary impulses found in both musics, but targeted at the white or *Pākehā* establishment in Aotearoa. They expressed Māori views that rarely had been so forcefully articulated in local popular culture. By the mid-1990s, a video of UHP's reggae cut, "Dread on a Mission" fronted by MC Wiya (Matt Hapeta) included what was probably the first unfurling of the *Tino Rangatiratanga* or Māori sovereignty flag (in front of the New Zealand parliament house) in a television pop clip.[4]

The commitment of reggae bands to Māori cultural expression was allied to declarations of affiliation with Rastafari and denunciations of Babylon. In addition to the use of Rasta terms and Jamaican patois by several Māori groups, the band Aotearoa made a decision to sing in *te reo Māori*, Māori language, memorably demonstrated in their 1985 single, "Maranga Ake Ai" ("Wake Up People") which quickly insinuated itself into homes, nightclubs and land rights marches. Whether as a soundtrack to recovering ancestral land, fighting cops or partying, reggae was made indigenous by Māori artists and audiences in the 1980s and arguably into *the* national music of Aotearoa in the new millennium. This development of reggae (as well as soul and hip-hop) in the Māori language was consistent with the broader campaign to rescue *te reo* from extinction, bolstered by the creation in 1982 of *kohanga reo* or total

Māori immersion language nests for pre-school children, a scheme followed two years later in Hawai'i.

The question of indigenous expression played out in somewhat different ways in Hawai'i, where adoption of reggae by island musicians happened initially in the mid- to late 1980s. This original wave of reggae-informed music came soon after the popularly known 1970s "Hawaiian Renaissance" of music and dance, in which modern (from the late nineteenth century onwards) Hawaiian language songs in the *hula ku'i* and *mele Hawai'i* styles and English language *hapa haole* songs were revived and accompanied by lyrics directly concerned with the unique and threatened aspects of Hawaiian culture and *aloha'aina*: love and defence of the land.

Jawaiian Style: Hybridization of Reggae

After Bob Marley's seminal concerts in Hawai'i on 5 and 6 May 1979, reggae was taken up locally with some attempts to approximate a Jamaican style in the mid-1980s by artistes like Butch Helemano, Brother Noland and Peter Moon. By the early 1990s, reggae was being hybridized with uniquely Hawaiian nuances – strong melodies, harmony vocals, a legato or smoother sense of rhythm (which is characteristic of music throughout the Pacific) and the occasional use of ukulele or ethnic Hawaiian arrangements. The style was readily marketed by the radio and recording industry as *Jawaiian* – conflating its Jamaican and Hawaiian characteristics.

Jawaiian music also localized reggae as a driver for a much needed popular dance music. Jawaiian songs were often covers of Jamaican reggae tunes, but with quicker tempos. Local musician Peter Moon said, "it is one of the first, if not the first danceable type of local music" (Weintraub 1998, 79). The music also was described as "cha-lang-a-lang" which refers to the foregrounding of ukulele and the "island strum" – a feature in much *hapa ha'ole* music, and present in Jawaiian (ibid., 82). Rather than meshing easily with a programme of indigenous Hawaiian cultural advancement, Hawaiian reggae and Jawaiian were greeted (and are still treated) by some guardians of things genuinely Hawaiian as another foreign incursion and principally a music for "locals", a term which encompasses ordinary or "grass-roots" Hawaiian-born people of mixed Polynesian and non-indigenous (often East Asian) backgrounds (ibid., 80). In 2002, music critic and *Honolulu Star-Bulletin* columnist John Berger noted the following: "The division between reggae-beat music and other styles of local music will continue to be the great divide of the music scene here. No type of music here evokes stronger feelings pro and con . . . the island culture represented is Jamaican, not Hawaiian."[5]

But, as Amy Ku'uleialoha Stillman points out, Jawaiian artistes express concerns for, and commentary on, everyday life in the islands. Songs such as "Hawaiian Lands", "Hawaiian Roots", "Island Reggae", "Jawaiian Wave" and "Sweet Lady of Waiahole" are clearly about subject matter unique to Hawai'i, dispelling any notions that Hawaiian reggae may be nothing more than imitations of Jamaican exemplars (1998, 97). This emphasis on local roots is a sign of the indigenization of reggae common to Pacific and Australian Aboriginal artistes, where disputes over land ownership and an evocation of a home-place (in Māori, *Turangawaewae* – or "a place to stand") are crucial themes.

Native Hawaiian Bruddah Walter's adaptation of the Marley song, "No Woman, No Cry" (addressed in the chorus to an "Hawaiian woman") is relocated from a government yard in Trench Town to the Hawaiian countryside and functions as a nostalgic remembrance of native autonomy and a call to protect locally owned land from rapacious outside development:

> I remember when we used to swim
> on a little beach down in the country.
> It's all yours from the hill to the sea, Hawaiian!
> We could go fishing a-plenty
> But observe all the hypocrites along the way.
> In this great future you can't forget your past
> Dry your tears I say.[6]

The affiliations and differences between "local" and "native" are sometimes expressed in the context of Hawaiian reggae, but the common factor is an overriding concept of *aloha'aina* or love of the land. Leader of Kupa'Aina (meaning "people who love this place"), a contemporary band which fuses Hawaiian language and reggae, Kevin Chang (whose ancestry includes Chinese and Irish) says: "Hawaiian music is a thing that talks about identity – maintaining or perpetuating our way of life. It doesn't necessarily pertain only to native people. We are trying to negotiate our identity. Local people are not just Hawaiian – it is the generation before us that was concerned with annihilation. Ours is trying to recapture what the generation before may have lost. That's something that's going on around the world – struggling with globalism and change beyond people's control" (quoted in Griffith 2006).

Reggae in Melanesia

Thousands of kilometres to the west of Hawai'i is Melanesia, a region frequently described by Australian politicos as an "arc of instability" seen to run from East Timor in the northwest to Fiji in the southeast. Melanesian adoption of reggae is now so ubiquitous, it is seen as being intrinsic to local culture.[7] But, to borrow Eric Hobsbawm's famous phrase, this "invention of tradition" in Melanesia is relatively recent (1992). In some parts of Melanesia, reggae's indigenization has meant merging with kastom[8] music and performance, deployed as a simultaneous expression of modernity and village level resistance to homogenous national identity.

In Vanuatu, a dance from the Pentecost Islands in Penama Province fits well with reggae. The language and style are called, interestingly, raga, and the songs sometimes deal with the nature of village kastom activities like pig killing. In 2004 the group Vanlal[9] from Central Pentecost Island came to the annual Fest' Napuan music festival in Vanuatu's capital of Port Vila and stunned and delighted the city audience with their adaptation of a local dance form to a reggae arrangement – the fit was electrifyingly right. Indeed, although Fest' Napuan is dominated by local and international reggae acts often playing distinctly Marley-style reggae, the kastom bands continue to excite the crowd like no others. This was certainly the case at the November 2008 festival when Nauten Band from the southern Vanuatu island of Tanna, dressed in traditional costumes and singing in their local language, was one of the very few bands to elicit any dancing from the otherwise attentive but relatively motionless Ni-Vanuatu audience of several thousand people.

In other parts of Melanesia, like Papua New Guinea and the Solomon Islands, most people retain connections to their land, but Westernization and the weakening of traditional village life has exacerbated problems like urban drift, poverty, gangsterism, and ethnic tensions between migrants and residents. Endemic government corruption, lack of infrastructure, unsustainable

13.3 Melanesian fans at Pacific Reggae Sounds, Gallery of Modern Art, Brisbane, 2009. Photo: Brent Clough.

logging of rainforest timber by foreign companies and associated environmental issues add to a perception, frequently advanced by the former conservative government of Australia, that these are weak nations teetering on the brink of becoming "failed states" and as such invite regional insecurity.[10]

The Solomon Islands are north of Vanuatu. There are nearly a thousand of them with some seventy languages spoken by around half a million inhabitants. The Solomons have been especially affected by civil strife with armed conflict breaking out in 2000 between migrants from the populous island of Malaita and residents living in and near the British-created capital, Honiara on Guadalcanal. Hundreds of people died in the internecine battles and thousands of lives were disrupted until peace was restored by the intervention of the Regional Assistance Mission of Pacific armed forces led by Australian troops and bureaucrats. In the period after the civil unrest there was an explosion of music production in the Solomon Islands, frequently in small home studios, as well as at established facilities like Unisound Studios, where numerous Rasta-inspired melodic roots reggae albums from the likes of Native Stoneage, Iron Bottom Sound, Jah Roots and Litol Rastas were recorded. The songs, mostly sung in English or Solomons *pijin,* were clearly influenced by 1970s style Jamaican music along with the South African roots-derived reggae of the late Lucky Dube (who performed several times in the Pacific before his death in 2007).

Mediating the journey from rural tribal life to urban uncertainty, popular music, and especially reggae, has been for many "grass roots" people a refuge, solace and key to imagining the future for their communities and an emerging sense of nationhood. Tapping into a Rasta worldview, some black inhabitants of contemporary Melanesia look to imagined, ancient African roots to guide them out of a neocolonial Babylon. This is clearly reflected in the use of dread language and titles of songs like "Jah People", "Rastaman Personality", "Shanty Town Dreads", "Rastaman Wake Up" and "Dready Image". Some Solomons reggae songs speak directly to local politicians on behalf of an electorate weary of cronyism and corruption. The 2008 piece, "Leaders Fighting" calls out to national figures to "stop your dreams and you'll be satisfied" over a slow reggae arrangement.[11] And in the midst of conflict and its social residue, a Solomons roots artiste like Marata Man, with little public profile, can emerge on a grainy YouTube video clip for viewing via the expanding Internet network in the Solomons and around the world, extolling the role of the universalized Rasta as observer of armed men fighting (in this case in the neighbouring island of Bougainville, the now-autonomous province of Papua New Guinea): a "Borderline Rastaman".[12]

If these glimpses of reggae's indigenization in Aotearoa, Australia, Hawai'i and parts of Melanesia have a common thread, it is in the value musicians and audiences place on "roots" as a metaphor for the vital expression of local cultural identity. Paradoxically perhaps, this means for many Rastafari in Melanesia, Hawai'i, Aotearoa and Australia, that reggae calls them "home" to Ethiopia. This creates a desire existing, not without tensions, alongside indigenous cultural nationalism and ongoing struggles to retain land and prepare for the worst of the omni-colonial future.

Reggae Culture in Oceania

Such visions of spiritual Exodus continue to be mediated by the sounds and feelings of contemporary Jamaica. In Hawai'i a slew of reggae artists play a form strongly influenced by modern Jamaican roots and dancehall. A number of them are committed Rastas or incorporate Rasta ideas and "bun fire" rhetoric into their lyrics. Most also identify with and defend indigenous Hawaiian sovereignty. As Ryan Rodrigues, otherwise known as Lion Fiyah, says: "I am a Hawaiian Rastaman. I am a Kanaka Maoli which means Native, true, indigenous, Hawaiian man of the soil. I love Jamaica and the people of Jamaica deep in my heart, even though I have not been there yet. Jamaica is a huge part of who I am, but Rastafari showed I to hold close to I&I culture" (e-mail to the author, January 2008).

While "roots and culture" is again enjoying some of the spotlight in Jamaica and elsewhere, there is a growing world interest in roots reggae played proficiently by bands – the tradition which still dominates in Oceania. Bands from Aotearoa are riding high on a tide of local and international interest in dub and all things organic and "roots". To a degree, indigenous political motivation has been replaced by an abstract concern for environmental sustainability, Rasta-guided philosophies and an increasingly central place in the national popular music culture. Bands include Unity Pacific, Katchafire, House of Shem, the Black Seeds, International Observer, Three Houses Down, Cornerstone Roots, Sons of Zion, the Yoots, the Native Sons, and the Wellington jazz-soul-reggae ensemble Fat Freddy's Drop. Artists like Te Kupu (Upper Hutt Posse), Che Fu, Opensouls, the Kingites, Kora, Samonella Dub, Pitch Black, Shape-shifter, Rhombus, Tiki Taane and others blend reggae elements with hip-hop, rock, or drum 'n' bass formats; and in a recent departure, online labels like High Stakes and Reality Chant have created successful dancehall and one drop rhythms for local and Jamaican vocalists.

In Australia there have been fewer reggae releases than across the Tasman Sea, although the live scene is burgeoning with bands in most major cities. Producer and musician Jake Savona and the Mista Savona band from Melbourne created the first substantial link-up between Australian musicians and contemporary Jamaican dancehall, featuring new and veteran roots artists in the 2007 album, *Melbourne Meets Kingston*. More recently, Savona has been producing tracks for Sizzla. Another contemporary Australian band, the Melbourne-based Blue King Brown led by Natalie Pa'apa'a (who has Samoan, Native American, Mexican and Basque ancestry), interpolates dancehall and reggae into their "urban roots" repertoire. The band has recorded in Jamaica, working with artistes such as Sly and Robbie, Queen Ifrica and Jah Mason, and their 2010 release *Worldwize Part 1: North and South* was in part mixed by Jamaican engineer, Collin "Bulby" York. Indigenous Australian bands like No Fixed Address, Mixed Relations, Blekbela Mujik, the Saltwater Band and many others have crafted a distinctive mix of rock, reggae and ska. Of the new generation of Aboriginal artists, many have been heavily influenced by hip-hop and rhythm and blues, but as the "bush band" scene in outback Australia demonstrates, reggae remains the dominant stylistic ingredient. The young group Zennith from Kuranda (guided by their father, Willie Brim) in far northern Queensland has created a lively, popular form of reggae, mixed with ska and hip-hop and they hope to travel the world with it. As Aboriginal youth of the Internet generation they say: "we suffer the same oppression and the same struggle as our brothers and sisters in Jamaica. . . . Reggae is the music message board of the world and the message of the Indigenous struggle . . . it is also a way for us to communicate with each other" (Aden Brim, e-mail to the author, January 2008).

In both Aotearoa and Australia there are now numerous sound systems, based closely on Jamaican and English models, using dubplates featuring Jamaican and occasionally local artistes. The original Australian-based sound was established in 1974 by St Catherine-born Jamaican, J.J. Roberts. The set is called Soulmaker and continues to play out in Sydney. As well, exclusively reggae and dancehall online forums[13] are flourishing in both countries, and international reggae artistes like Luciano, Mikey General, Inner Circle, Third World, Ziggy Marley, Jimmy Cliff, Shaggy, Junior Reid, Lee "Scratch" Perry, Mad Professor, Lady Saw, Horace Andy, Michael Rose, Sly and Robbie, Jah Mason, Burning Spear, Junior Kelly, Bushman, Ernest Ranglin, Chaka Demus and Pliers, Midnite, Turbulence, Lukie D, Ce'cile, Anthony B, Gyptian, Papua New Guinean–Hawaiian performer O-Shen, Fijian-Hawaiian singer Fiji, and the Samoan-American singer Jerry Afemata (known as J Boog) have toured Australia and Aotearoa, often as part of multiband events or festivals like Ragamuffin, Womadelaide, Big Day Out, Sydney Arts Festival, Reggaetown, Byron Bay Reggaefest and Soundsplash.

These are all signs of Jamaican culture's propensity to spread through international circuits, colonizing in reverse, mutating in unexpected ways as it is absorbed, yet also requiring local artists who get involved to sometimes seek guidance from "the root" of the culture. For certain sound system crews in a city like Sydney strict verisimilitude is the order of the night. It is not uncommon to find a DJ booth of fanatical "bad men", of numerous ethnic origins, furiously screaming Jamaican "bad wuds" at one another over the latest special from Kingston. Of course, similar events take place regularly at dancehall clashes in cities like Berlin, Osaka and San Francisco. Nowadays, the borders of digital Jamaica expand ceaselessly.

Questions about mimesis and authenticity in such situations are almost irrelevant. Through its sheer mutability Jamaican music has long ventured

13.4 Natalie Pa'apa'a, lead singer of Melbourne "urban roots" band Blue King Brown. Photo: Polly Armstrong.

down the cyber byways detailed by Louis Chude-Sokei (1994), and for several decades it has slipped well beyond the black Atlantic into the polyglot Oceanic realm, where local reggae practitioners mostly determine their own indices of authenticity and the effectiveness of Jamaican-derived music to meet their needs – spiritual, political or aesthetic. In a revealing mapping of reggae routes, producer from the Aotearoan High Stakes label[14] Tiopira McDowell relates the circumstances of a single he worked on called "Drums of War". Voiced by MC Flowsion, who like McDowell is Māori, the track denounces controversial police raids on homes of activists and an alleged "terrorist camp" near a rural Māori community in 2007.[15] McDowell says:

> Our Jamaican friends heard about the raids all the way over there in the West Indies and made fun about it. One friend jokingly asked if we were one of the ones arrested. That was embarrassing because Māori are proud people who hold Jamaicans in high esteem for the contribution of their music to our struggles: it was sad to think that all they know about us is that we are supposedly terrorists. . . . We

added the *haka* sounds in the background to make it different, add our own culture in there alongside the elements of hip-hop and bashment dancehall. (E-mail to the author, January 2008)

The response from Jamaican artistes was to use the same riddim to voice their own "conscious tunes" and post them back. This, a gratified Tiopira McDowell acknowledges, is "cool because hopefully they realise where we are coming from". The High Stakes example hints at the possibilities of what Hannah Appel calls "poly-lateral dialogue among aggrieved populations . . . making the relationship between 'margins' and 'centre' dramatically different" (2004, 72–73).

Another Pacific artiste who embodies emerging flows of cultural exchange in a post-national world has the appropriate sobriquet of O-Shen. Born Jason Hershey, O-Shen is the son of white American medical missionaries, and he grew up in the village of Butaweng, Morobe province, in northeastern Papua New Guinea, speaking the local language of Yabim and the country's widely accepted creole, Tok Pisin. When he was fifteen, his parents returned with him to live in the United States. By age nineteen Hershey was in jail for a three-year stretch. Upon release he fled to his birthplace. He eventually wound up in Honolulu, renewed his interest in music, and by 2000 had one of his Tok Pisin raps included on an album by the Fijian-Hawaiian singer, Fiji (George Veikoso). Since then O-Shen has recorded six albums, mostly reggae based but also incorporating dancehall, rhythm and blues, hip-hop, and traditional Papua New Guinea string band and tribal music. He has recorded with Bunny Rugs, Don Carlos and Elephant Man. In a single album he might employ American English, Hawaiian, Tahitian, Spanish, Tok Pisin and Jamaican patwa. He is a star thoughout the Pacific, especially in his homeland of Papua New Guinea.

Although O-Shen is cosmopolitan he does not carry the "whole baggage of liberal universalism" which Stuart Hall notes is, "broadly speaking, assimilationist in its thrust" (2003, 27). O-Shen maintains a *Pasifikan* particularity, and affirms his affiliation with the indigenous islander, the *kanaka*, whether from Hawai'i or Papua New Guinea. In the 2007 album, *1 Rebel*, O-Shen sings "Revolutionary Soldier" over a digital roots rhythm in a Jamaican-accented voice:

> History is full of lies that they teach us
> Government don't want reality to reach us
> The Kingdom that we livin' is a nation
> Illegally overthrown occupation.

13.5 O-shen at Pacific Reggae Sounds, Gallery of Modern Art Brisbane, 5 December 2009. Photo: Natasha Harth.

This is a direct reference to the US overthrow of the Hawaiian monarchy of Queen Lili'uokalani in 1893. As well as being a supporter of Hawaiian sovereignty, Kanak self-determination in New Caledonia, ganja legalization and Rastafari, O-Shen is a hunky, blonde, good-looking guy who enjoys swimming and surfing. But even in his role as a sexy lover man he rejects the United States. As he sings in the song "Beautiful Island Princess", also from *1 Rebel*: "Don't want no Yankee chick / don't want no skanky chick / cos island girl's my pick."

On being displaced in the United States as a teenager, one Hawaiian article notes, "O-Shen found himself in a world where it was far easier to get by by burying his identity instead of celebrating it" (Paiva 2006). Rather than expecting a naïve equivalence between black and white, O-Shen is a proud, even chauvinistic local "island boy" whose only commitment to his parents' language is pragmatic: "I use English because I have to. But if I could choose to eliminate English I might not do it completely, but I would probably not use it very much" (ibid.). A dreadlocked, white-skinned Pasifikan who is able to shout out to *bredren* in Honolulu and Spanish Town *and* Port Moresby suggests another kind of Oceanic reggae culture that is neither necessarily global nor *glocal*, but complex, lateral and specific.

Of course, the Pacific and the Caribbean are very different stretches of land and ocean, but with ever expanding means of communication, the links become clearer. Widely separated peoples are learning about the specificities of other locations and feeling deeper connectedness with cultures that share existing and emerging affinities. And here it is necessary to remember that a "flat world" (after Thomas Friedman's brutalist 2005 depiction) in which accessible, ubiquitous telecommunications encourage ever more competitive, increasingly unstable economies and cultures is only one version of a nervous present. Actually, what might be perceived as an homogenizing mash-up of disparate, even antagonistic styles can also be a gathering of far distant cousins, where the differences and links between, say, Jamaican dancehall, UK drum 'n' bass and *kapa haka* or Māori posture dance and chant from Aotearoa can be elided *and* highlighted by a heavily tattooed young man reclaiming *taha Māori*, an indigenous perspective on history and the environment.

According to its creator, vocalist and producer Tiki Taane, the song "Tangaroa" expresses "the anger and rage Tangaroa [the Māori god of the sea] had towards mankind as we have shown no respect for the ocean and its inhabitants" (http://www.tikidub.com). One time front man with the predominantly

Pākehā New Zealand dub and drum 'n' bass group Salmonella Dub, Taane released his debut solo album, entitled *Past, Present, Future* to acclaim in his homeland in 2007, a sign that his previously somewhat occluded Māori identity has now become desirable as a local cultural commodity. Perhaps like the original founders of Jamaican post-war popular music, Tiki Taane is finding success among his people because his style is recognized as "island style" that is willing to be mixed with world culture. In "Tangaroa", from the debut, a defiantly traditional Māori presence rubs up against cosmopolitan sensibilities as Jamaican dancehall's electronic pulse is mutated into a striking example of modern *waiata* (song).

Surrounded by the Caribbean Sea, and operating with a similarly *faas-tie* intent, Jamaican scholar of local dancehall expression, Carolyn Cooper reminds dry-land commentators of a few home-truths in the introduction to her book *Sound Clash: Jamaican Dancehall Culture at Large*: "the local is decidedly not conceived as a narrowly insular, uniformly flat landscape cut off from currents of thought beyond its shores. Indeed an island is a frontier. Seemingly bounded on all sides by the sea, it does have porous borders and remains open to multiple influences" (2004, 2).

One dignified denizen of that outernational maritime frontier is octogenarian singer and composer, Henry Gibson "Seaman" Dan from Thursday Island at the northernmost tip of Australia in the Torres Strait. Seaman Dan has created his own genre of music which he terms "Hula Jazz", mixing blues, hula, calypso, reggae, jazz, local music and songs from the pearling industry which he worked in as a diver for many years. In 2006 he recorded a reggae tune with his grandson Patrick Mau. The song, called in local pijin "Ailan Man", proudly acknowledges Seaman Dan's great-grandfather, Jamaican seafarer and pearl-diver Douglas Pitt – a Caribbean pioneer who sailed with his *Lifou* (New Caledonia) wife to the Torres Strait in 1870 (a year before the missionaries) and is said to give his many descendants in the region a special love of reggae. As well as his prodigious Jamaican forbear, Dan also recalls hardy ancestors who came from all over Melanesia and Polynesia and those who were indigenous to the islands of the Strait.

The epigraph to Seaman Dan's 2006 album *Island Way* is taken from a book by Aboriginal writer Terri Janke. The words remind listeners that although Seaman Dan is by genealogy and inclination a cosmopolitan man who has loved to move around, he also has a much-loved home-place, a place to stand.

Janke writes: "They say if you live on an island too long, you merge with it. Your bones become the sands, your blood the ocean. Your flesh is the fertile ground. Your heart becomes the stories, dances, songs. . . . It will beg for you to dream it, and know it, forever. No matter where you or your children travel, the island is home" (2005, 3).

In Oceania the dreams of different but long-connected island peoples hold uncertain visions of Bob Marley's "great future". Facing literal rising tides due to global warming, the jockeying by continental states and transnational corporations for resources and influence, fraying governmental, economic and social structures, as well as the subversion of traditional land tenureship and the subsequent depredations of real estate speculation (Stefanova 2008), local people have no assurance that "home" will remain familiar or even continue to exist in years to come. But, in the face of the worst that Babylon can deliver, Bob Marley's injunction in his song "Rat Race" on *Rastaman Vibration*, "Don't forget your history / know your destiny" reminds those who love their island homes that reggae has always been and will continue to be a crucial technique of cultural navigation, a way to stay afloat in the dangerous currents of modernity.

Notes

1. "[Bob Marley] would have turned 64 yesterday if he was still alive, and Jamaican flags dotted the crowd. They fluttered alongside Tino Rangatiratanga [Māori sovereignty] ensigns as the sun shone down" reported Simon Wood in "Peace and Harmony Prevail at Local Waitangi Day Celebrations", *Wanganui Chronicle*, 7 January 2009.
2. For an example of a young indigenous band from Central Australia, the Tjupi Band, utilizing reggae, see Ronan Sharkey, "Hack: Bush Bands Bash Pt. 2", *Triple J TV*, 29 September 2008, http://www.abc.net.au/triplej/media/s2359990.htm.
3. For more information see "Religion of Reggae", *Evening Post*, 29 November 1980, 16. The article contains an interview with seminal Wellington-based Māori reggae band Chaos, who describe being raided by police, embracing Rastafari, and Māoritanga (Māori culture). Band member, Alma, states, "We're not African, we got roots here. We are the tangata whenua, the original people."
4. "Dread on a Mission" video at http://www.filmarchive.org.nz/readytoroll/view.php?id=65.
5. John Berger, "'02 Not the Year Jawaiian Dies, but Watch Out", *Honolulu Star-Bulletin*, 1 January 2002.
6. Song found on *Everybody Loves Bob Marley*, 2006.

7. Fijian radio presenter Griffin Carter says of reggae, "It's huge. . . . It's a Melanesian thing. . . . That's why it took so long for rock to catch on here" (interviewed by Jennifer Cattermole, 3 May 2007, from unpublished manuscript on Fijian reggae, Macquarie University, Sydney, e-mail communication, January 2008).

8. The term *kastom,* a *pijin* word from the English "custom" is common to the Melanesian archipelago and is much debated by anthropologists. For a definition by a Melanesian, I cite cultural worker Jean Tarisesei, from the Vanuatu Cultural Centre in Port Vila: "Kastom is a term we use in Vanuatu, in our language Bislama, to mean the way of life in which we grew up and still practice. This is the way of life which comes from our own place. . . . This is a hard thing to explain in any language, but especially in English. People today are trying to find ways to fit kastom together with the new things that have come into our lives. So the kastom that we now practice on Ambae is not the same as it was before. Now people are changing it and adding new things" (1998).

9. See "Vanlal Launch Their Second Album, *Situation*" from Vanuatu Cultural website, http://www.vanuatuculture.org/contemporary/20070330_vanlal.shtml.

10. For a scathing attack on the achievements of Pacific governance and development see Hughes 2003.

11. Izzy featuring LG and PLO, "Leaders Fighting", Onehaus Productions video, 2008. Seen on One TV, Honiara, November 2008.

12. See clip at http://www.youtube.com/watch?v=vYvvhMPO7PE.

13. See http://www.ozreggae.com and http://www.niceup.org.nz.

14. See High Stakes website, http://profile.myspace.com/index.cfm?fuseaction=user .viewprofile&friendid=226017689.

15. See "New Zealand Anti-Terrorism Laws Branded Incoherent After Raid Fiasco", *ABC News On-Line*, 18 November 2007, http://www.abc.net.au/news/stories/2007/11/18/ 2094044.htm.

References

Appel, Hannah. 2004. "Dancehall, Hip Hop and Musical Cross-Currents". *Glendora Review: African Quarterly on the Arts* 3 (3–4): 72–73.

Blue King Brown. 2010. *Worldwize Part 1: North and South.* Lion House Records, BKB 007.

Bob Marley. 1976. *Rastaman Vibration.* Island, L 35853.

Bob Marley and the Wailers. 2002. *Legend.* Island, CD 314 548 904-2.

Chude-Sokei, Louis. 1994. "Post-nationalist Geographies: Rasta, Ragga and Reinventing Africa." *African Arts* 27 (4): 80–84.

Cooper, Carolyn. 2004. *Sound Clash: Jamaican Dancehall Culture at Large.* New York: Palgrave Macmillan.

Friedman, Thomas L. 2005. *The World Is Flat: A Brief History of the Twenty-first Century*. New York: Farrar, Strauss and Giroux.

Griffith, Lesa. 2006. "The New Face of Hawaiian Music: Paula Fuga and the Bands Kamau and Kupa'aina Buck Tradition and Find Freedom in Musical Exploration". *Honolulu Weekly*, 4 January.

Hall, Stuart. 2003. "Political Belonging in a World of Multiple Identities". In *Conceiving Cosmopolitanism: Theory, Context, and Practice*, ed. Steven Vertovec and Robyn Cohen, 25–31. New York: Oxford University Press.

Hebdidge, Dick. 2003. "Roots in the Airwaves: Popular Culture in a Global Context". In *Bob Marley: The Man and His Music*, ed. Eleanor Wint and Carolyn Cooper, 1–11. Kingston: Arawak.

Herbs. 1981. *What's Be Happen?* WEA/Warrior Records, Z20012.

Hobsbawm, Eric, and Terence Ranger, eds. 1992. *The Invention of Tradition (Canto)*. Cambridge: Cambridge University Press.

Hughes, Helen. 2003. "Aid Has Failed the Pacific". *Issue Analysis* 33 (7 May).

Janke, Terri. 2005. *Butterfly Song*. Melbourne: Penguin.

Lipsitz, George. 1994. *Dangerous Crossroads: Popular Music, Postmodernism and the Poetics of Place*. London: Verso.

Mista Savona. 2007. *Mista Savona Presents Melbourne Meets Kingston*. Elefant Tracks, ACE029.

O-Shen. 2007. *1 Rebel*. Sharpnote Records, SNR0024.

Paiva, Derek. 2006. "O-Shen Goes Back to His Roots on New Album". *Honolulu Advertiser*, 7 February.

Seaman Dan. 2006. *Island Way*. Steady Steady Music, TI 1001.

Stefanova, Milena. 2008. "The Price of Tourism: Land Alienation in Vanuatu". *Justice for the Poor* 2 (1).

Stillman, Amy Ku'uleialoha. 1998. "Hula Hits, Local Music and Local Charts: Some Dynamics of Hawaiian Popular Music". In *Sound Alliances: Indigenous Peoples, Cultural Politics and Popular Music in the Pacific*, ed. Philip Hayward, 89–106. London: Cassell.

Tarisesei, Jean. 1998. "Today Is Not the Same as Yesterday, and Tomorrow It Will Be Different Again: *Kastom* on Ambae, Vanuatu". Paper presented at the conference "Women, Christians, Citizens: Being Female in Melanesia Today", Oceanic-Whitehall Guesthouse, Sorrento, Victoria. http://rspas.anu.edu.au/melanesia/kastom.htm.

Tiki Taane. 2007. *Past, Present, Future*. Tikidub Productions, tiki002.

Various Artists. 2006. *Everybody Loves Bob Marley*. Neos Productions, CD V104.

Weintraub, Andrew N. 1998. "Jawaiian Music and Local Cultural Identity in Hawai'i". In *Sound Alliances: Indigenous Peoples, Cultural Politics and Popular Music in the Pacific*, ed. Philip Hayward, 78–88. London: Cassell.

CHAPTER 14

DUB
ELECTRONIC
MUSIC AND SOUND
EXPERIMENTATION

MICHAEL VEAL

All things, in a constant state of flux, evolve from
nothing and devolve back to nothing. Within
this perpetual movement nature leaves arbitrary
tracks for us to contemplate, and it is these random flaws and irregularities that offer a model for the modest
and humble wabi sabi expression of beauty. Rooted firmly
in Zen thought, wabi sabi art uses the evanescence of life to
convey the sense of melancholic beauty that such an understanding brings.

– Andrew Juniper, *Wabi Sabi: The Japanese Art of Impermanence*, 2003, 2–3

With the dubs, you're working with a rhythm that's hang-
ing on the verge of collapse all the time. You're putting it to

pieces, holding it together with delays and adding and spinning the rhythm, taking out . . . one bar blurs into another or distorts into the end of the four-bar figure, and then you pull it back, just when you think it's gonna collapse. You soothe people by bringing back the bass when you've taken it out. There's more space in it than anything.

– Adrian Sherwood, interview, November 2001

The date: 1979. The place: Admiral Town, Kingston. The sound system: Virgo International. Gregory Isaacs's lovers rock tune "Always Loving You" is playing from the speakers, as deejay Brigadier Jerry interjects his own lines in between Isaacs's recorded lyrics. The song sails along on a one-drop rhythm taken at an easy pace that feels like it could go on forever: intro, verse, refrain, verse, refrain. Then the band vamps along on the tag as Isaacs sings to the end of the track:

> I've got to tell everyone
> That you're my girl
> No one co-o-o-o-o . . .
> Oh, yeah
> I got-ot-ot-ot-ot-ot-ot

An echoing fragment of Isaacs's final line sails through the air and signals the end of the song proper and the beginning of the dub side. After a two-second pause, the dub version begins. With fragments of piano and guitar chords intermittently echoing across a stripped-down remix of the "Loving Slow" riddim, Briggy steps up to the microphone to chant his "Two Bad Deejay Haffi Chat" lyric. The theme is completely unrelated, but that is the beauty of it: the potential meaning of the lyrics expands with each disjunction, and that disjunction is intensified by all of the sounds zipping across the soundscape – fragments of the lyrics, delay units creating streams of liquefied sound, synthetic reverberation implying cavernous spaces, instruments sliding in and out of the mix, filter units manipulating the sonic frequencies. It is like jazz in a way, with a vocalist improvising over a constantly changing relationship between the various instruments – mostly drum and bass, sometimes with echoing bits of guitar, organ or piano added. It is also like electronic music, with all of the sonic manipulations that make the music sound at times like psychedelic music and at other times like experimental music. But in the end it is dance music, all united around the lilting groove and suffused with the culture of the streets; the sound processing can make the political songs seem heavier and harder, the cultural songs deeper and more rootsy, and the spiritual songs more sublime. On this night in Admiral Town, it makes Isaacs's romantic song seem warmer and more inviting, so everyone is rocking coolly and slowly, the neighbourhood momentarily transformed into one of the world's most distinctive electronic soundscapes.

With *Time* magazine voting Bob Marley and the Wailers' *Exodus* as the "album of the twentieth century", Jamaica is beginning to be recognized for its influence on world popular music.[1] Like Cuba, Jamaica is a small island culture of the Greater Antilles that has exerted a tremendous influence on the global development of post–World War II popular music. But although Jamaica has been making its musical presence felt in mainland American music, at least since Louis Armstrong's 1927 recording "King of the Zulus", the sonic innovations of its music – unlike Cuba's – have yet to be widely acknowledged.[2]

My 2007 book *Dub: Soundscapes and Shattered Songs in Jamaican Reggae* presents a historical, analytical and interpretive study of the subgenre of Jamaican dub music, a form pioneered by recording studio engineers such as Osbourne "King Tubby" Ruddock (1941–1989), Lee "Scratch" Perry (b. 1935) and Errol "Errol T." Thompson (1941–2005). Dub music flourished during the era of "roots" reggae (approximately 1968 through 1985),[3] and its significance as a style lies in the deconstructive manner in which these engineers remixed reggae songs, applying sound processing technology in unusual ways to create a unique pop music language of fragmented song forms and reverberating soundscapes.

Today, the sounds and techniques of classic dub music have been stylistically absorbed into the various genres of global electronic popular music (such as hip-hop, techno, house, jungle, ambient, and trip-hop), and conceptually absorbed into the now-commonplace practice of song remixing. Few people are aware that dub – a style built around fragments of sound over a hypnotically repeating reggae groove, was a crucial forerunner of these genres and that much of what is unique about contemporary dance music is directly traceable to the studio production techniques pioneered in Kingston beginning in the late 1960s. Dub's "aesthetic of fragmentation" has become one of the stylistic cornerstones of popular dance music in the digital age, and its fluid reinterpretation of song form laid one important foundation for the amorphous remix culture that is so central to contemporary pop music. It is not overstating the case to suggest that this music has helped change the way the world hears the popular song. Thus, in the same way that the themes of exile and spiritual conviction sung by musicians such as Bob Marley have inspired audiences around the world, so has the production style of Jamaican music helped transform the sound and structure of world popular music. And what this ultimately demonstrates is how the site of the recording studio – despite its hermetic remove from the rest of "society" – can often function as a potent site for the sublimation of a cultural mood into musicalized sound.

Jamaican music had not always been on the sonic cutting edge of global popular music. The foundations for the 1970s success of musicians like Marley had been laid firmly in place during the 1960s by the producers, singers and musicians associated with Jamaica's two dominant recording companies: Clement Dodd's Studio One and Duke Reid's Treasure Isle. In terms of sound, their work was more conservative in conception, while always innovative in the unique slant it gave to the evolving language of global popular music (particularly in the sphere of rhythm). From the time of Jamaica's independence from England in 1962, Dodd and Reid had charged the session musicians in their employ with the task of using their jazz skills to adapt black American rhythm and blues into a new local popular music. In response, these musicians had blended accomplished musicianship and meticulous songcraft in the synthesis of so-called ska and rocksteady music. Their efforts resulted in the creation of what some consider the era of Jamaica's "perfectly formed pop song", strongly influenced by the American model. Ska and rocksteady were very influential outside of Jamaica (particularly in England) in their own ways, but they were ultimately locally based island styles, not necessarily more influential outside of Jamaica than other regional styles such as *calypso*, *mambo*, *merengue* or *konpa*. And certainly, less so than the Cuban genres such as *mambo* and *son* that had already transformed world popular music in the years following World War II.

Nevertheless, the sonic and conceptual elements that would come to define dub were still evident in the formative years of reggae. It was due to a configuration of social, political and technological factors that the neat conception of the pop song presented in ska, rocksteady and early reggae would undergo a strange and dramatic transformation during the 1970s, electronically deconstructed and reconfigured by a generation of studio engineers who had variously tuned into the potentials of African heritage, psychedelia, the space race, nature, and the late modernist machine. Like the generative moments of other styles, the radical departures of dub in the 1970s were also a potent reflection of the society and times within which it emerged and later, as it influenced music making beyond Jamaica, a potent agent within global sonic culture at the turn of the twenty-first century.

Recording engineers have certainly never been the star personalities of popular music and, consequently, dub mixes seemed to exist simultaneously in the middle and at the fringe of the reggae mainstream. They were in the middle, given that they are absolutely central to the sound system dances, at which deejays use them as backgrounds for rapping and toasting. And they were on the fringe, because it is a music of studio-ensconced knob-twiddlers and sound equipment enthusiasts, a music cast as shadow versions of popular themes, anonymous-sounding in their skeletal spookiness. Who created this strange music, and where was it being created?

In fact, the music was created by, and operated among, a complex of musicians, music professionals and music lovers. Foremost among these were the engineers: Osbourne "King Tubby" Ruddock, the studio engineer who, in the back of his home in one of Kingston's roughest ghettos, had turned remixing into a new and dramatic form of composition which used sound processing to melt the reggae song form into ambient soundscapes. There was also Lee "Scratch" Perry, eccentric master dancer, producer, engineer and songwriter, mentor of Bob Marley and the Wailers, the so-called Dali of Reggae, who had progressed from funky, soul-inspired reggae rhythms to swirling, psychedelic soundscapes and (allegedly) on to madness. Also, there was Sylvan Morris, who forged the sound of Jamaica's most legendary recording company, Studio One. Another producer was Errol Thompson, student of Morris, who worked in the legendary recording outfits of Randy's Studio 17 and Joe Gibbs's studio, and used the reggae groove as the basis for his unique brand of sound collage. Overton "Scientist" Brown, also a dub producer, was an apprentice of King Tubby, who blasted the hard rhythms of the Roots Radics band into the sci-fi future with a language of electronic sounds. And finally, there was Lloyd "King Jammy" James, another apprentice of King Tubby, who would mix hundreds of dub sides before transforming himself into one of Jamaica's most legendary producers of the ragga and dancehall era.

Then there were the producers who put their money behind the new sound: businessmen like Clement "Coxsone" Dodd (founder of Studio One),

Joe Gibbs, Lee "Scratch" Perry, Bunny Lee, Clive Chin, Jack Ruby and others who would record the emerging musicians. It is impossible to talk about the music without mentioning these figures, and the story of dub music in particular is a collaborative story between these producers and the studio engineers they worked with – of Bunny Lee and Augustus Pablo with King Tubby, of Clive Chin and Joe Gibbs with Errol Thompson, of Linval Thompson and Junjo Lawes with Scientist, and other similar partnerships.

Then there were those who were not engineers or producers, but were musicians devoted to the dub sound because that sound provided a sonic corollary to the devotional spirituality of Rastafari, or the political struggles of the times. These were dub's guiding mystics, Augustus Pablo and Yabby You – the first, an elusive and introspective Rasta producer and session musician whose heavy dub rhythms were graced with his wistful melodica improvisations and whose devout faith imparted to his dub music a feeling of meditation and devotion. The second, a vocalist possessed by postcolonial visions of biblical apocalypse who found in dub a sonic complement to his excoriating sermonizing.

As the legendary bassist Robbie Shakespeare acknowledged:

> Everytime you mention dub, you have to get to so many people. Tubby's have to come up. Bunny Lee have to come up. Niney, Scratch, Channel One, Coxsone, Treasure Isle. You have to name the musicians. The sound operator with him dub plate. You have to name the little man who used to believe inna it and walk and sell [cassettes of the music] on the street. So much people fe get credit. You have to just give the whole music fraternity – the old school – the credit. (Personal interview, March 2002, Kingston, Jamaica)

Electronic Music in Jamaica

As a genre of reggae music particularly associated with the recording studio, dub music can be understood in the context of the global evolution of sound recording technology in the twentieth century. Recording studios – the primary site for the manipulation of magnetic sound recording tape – have existed since just after 1900. As far back as phonograph inventor Thomas Edison and early recording pioneers like Fred Gaisberg, Walter Legge and John Culshaw, studio engineers have had to make aesthetic as well as technical judgments in their translation of musical performances onto a recorded format that was, from its earliest years, understood in some quarters to hold more creative potential than a mere passive documentation of a "traditional" musical performance (Lastra 2000, 84–91).

It was in tandem with the technical advances in sound recording that the engineer began to play a more prominent creative role in the studio-based creation of popular music. By the mid-1960s, aspects of the studio production process began to consolidate into the signature styles of various producers and engineers of popular music in England and America. These were the years in which the acknowledged masters and innovators of studio craft began to emerge: George Martin, Tom Dowd, Eddie Kramer, Phil Spector, Geoff Emerick, Joe Meek and others. The Jamaican producer/engineers who created dub music belong to this group of post-war sound innovators. Their closest English and American counterparts would be multitasking producer-engineer-inventor-entrepreneurs such as Joe Meek, Sam Philips, Norman Petty and Les Paul, who, despite various technical, institutional and economic limitations, created the aesthetic foundations of entire pop music cultures. Jamaicans such as Sylvan Morris, King Tubby, Errol Thompson and Lee Perry created dub music at a time when American record companies were expanding their markets into the Caribbean (Bradley 2000, 22), and recording technology was being gradually adapted outside of the overdeveloped nations in the service of budding local record industries. It also developed at a time when the introduction of stereo radio transmission into Jamaica led to a rise in the broadcasting of foreign music "deemed to sound good in stereo" (Malm and Wallis 1992, 47). This in turn gradually opened a space for the appreciation of Jamaican music with more sophisticated production values.

But this is not merely a matter of studio technology and insider jargon. Local politics and global economics have extracted a heavy toll in Jamaica, and it takes a powerful music to transform the harsher aspects of this reality. That is exactly what King Tubby, Lee Perry and other producers of dub music accomplished during the 1970s. All the talk of circuits, knobs and switches can distract one from the fundamental reality that what these engineers were doing was synthesizing a new popular art form, creating a space where people could come together joyously despite the harshness that surrounded them. They created a music as roughly textured as the physical reality of the place, but with the power to transport their listeners to dance floor nirvana as well as the far reaches of the cultural and political imagination – Africa, outer-space, inner-space, nature and political as well as economic liberation. Focusing on the contributions of these engineers allows us to develop an understanding of the role of sound technology, sound technicians and sound aesthetics within larger cultural and political realities.

Dub also presents a compelling example of what we often think of as "electronic music", provided that we give a suitably localized inflection to the term. Originally, the term "electronic music" was quite restrictive, coined after World War II in the studios of Köln, Germany to refer to music composed from electronically generated sound signals (*elektronische musik*). Later, the term was broadened to include the tape-based *musique concrète* composition associated with French composers such as Pierre Henri and Pierre Schaeffer, and still later broadened to include works realized with electronic synthesizers. Clearly, dub cannot be defined as "electronic music" in the specific sense that we define the term in the context of these traditions of post–World War II Euro-American experimental art music. If, on the other hand, we define the term "electronic music" broadly as encompassing either any musical form relying on the electronic generation, processing, amplification or storage of sound signals or as any pre-recorded work intended solely for transmission via loudspeakers, a huge majority of contemporary music making could then be classified as "electronic".[4]

The significance of dub music can be located somewhere between these two definitions. On one hand, it can be generically discussed as "electronic" in the same way that we discuss other musical forms that make use of any electronic technology. But it can also be discussed in more narrowly "electronic" terms, due to the degree to which Jamaican producers and engineers foregrounded the experimental use of sound technology within the genre. In varying ways, similarities can be drawn with *musique concrète* and minimalism (in fact, the music was adopted as an aesthetic template in the 1990s by a generation of German electronic music composers who had themselves been influenced by minimalism). Dub's electronic manipulation of spatiality can be compared with certain spatially conceived works of composers like Karlheinz Stockhausen and John Cage. In purely sonic terms, it bears comparison with certain works of composers such as Stockhausen, Cage and Vladimir Ussachevsky, who subjected pre-recorded musical materials appropriated from mass media (such as commercial recordings or radio broadcasts) to elec-

14.1 *Tribute to Dub*, by Alon Braier, first-place winner of the First International Reggae Poster Contest, 2012. Courtesy of Alon Braier.

tronic manipulation.[5] Conversely, the Jamaican practice of deejays toasting over pre-recorded music fits into a body of work composed for electronics and live musicians, which in its broadest sense encompasses everything from pieces like Mario Davidowsky's *Synchronisms #1* (composed for live flautist and tape) to karaoke singing.

Any sonic similarities between these very different musical areas probably reflect the fact that, to the ear, electronic and tape compositions (many of which were only notated after the fact) seem to share a sonic and conceptual space with popular forms that developed out of traditions of performance and improvisation (see Schwartz 1973, 253). It also reflects the rarely discussed fact that composers of the experimental tradition were often influenced by concepts of form, sound and process found in various types of jazz, both popular and non-Western traditions.

In the same way that it would be fascinating to hear how composers such as Pierre Schaefer, Pierre Henri or John Cage might adapt their "pure" sound experimentation to the stylistic demands of popular or dance music, it would be equally fascinating to hear the way Jamaican studio engineers like Scientist or Sylvan Morris would utilize venues specially designed for the performance of spatially oriented or "pure sound" works (such as the building constructed for Stockhausen at the 1970 World's Fair in Osaka, Japan), or studios specifically equipped for the realization of electronic works (such as the Nordwestdeutscher Rundfunk in Cologne, Radiodiffusion Française in Paris, or the Columbia-Princeton Electronic Music Center in New York City). The truth, of course, is that Jamaican engineers never had access to such elaborate technology, and what makes their work particularly provocative is what they were able to achieve by pushing the limits of the equipment at their disposal. In any case, Jamaica's musical innovations provide a fascinating example of the way in which similar forms of technology have been applied in different cultural areas, as well as a localized example of what constitutes musical "experimentation", in a Jamaican popular context.

In light of all this, it follows that the application of the "experimental" idea in relation to Jamaica must remain grounded in Jamaica's cultural reality since although there is a local tradition of modern jazz (typified by musicians like Joe Harriott, Monty Alexander, Ernest Ranglin and Don Drummond), the culture has no tradition of a musical avant-garde in the Euro-American or African-American sense of the term.[6] There is, however, a vibrant tradition of electronic music, best typified by dub. The creators of this music certainly viewed themselves as experimentalists, as their comments and professional monikers indicate: Scientist, Peter Chemist, Professor and so on. Their work represented the sonic vanguard of Jamaican music in the 1970s and early 1980s, and also one sonic vanguard of global popular music.

The Jamaican Sound System

Ultimately, the most relevant and organic context in which to ground any discussion of an electronic aesthetic within Jamaican music (besides the recording studio) is clearly the local institution known as the sound system, asserted by many observers as the site of most that is unique to Jamaican music.[7] It seems plausible to speculate that due to the relative dearth of performing ensembles in Jamaica, emphasis has tended to be placed on verbal and electronic creativity. But the significance of the sound system, which has received thorough cultural grounding in works by Carolyn Cooper and Norman Stolzoff, transcends mere entertainment; it is arguably one of the most powerfully resonant metaphors for post-colonial Jamaica. It has been described as the "community's heartbeat" (Bradley 2000, 4) – the place where "a discourse of specifically black identity was celebrated and articulated" (Chude-Sokei 1997, 188) in a particularly powerful way. Like the stereotypical village clearing in sub-Saharan Africa or the block party in urban black America, the sound system is a communal space in which many of the nation's most potent myths, tropes and emotions are dramatized in the act of communal dance. The soundscape innovations of dub music, composed in the recording studio with the 1970s sound system experience in mind, are intimately implicated in these same myths despite the largely non-literal (meaning instrumental) nature of the music.

As such, any "experimental" tendencies evident in dub remained predicated upon the capital-driven setting of the Jamaican recording studio, which was a radically different setting than the radio and university studios which have provided the technical and institutional framework for electronic composition in Europe and America. These tendencies also remained predicated upon the communal imperatives of the sound system and the dancehall, which were themselves radically different settings than the concert halls, galleries and other spaces we usually associate with the performance of experimental music in Europe and America. Despite its experimental aspects, dub music remained solidly grounded in the reality of Kingston life in the 1970s.

The social polar opposite of the recording studio in its hermetic isolation, the sound system is significant as the site in which studio experimentation acquires its cultural grounding. In his insightful essay on Orientalism in the Western experimental tradition, John Corbett observes how "the notion of experimentation rhetorically carries into the musical process a connotation of science – of laboratory experimentation" (2000, 164). He goes on to mention how the hermetic setting of the laboratory implicitly divested such experimentation of its potential political or ideological import. Dub, however, was composed with the sound system audience in mind and it is because of this that the experimental impulse remained connected to the general social mood in Jamaica. In many ways, in fact, it was a particularly accurate articulation of this mood (Corbett 2000).

How did such a technologically dependent style develop to such an advanced extent under these circumstances, in a nation of extremely limited economic resources, within a region marked by a diversity of traditional performing ensembles? The easiest explanation would be that Jamaica's proximity to the United States provided a convenient physical and economic conduit for what Malm and Wallis have described as a "remarkable influx of electronic hardware" (1992, 39). Industrious Jamaicans then used this technology to supplant the dominance of more expensive performing ensembles that the economy was incapable of supporting. But physical proximity can only be part of the answer, since dub-like genres did not develop on other islands in the region with dynamic music cultures, such as Haiti, Cuba or Trinidad. There are no definitive answers, but several likely factors. One fundamental factor is that, historically speaking, Jamaica was the most technologically advanced of the British colonies in the Caribbean. Another may be the tradition of seasonal migration to the southern United States that employed thousands of Jamaicans who purchased American records, sound equipment and musical instruments, and brought them back to Jamaica. A third might be the currents of commerce during the Cold War; Cuba has an arguably more diversified music culture than Jamaica, but during the same period that sound equipment was developing in the United States, Cuba itself was economically alienated from the United States. Finally, there is the language factor – Jamaica is an English-speaking country and, as such, had a closer economic and cultural relationship with both England and the United States, two important centres of developing musical technology.

Any other explanation for Jamaica's vigorous musical culture must lie in the elusive and unquantifiable "character" of the Jamaican people, and in the rural folk forms which were transplanted to Kingston and which guided Jamaica's adaptations of foreign music. Unfortunately, as Ken Bilby mentions, the class divide in Kingston meant that the rural-based cultural expressions of "downtown" culture were never considered worthy of serious study, and have gone mostly undocumented until fairly recently (Manuel, Bilby and Largey 1995, 151–59).[8] This began to change as the music moved beyond Jamaica, and especially as foreigners became intensely interested in Jamaican reggae beginning in the late 1960s. By the 1970s, dub music was making a substantial impact beyond Jamaica, with its influence beginning to show in the spheres of rock music, early hip-hop and disco. And today, it is one of the influences at the heart of the digitally produced genres collectively referred to as "electronica" – trip-hop, techno, house, ambient, jungle and drum 'n' bass, grime, dubstep, hip-hop, and other genres.

It is in this global setting that we can see the music's profound influence in the shaping of sonic concepts in contemporary music. In James Lastra's thinking, the experience we describe as "modernity" has been fundamentally shaped by the technological media of the modern era (Lastra 2000, 4). Within divergent experiences of modernity, then, these technologies become implicated in various local dynamics of cultural redefinition, while ultimately remaining a complementary part of modernity, newly understood (per Gilroy 1993) in global terms. The composite idea of technology being developed according to differing cultural priorities in different settings helps nuance the stereotypical "impact" model in which technology is seen to flow uni-directionally from technologically advanced to technologically marginal cultures.[9]

Thinkers from Fanon to Gilroy have long argued for an understanding of the experiences of colonizer and colonized as symbiotically intertwined, and this inevitably implies a cross-cultural renegotiation of our understanding of modernity and modernist art. The result is that the constellation of formerly colonized cultures (including those of the African diaspora) are understood not *in opposition* to modernity, but as modernity's *many local conjugations*. The particular local conjugation I address in *Dub: Soundscapes and Shattered Songs in Jamaican Reggae* differs from typical understandings of Western artistic modernism, which is often considered as either a deliberate break from the past, or a depiction of the alienation of artists from the rise of the corporate and industrial state (see Sims 2005). Modernism for artists of Africa and the African diaspora, rather, often represented an opportunity to seize the reins of self-definition and to position themselves as agents in the postcolonial transformation of society (ibid.). Their rescuing of the definitions of black subjectivity from Eurocentric discourses was essential to the postcolonial moment and permanently altered the terms of debate on both sides.

What might be thought of as Jamaica's period of musical modernity was, arguably, bookended by the tragic, lone-genius figure of trombonist-composer-bandleader Don Drummond on one hand, and the techno-deconstructionist figures of Lee Perry and King Tubby on the other. The advent of dub created a space in Jamaican music (and later world pop) for the post-song, for linguistic, formal and symbolic indeterminacy. Nevertheless, dub was very much a reflection of the particular society and historical moment in which it arose. If the resounding bass drum patterns of the Kumina traditional healing ceremony were considered sonic "heart strings" which connected the worlds of the living and the dead (Manuel, Bilby and Largey 1995, 147), the thunderous patterns of the reggae electric bass would similarly serve to reawaken postcolonial Jamaicans to their "dead" past as a people of African descent, as a British slave colony and their uncertain future as a neocolonial satellite of the United States. The emergence of what Lloyd Bradley described as the "nationalistic swagger" of "drum & bass" (2000, 199) to Jamaica's musical forefront paralleled the full flowering of postcolonial political consciousness and pro-African cultural nationalism which formed roots reggae's symbolic fibre. Within this potent moment of cultural redefinition would be contained the first glimpses of a new musical language, which at once hearkened backwards in cultural time to ancestral Africa and forward to a pan-cultural, cyber-sonic future of virtual environments, human-machine interfaces and digitized sensuality.

In *Dub: Soundscapes and Shattered Songs in Jamaican Reggae* I demonstrate the role that musical technology and local concepts of experimentation played in this redefinition. When we blend the parallel significance of dub's role within and outside of Jamaica, it becomes clear that the central artistic revolutions of the late twentieth century were not only accomplished in the intellectual and cultural centres of Europe and America. They were also accomplished on the margins of Europe and America, where Western cultural forms mixed, mingled or collided with a variety of non-Western forms in the creation of new aesthetic, cultural and technological centres.

Acknowledgement

Excerpt from Michael Veal, *Dub: Soundscapes and Shattered Songs in Jamaican Reggae,* © 2007 by Michael Veal. Reprinted by permission of Wesleyan University Press.

Notes

1. For example, see "Best of the Century", *Time*, 31 December 1999. Lee Perry was awarded a Grammy for his album *Jamaican E.T.* (Trojan/Sanctuary Records, 2002).
2. Armstrong's "King of the Zulus" features a skit midway through the performance that includes a Jamaican voice. See *The Best of Louis Armstrong: The Hot Five and Hot Seven Recordings* (Sony, 1999).
3. The terms used in the stylistic periodization of Jamaican popular music have differed in different accounts. To take two examples: Barrow and Dalton use the term "early reggae" to indicate music created between approximately 1968 and 1972, "roots reggae" to indicate music created between approximately 1973 and 1980, and "dancehall" to indicate music created between approximately 1980 and 1985 (in this account, dub music is discussed as a subgenre of the roots reggae and dancehall periods). These authors use the term "ragga" to indicate the digital music that began to be produced in 1985 (see Barrow and Dalton 1997, 82–324). Stolzoff, on the other hand, uses the term "reggae" to indicate all of the music produced between 1968 and 1985, and uses the term "dancehall" to indicate the digital music that began to be produced in 1985 (Stolzoff 2000, 65–114). Stolzoff also uses the term "dancehall" in a broader sense, to refer to any historical site in which Jamaicans enjoyed music communally. For my purposes in this chapter, the most important distinction to be made is between music performed by ensembles using standard popular music instrumentation (that is, voice, electric guitar, electric bass, drum set, keyboards, wind instruments, percussion, and so on), and music created by digital means (that is, digital keyboards, samplers, drum machines, computers, and so on). Thus, I use the terms "reggae" and "roots reggae" interchangeably to refer to the music produced between approximately 1968 and 1985, and "ragga" to refer to the digital music produced thereafter. I believe this is consistent with the general usage of these terms in Jamaica.
4. These two definitions of "electronic music" are offered in Schwartz 1973, 4–6. See also Chanan 1995, 146.
5. For example, see Stockhausen's *Hymnen* (1969) and *Kurzwellen* (1969), Cage's "Williams Mix" (1953), or Ussachevsky's "Wireless Fantasy" (1960).
6. See Robert Witmer (1989) for a survey of the colonial-era traditions of live musical performance in Jamaica which included jazz and blues.
7. For example, see producer Prince Buster's comments in Bradley (2000, 11).

8. Witmer also refers to "a rich and vibrant – but almost entirely undocumented – Afro-Jamaican folk or traditional music culture" (1989, 17).
9. See Sterne for a discussion of this "impact" model of technological encounter (2003, 7).

References

Barrow, Steve, and Peter Dalton. 1997. *The Rough Guide to Reggae*. London: Rough Guides.

Bradley, Lloyd. 2000. *Bass Culture: When Reggae Was King*. London: Penguin.

Chanan, Michael. 1995. *Repeated Takes: A Short History of Recording and Its Effects on Music*. London: Verso.

Chude-Sokei, Louis. 1997. "The Sound of Culture: Dread Discourse and the Jamaican Sound Systems". In *Language, Rhythm and Sound: Black Popular Cultures Into the Twenty-first Century*, ed. Joseph K. Adjaye and Adrienne R. Andrews, 185–202. Pittsburgh, PA: University of Pittsburgh Press.

Corbett, John. 2000. "Experimental Oriental: New Music and Other Others". In *Western Music and Its Others: Difference, Representation and Appropriation in Music*, ed. Georgina Born and David Hesmondhalgh, 163–86. Berkeley: University of California Press.

Gilroy, Paul. 1993. *The Black Atlantic: Modernity and Double Consciousness*. Cambridge, MA: Harvard University Press.

Juniper, Andrew. 2003. *Wabi Sabi: The Japanese Art of Impermanence*. Boston: Turtle Publishing.

Lastra, James. 2000. *Sound Technology and the American Cinema*. New York: Columbia University Press.

Malm, Krister, and Roger Wallis. 1992. *Media Policy and Music Activity*. New York: Routledge.

Manuel, Peter, Kenneth Bilby and Michael Largey. 1995. *Caribbean Currents*. Philadelphia: Temple University Press.

Schwartz, Elliott. 1973. *Electronic Music: A Listener's Guide*. New York: Praeger.

Sims, Lowery Stokes. 2005. "The Post-Modernism of Wifredo Lam". In *Cosmopolitan Modernisms*, ed. Kobena Mercer, 86–101. Cambridge, MA: MIT Press.

Sterne, Jonathan. 2003. *The Audible Past: Cultural Origins of Sound Reproduction*. Durham, NC: Duke University Press.

Stolzoff, Norman. 2000. *Wake the Town and Tell the People: Dancehall Culture in Jamaica*. Durham, NC: Duke University Press.

Veal, Michael. 2007. *Dub: Soundscapes and Shattered Songs in Jamaican Reggae*. Middletown, CT: Wesleyan University Press.

Witmer, Robert. 1989. "A History of Kingston's Popular Music Culture: Neo-Colonialism to Nationalism". *Jamaica Journal* 22 (1): 11–18.

CHAPTER 15

REGGAE STUDIES
AT THE UNIVERSITY
OF THE WEST INDIES

CAROLYN COOPER

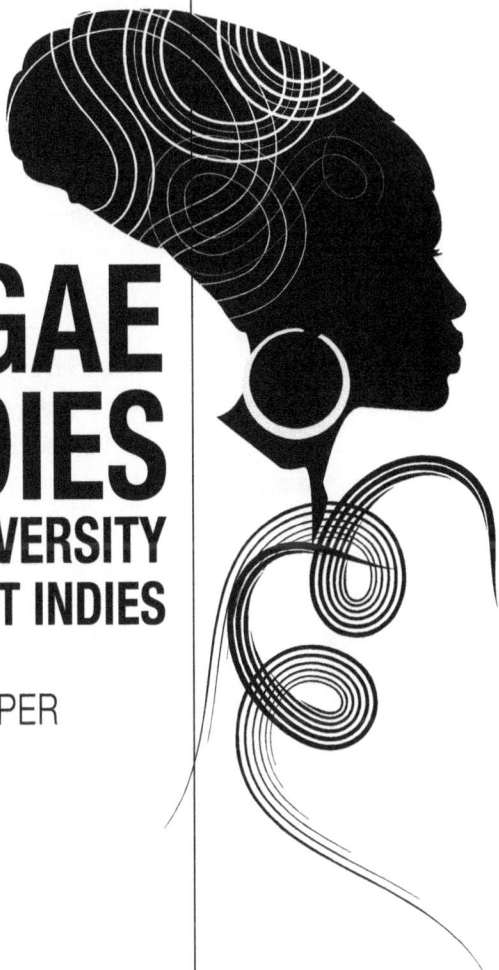

The ambitiously named International Reggae Studies Centre (IRSC) at the University of the West Indies, Mona, Jamaica, has its genesis in a long tradition of regional scholarship that focuses on populist consciousness in all its multifariousness. A classic articulation of this empowering consciousness is Marcus Garvey's authoritative exhortation (1938, 9), "We are going to emancipate ourselves from mental slavery because whilst others might free the body, none but ourselves can free the mind." This metaphorical representation of the liberation process as freedom from ideological shackles is an artful, streetwise restatement of a familiar academic concept: the cultural politics of decolonization. Transposed by Bob Marley into the moving "Redemption Song", Garvey's injunction is amplified by the resounding reggae beat.

The overtones of "redemption" are potent, as the *Oxford English Dictionary* definitions make clear: there are the pacifist echoes of Christian "redemption" – "deliverance from sin and its consequences by the atonement of Jesus Christ". There are, as well, the militant reverberations of Caribbean slave history: "redemption" as "the action of freeing a prisoner, captive, or slave by payment; ransom". Somewhat ironically, "redemption" in this latter sense of the word – buying out of the slave system – often means liberation from the epistemological weight of conservative Christian traditions that do valorize the passive acceptance of one's lot in life, with the promise of deferred gratification in the life to come.

The reggae musician, himself, thus expresses in song a tradition of visionary insight that is not always acknowledged as knowledge by the academy. Thus, one of the primary projects of the IRSC at Mona is to establish the social history of reggae as a distinctly Jamaican cultural formation. This process of revalorization of nativist discourses is intended to reinforce the ideological underpinnings of the music itself and thus facilitate analysis of the continuities and discontinuities between the knowledge on the street and the knowledge in the academy.

An equally important project of the centre is foregrounded by the modifier "international". The centre focuses on the evolution of international reggae – both the "pure" and "hybridized" forms of reggae that have emerged from the cross-fertilization of Jamaican reggae with other world musics. Reggae is itself a hybridized music, evolving, in part, out of the fusion of Jamaican mento and African-American rhythm and blues. The role of transnational recorded music corporations in the globalization of both Jamaican reggae, and its "world beat" analogues must be interrogated. For example, the emergence of Jawaiian in Hawai'i illustrates this globalizing process. The portmanteau word "Jawaiian" embodies the blending of Jamaican and Hawaiian musical forms, described by Brent Clough as "the fusion of cha-lang-a-lang, ukelele-dominated Hawaiian song with bass-and-drum-heavy reggae".[1]

The "international" in IRSC bears a dual burden: it modifies both the music, reggae, and the fledgling institution, the centre. It is anticipated that the centre will indeed become an international centre of excellence in research on reg-

15.1 Marcus Garvey, by Michael Thompson.
Courtesy of Michael Thompson.

gae, attracting scholars from around the world who wish to contribute to the body of knowledge that we are attempting to generate at the centre of origin of this New World music.

Reggae studies is a multidisciplinary enterprise; it requires the collaboration of a wide range of academics within the university and a diverse group of practitioners in the field. Thus, the centre seeks to close the perceived gap between the purely "academic" preoccupations of the university and the rather practical concerns of the reggae music industry. The challenge the centre faces in fulfilling the mandate of emancipation from mental slavery is pointedly stated by Bob Marley:

> Babylon system is the vampire
> Sucking the blood of the sufferers.
> Building church and university
> Deceiving the people continually.

This representation of the university in the popular imagination as an agent of the vampirish state is one of the barriers that must be negotiated. Indeed, there is a long established Rastafari inversion of the original name of the University of the West Indies – University College of the West Indies – abbreviated as UC. In dreadtalk, "you see", the homonym of UC, becomes "you blind". The vision that is so grandiloquently pronounced in the university's motto, "Lux oriens ex occidente" – "A light rising from the West" – is eclipsed in cynical, populist discourse.

Institutional Antecedents at the University of the West Indies, Mona

The late Rex Nettleford, former vice-chancellor of the University of the West Indies, defined the study of Caribbean popular culture as a process of "rethinking the classics" (interview with the author). This rethinking requires a revaluation of the privileged cultural hierarchy of aesthetic values in the contemporary Caribbean. Conventional wisdom constructs a pyramid of aesthetic forms and practices at the top of which is the "classical". The centre is occupied by the "contemporary/popular". At the very base is the "folk". Given the racialized history of the Caribbean, it is not surprising that the pyramid is colour-coded. The "classical" peak is Eurocentric/white; the "folk" base is Afrocentric/black;

the "contemporary/popular" centre is a grey area. Though one could very well argue that the base as foundation is the most important structural element of this pyramid, one must, nevertheless, concede the historical devaluation of the base folk in the Caribbean.

On the Mona campus of the University of the West Indies, Mervyn Alleyne, former head of the Department of Language and Linguistics, was the first to formally propose an Institute of Caribbean Studies that would seek to understand how Caribbean people, "the folk", interpret the universe and express their insights in various ways. Language is obviously a primal facilitator of this process of self-definition and articulation. Alleyne's distinguished career as a Caribbean linguist committed to theorizing Caribbean Creole languages has contributed in no small measure to our understanding of Caribbean folk epistemology.

As dean of the Faculty of Arts and General Studies in the late 1970s and early 1980s, Alleyne was instrumental in laying the foundation of the Institute of Caribbean Studies at Mona. The first project was the institutionalization of a Folklore Studies Committee in the faculty. From the very beginning, this committee recognized that interdisciplinarity was a key factor in the success of a broad-based project such as this. The pioneering folklore studies researchers knew that a wide range of the traditional and classical disciplines had to be brought into creative play in order for them to be able to fully theorize and analyse Caribbean folk forms and popular practices. This meant that the Folklore Studies Project had to be extended beyond the boundaries of the Faculty of Arts and General Studies. It had to cross borders.

Indeed, just as the project of folkore studies challenged canonical notions of what the appropriate subjects of classical scholarly research are, interdisciplinarity itself raised questions about the hegemony of the classical disciplines. A university in a postcolonial society ought to be actively engaged in this exciting process of cultural redefinition. But, too often, timid academics, who have career investments in particular disciplinary definitions of scholarship, find it difficult to function in what appears to be destabilizing circumstances.

Fortunately, at Mona there has always been a core group of scholars who valorize the creative possibilities of "chaos". Even before "chaos theory" became fashionable, academics who were actively trying to emancipate themselves from mental slavery willingly engaged in judicious risk management. The establishment of the Folklore Studies Project made later developments possible. For example, Maureen Warner-Lewis, a foundation member of the Folklore Studies Committee, has done extensive work on Caribbean orature and designed three non-traditional courses for the Department of Literatures in English: "Introduction to Orature", "Folktale and Proverb" and "Myth and Epic".

In the late 1980s, under the direction of the dean of the faculty, Joseph Pereira, the Institute of Caribbean Studies was formally established, and a board appointed, to be chaired by the dean or his nominee. Mervyn Morris served as the first chairman, and was succeeded by Kamau Brathwaite. On the latter's resignation from the university, Pereira assumed the chairmanship. During his administration, three research fellowships became available and projects in oral history, comparative Caribbean literature, and linguistics were funded. A lively lecture/seminar series is an ongoing public education activity of the institute.

The institutionalization of the IRSC marks a logical extension of the borders of the "folk" to include "popular" culture. Of course, one generation's popular culture becomes the next generation's folk culture. But the popular, in the present, appears to some purists to be even less worthy of serious academic study than its "folk" antecedent. Like the earlier folklore studies, cultural studies is now a well-developed discipline and an established department, programme and institute designation in universities all over the world. At the University of Birmingham, England, in the 1970s, Stuart Hall, that iconoclastic Jamaican intellectual, was a leading figure in the institutionalization of cultural studies in the United Kingdom and internationally.[2]

At the Cave Hill (Barbados) and St Augustine (Trinidad) campuses of the University of the West Indies, the study of popular culture is now institutionalized. James Millette, a former dean of the Faculty of Arts and General Studies at St Augustine, was a prime mover in the establishing of the Institute of Caribbean Studies there. Gordon Rohlehr, a former director of the St Augustine institute, has done exemplary scholarly work on the Trinidad calypso and the steel pan. The more recent formalization of "Carnival studies" at St Augustine, linked to the development of heritage tourism, is a classic example of the collaboration of the university with the public and private sectors in the marketing of indigenous cultural products.

At Cave Hill there is no formal Institute of Caribbean Studies. But, individuals are doing important popular culture research there. Sir Hilary Beckles, campus principal, has been instrumental in advancing the academic work on cricket that was begun so brilliantly by C.L.R. James in *Beyond a Boundary*. Under Beckles's leadership, the Centre for Cricket Research has been established within the Department of History. A course on the history of cricket is being taught at both Cave Hill and Mona. Reggae in Jamaica; calypso in Trinidad; cricket in Barbados. These three pulse beats of the Caribbean body politic loudly declare that the "folk" are very much alive. What is now needed at the University of the West Indies is a formal institutional structure that will link the various initiatives in popular culture scholarship. Such an institution would function as a coherent centre from which to establish wider linkages with similar centres of research and teaching on popular culture in the Caribbean and the diaspora.

The Catalytic Moment

Having defined the institutional context, I will now outline the confluence of wider social forces that resulted in the conception of the IRSC. In December 1992, a seminar on "Reggae Music as a Business" was convened at the Jamaica conference by Specs-Shang Muzik Incorporated and Sandosa Limited, in collaboration with the Eagle Merchant Bank, the National Commercial Bank and the Trafalgar Development Bank. I was invited to present a paper which I entitled "Cultural Implications of Marketing Reggae Internationally".[3] I focused on the mixed reception of Buju Banton's anti-homosexuality song "Boom Bye Bye". The resonant boom of this song has echoed across continents, generating much public debate. In my presentation, I analysed and contextualized popular Jamaican cultural values that have increasingly come under attack in the international community.

I argued that the fate of Buju's song in the "outernational" market, particularly in the United States and the United Kingdom where highly politicized gay, lesbian, bisexual and transgender activists wield substantial power, was a test case of the degree to which local Jamaican cultural values can be exported, without censure, into a foreign market. I raised the issue of language in deejay culture and the separation of aesthetic and ideological issues that can arise in the exporting of Jamaican music. Non-Jamaicans can appreciate the aesthetically appealing noises of the music without understanding the words.

Once they understand the words they may be unable to accept the cultural message in the music. They may reject the music altogether.

I asked a number of questions: How, then, should the reggae artiste respond to this marketing problem? Adapt the message to suit the export market, sacrificing authenticity for airplay? Should the artiste do one kind of song for the local market and another for export? Admittedly, in the age of the Internet, the distinction between local and international markets is subject to constant erasure. Should the reggae artist risk censorship in order to maintain the cultural integrity of the Jamaican way of seeing the world? In my role of cultural critic I assumed the burden of communal responsibility for the youthful deejay who had put himself at risk by running up his mouth.

There are well-defined Caribbean cultural codes that justify this acceptance of communal responsibility. Consider the cultural rules that are at work when the man with mouth is confronted by the man with muscle. The man with mouth bawls out to the community, "Unu huol mi yaa, huol mi yaa, ar mi a go kil him" (Hold me back, you hear, or I am going to kill him). The man with mouth is depending on the community to hold him back because he knows that he dare not attack this formidable enemy he has verbally challenged. And so the man with mouth gets to save face. It is the community, not his cowardice, that has restrained him.

I concluded my presentation with a clear injunction: the deejay must learn to censor herself or himself, otherwise somebody else will do the censoring. Nevertheless, my talk was scathingly indicted in a review of the seminar published by the *Village Voice*:

> By all reports Cooper's speech was the most enthusiastically received of the conference. A room full of 300 lawyers, bankers, and music businesspeople greeted references to "buttocks" and a Jamaican proverb that goes "Two pot cover can't shut" by whistling and banging on tables and gave the professor a standing ovation when she concluded. . . . According to Payday Records' Patricia Moxey, the Americans stood around afterward saying, "Jeez, these people are pretty out there", but saw no way to convey their reaction to their hosts. "I don't agree with her views," Moxey told us, "but I think she was right about what she was saying about Jamaica – that everyone is completely homophobic." (Christgau 1993)

That is decidedly *not* what I was saying. Furthermore, explication of the biblical genesis of homophobia in Jamaica is not synonymous with endorsement of fundamentalist Christian ideology.

The Bureaucratic Process

The reception of my presentation by the local Jamaican audience was so positive that it occurred to me that the University of the West Indies ought to become more actively involved in the reggae music industry by functioning as a clearing-house of ideas. And that was the genesis of the IRSC. I canvassed then chairman of the board of the Institute of Caribbean Studies at Mona, Joe Pereira, since it appeared to make sense to locate the reggae studies project within an existing institution rather than trying to start from scratch. His enthusiastic support precipitated action. I conferred with Hubert Devonish, of the Department of Language, Linguistics and Philosophy, who developed the first draft of the proposal for what has become the IRSC.

The process of institutionalization was relatively painless, given the rigidity of the university's bureaucracy. Within a year, the proposal had passed through all the relevant committees: first, the board of the Institute of Caribbean Studies; then the board of the Faculty of Arts and General Studies, within which the institute is located; then the academic board, Mona; and, finally, the University Academic Committee. There was some initial resistance to the idea of reggae studies as an academic project, but good sense quickly prevailed.

And there were minor quibbles of nomenclature. At the meeting of the Board of the Institute of Caribbean Studies where the proposal was first reviewed, the original name of the centre, the "International Reggae Institute", was changed when a pedant insisted that an institute could not be located within an institute. So "institute" was changed to "centre". At the Faculty Board meeting, it was recommended that the word "Studies" be inserted in the title, presumably to signal academic rigour, not performance. Somewhat anomalously, the centre was institutionalized as a "unit", despite its name, and I was appointed as its first coordinator in 1995.

In the 1995–96 and 1996–97 academic years, the process of institutionalization, particularly the drive for external funding, was decelerated because I went on leave for three semesters. On my return from leave, efforts were intensified to secure substantial external funding to establish a chair in reggae studies as well as a multimedia archive. The reggae music industry, itself, is an obvious potential source of funding. But the major players in the industry do not always fully appreciate the long-term benefits of investment in the development of intellectual capital.

In a sense, the institutionalization of the IRSC is a classic case of fool-hardy academics agreeing to "tek basket carry water". But since folk wisdom confirms the efficacy of tar as a stopgap measure, we bravely soldiered on. Approval of the centre at the levels of the Mona Academic Board and the University Academic Committee was granted on the clear understanding that the centre would be self-financing. Given this major limitation, we initially concentrated our efforts on "no-cost" activities.

Academic Initiatives

The first public event of the centre in its inaugural academic year, 1994–95, was a lunch-hour concert at the Philip Sherlock Centre for the Creative Arts, featuring Bigga Haitian, a New York–based deejay and Sandra Lee, a local dub poet, both of whom performed free of cost in support of the work of the centre. After that performance, an enthusiastic member of the university's administrative staff said that Bigga Haitian had inspired her to try to learn *kreyol*. The potential for cross-regional, multilingual dialogue is clearly one of the compelling features of the study of Caribbean popular culture, broadly defined.

A successful lecture series on popular culture was also launched that year. This was the beginning of a long-running programme in which reggae and dancehall artists, producers, managers and other industry experts have given talks at the university, narrowing the distance between town and gown. Luciano, Tony Rebel, Lady Saw, Queen Ifrika, Ninjaman, Capleton, Bounty Killa, Judy Mowatt, Louise Fraser-Bennett, Christine Hewitt, Jeremy Harding and Gentleman are just a few of the participants in the series. Recordings of these and other lectures on reggae are housed in the Library of the Spoken Word, Radio Education Unit, University of the West Indies, Mona, which has produced a bibliography of the unit's reggae recordings.

In 1995, the Bob Marley Foundation, in collaboration with the IRSC, hosted an international conference at the University of the West Indies, Mona, on "Reggae, Rastafari and Jamaican Culture", to mark the fiftieth anniversary of Bob Marley's birth. In his keynote lecture, "Roots in the Airwaves: Popular Culture in a Global Context", Dick Hebdige paid tribute to the dub aesthetic: "my whole approach to thinking and writing owes a lot to dub's loopy, dense and trailing way of doing logic". This conference was a defining moment for the IRSC, loudly proclaiming from a variety of disciplinary perspectives the legitimacy of reggae studies as a viable academic enterprise. A selection of papers from that historic conference has been published (Wint and Cooper 2003).

In the 1995–96 academic year, a junior research fellowship in the Social History of Jamaican Music was awarded to the Institute of Caribbean Studies by the university. Garth White, formerly of the African-Caribbean Institute of Jamaica, was appointed to undertake the research project. Five papers, a bibliography and a fifty-tape selection of representative music of the period 1960 to 1980 resulted from the fellowship, adding to the body of locally produced scholarship in the field. Michael "Ibo" Cooper was later appointed as another research fellow in the Institute of Caribbean Studies but the results of his attachment were disappointing.

In November 1997, the centre was formally launched with a public lecture, "'Dr Satan's Echo Chamber': Reggae, Technology and the Diaspora Process", delivered by Louis Chude-Sokei, then a faculty member at Bowdoin College, now at the University of Washington. His visit was substantially funded by his home institution. The launching of the centre was also the occasion on which the Bob Marley Foundation announced its further collaboration with the University of the West Indies in licensing us to use the name "Bob Marley" to establish an annual lecture series on reggae, the "Bob Marley Lecture". Chude-Sokei's lecture was the first in what has become a distinguished series to honour the name of an extraordinary reggae musician who "performed" globalization as cultural praxis. The 2012 lecture, the fifteenth, was "For the Record: Bob Marley's Island Albums and the Fortieth Anniversary of *Catch a Fire*", delivered by Mike Alleyne of the Department of Recording Music, Middle Tennessee State University.

Curriculum Development

Long before the establishment of the IRSC, undergraduate students at the University of the West Indies engaged in independent study of reggae through the compulsory final-year Caribbean studies research project. In recognition of the value of this body of work, the centre published a select bibliography of these research papers in 1997. The Bob Marley Foundation agreed to sponsor an annual prize for the best Caribbean studies research paper on reggae.

But the Caribbean studies research paper was being phased out. It therefore became even more urgent for undergraduate courses in reggae to be developed across the disciplines to satisfy the need of students who wanted to do academic work on reggae but no longer had the option that the independent Caribbean studies research paper provided.

Political scientist Clinton Hutton introduced the course "Jamaican Music 1962–1982" through the Department of Government. Anthropologist Kingsley Stewart designed the course "Identity and Conduct in the Dancehall Culture", taught in the Department of Sociology, Psychology and Social Work. The teaching programme of the IRSC was much enhanced with the securing of a lecturer post to enable delivery of the innovative undergraduate degree in entertainment and cultural enterprise management that the centre had pioneered under the leadership of Kam-Au Amen.[4] Donna Hope was appointed as the first lecturer in reggae studies in 2007. From the perspective of cultural studies, she introduced courses such as "Culture, Gender and Sexuality in Jamaican Popular Music" and "Performing Culture: Dancehall as Ritual and Spectacle".

Conclusion

C.L.R. James's classic account of cricket and the not so sporting politics of decolonization that is given in the exemplary cultural studies text *Beyond a Boundary* provides a useful model for cultural transformation in the region. Movement beyond boundaries is essentially what the study of Caribbean popular culture is about. The boundaries are many. Rethinking the classics is the first leap. In terms of Marcus Garvey's model of emancipation from mental slavery, it is not only the content of the curriculum that must be transformed in the academic institution. Disciplinary boundaries themselves constitute barriers to full freedom.

Furthermore, bureaucratic structures that are designed to ensure stability can often function as barriers of institutionalized resistance to change. In circumstances where open hostility to new academic projects such as reggae studies is not politic, funding decisions about programmes that are "essential" and others that are "peripheral" indirectly assert hierarchies of value. Like a dub track, this narrative of the institutionalization of the IRSC at the University of the West Indies, Mona, allows spaces for textual improvisation. It privileges reading between the lines.

In frustration at institutional politics that resulted in the appropriation of the centre's Entertainment and Cultural Enterprise Management degree programme by its host, the Institute of Caribbean Studies, I resigned as coordinator in 2008. I have concentrated my efforts on developing reggae studies courses in the Department of Literatures in English, such as "Reggae Poetry", which focuses on song lyrics, returning poetry to its roots in oral performance. Other pioneering courses of the department are "Reggae Narratives", "Reggae Romance" and "Reggae Films: Screening Jamaica", the latter designed by Rachel Moseley-Wood. In addition, the department has launched a series of public forums on reggae and dancehall such as the February 2012 interactive session with Damian "Jr Gong" Marley and Vybz Kartel's infamous 2011 lecture.

The case study of the IRSC at Mona is not unique. Having invested more than a decade in the arduous, collective process of institutionalizing the programme in Gender and Development Studies at the University of the West Indies, I am comforted by the knowledge that the race is not to the swift. The cunning tortoise often outdistances the gullible hare. The Anansi pragmatism that is ubiquitously encoded in African/diasporic folktales provides the reassurance that marginalization is, indeed, often a site of empowering resistance to, and radical transformation of, hegemonic institutions. In the words of Bob Marley (1979):

> We refuse to be
> What you wanted us to be.
> We are what we are
> That's the way it's going to be.
> You can't educate I
> For no equal opportunity
> Talking about my freedom
> People freedom and liberty.
> Yeah!
> We've been trodding on the winepress
> Much too long
> Rebel, rebel.

Notes

1. See, for example, Liza Simon, "Roots, Rock Jawaiian?", *Honolulu Weekly*, 6 November 1991, 4, where she quotes John Sexton, drummer of the Simplisity band: "People are blaming it for keeping Hawaiians away from their heritage." This issue is comprehensively addressed in Brent Clough's essay "Oceanic Reggae", chapter 13, this volume.
2. Stuart Hall's reader *Resistance through Rituals*, co-edited with Tony Jefferson, includes an essay by Dick Hebridge (1975) that is one of the earliest scholarly treatments of the subject "reggae studies" that is the *raison d'être* of the IRSC.
3. A "dub" version of that paper was published soon after in the *Massachusetts Review*. A later version was published in *Sound Clash*.
4. The story of the institutionalization of the entertainment and cultural enterprise management degree is told by Kam-Au Amen in chapter 16 of this volume.

References

Christgau, Robert. 1993. "Africanist Abomination: Homophobia as a Business", *Village Voice*. http://www.robertchristgau.com/xg/music/rbjaho-93.php.

Cooper, Carolyn. 1994. "Lyrical Gun: Metaphor and Role Play in Jamaican Dancehall Culture". *Massachusetts Review* 35 (3–4): 429–47.

———. 2004. "Lyrical Gun: Metaphor and Role Play in Jamaican Dancehall Culture". *Sound Clash: Jamaican Dancehall Culture at Large*. New York: Palgrave Macmillan, 145–78.

Garvey, Marcus. 1938. "The Work That Has Been Done". *Black Man* 3 (10): 9.

Hebdige, Dick. 1975. "Reggae, Rastas and Rudies". In *Resistance through Rituals: Youth Subcultures in Post-War Britain*, ed. Stewart Hall and Tony Jefferson, 135–53. Birmingham: HarperCollins.

Marley, Bob. 1979. "Babylon System". *Survival*. Island Records, ILPS 9542.

Wint, Eleanor, and Carolyn Cooper, eds. 2003. *Bob Marley: The Man and His Music*. Kingston: Arawak.

CHAPTER 16

ENTERTAINMENT AND CULTURAL ENTERPRISE MANAGEMENT

KAM-AU AMEN

The Entertainment and Cultural Enterprise Management (ECEM) degree programme at the University of the West Indies, Mona, was developed in the context of a personal academic quest to understand the nature of our collective identity as a Caribbean people. It evolved as more knowledge was unearthed to inform that understanding. Much of my thought, and the paradigm through which I analyse the Caribbean context, drew heavily upon the regionalist (not global in this instance) perspective of Jamaica's national hero the Right Excellent Marcus Mosiah Garvey. It was, therefore, very important that a programme such as this, while including the content that is necessary to function in the international arena, also grounds its majors in the unique demands that face our Caribbean region. In the original document that elaborated my vision in 2000, I wrote the following: "The specific goals are to produce graduates who will become innovative business and industry leaders. A major focus of the programme is entrepreneurial development and innovation. Graduates will have gained a full appreciation of the importance of the convergence of media, computer based technology and culture within the global context and be prepared to harness their benefits for the Caribbean."

These goals were not arrived at arbitrarily, but were informed by articulated sector needs. Up to that point, scholars such as economist Keith Nurse, first operating out of the University of the West Indies at St Augustine, Trinidad and Tobago, and now the University of the West Indies campus at Cave Hill, Babados, had done commissioned research on the way forward for some of the Caribbean entertainment sectors. Attorney Lloyd Stanbury and cultural entrepreneur Andrea Davis were also among those who had put out work on this subject. The United Nations Council on Trade and Development, the World Intellectual Property Organization, Jamaica Promotions Corporation, the Tourism and Industrial Development Company of Trinidad and Tobago and the Caribbean Export Development Agency were among the funders for some of these studies. The results of these several research projects remain shelved waiting on an elusive government buy-in. After more than ten years, many regional governments have still not moved to take these sectors seriously. With the benefit of hindsight, one is forced to acknowledge that conducting the research for presentation to government representatives has failed miserably. We have little meaningful progress to show for it. It would appear, then, that the current approach needs review, albeit the research is necessary.

The Informing Moment

The story of the present ECEM bachelor's degree programme began in November 1999 when, as a graduate student at the University of the West Indies, Mona, I attended the inaugural Caribbean Music Expo in Ocho Rios, Jamaica. It was there, while listening to the quite legitimate complaints of Jamaican and Caribbean music sector players about the lack of support for the industry, the idea of offering a training programme for the sector began to germinate. I asked myself the question, "Why didn't the University of the West

Indies have a programme that prepared personnel for this sector, which on the surface was so definitive of what it meant to be Jamaican or Caribbean?"

Shortly after my return from the expo, I ran into Carolyn Cooper, then coordinator of the university's Reggae Studies Unit. I posed the question to her about the absence of a programme at the University of the West Indies to service the entertainment industry. Her response was that I should take the initiative to develop such a programme to fill the gap in the curriculum. That was all I needed.

Institutional Precedents

I immediately set about researching similar degree programmes from other universities. My main inspiration came from New York University's Entertainment, Media and Technology programme, which had both an MBA and an undergraduate component. I also looked at other US university programmes such as Columbia University's and a few in the United Kingdom. At the time, there were not that many on which I could draw. In developing the academic programme for the University of the West Indies, I enlisted the support of Carolyn Hayle, who was then the special programmes coordinator. She was extremely supportive and allowed me access to resources that would have otherwise been difficult to obtain.

My initial approach was to use the model that had been followed for the African and African diaspora studies major offered by the University of the West Indies. The programme had been designed by Maureen Warner-Lewis and Rupert Lewis, who brought together existing African and African diaspora courses within the university's system to create the innovative major. The programme has been a success and I am proud to stand as its first graduate.

This precedent was to serve the ECEM initiative well. I combed through courses offered on all the campuses of the University of the West Indies (Mona, Cave Hill and St Augustine). We knew that if a course that could serve the ECEM programme were already on the books at Cave Hill or St Augustine, then the hurdle of course approval would already be overcome. Hence, the major concern would become provision of staffing for its delivery at Mona. Much to my surprise, I found a fair number of courses on both campuses that would have been beneficial, some of which did not make their way into the ECEM degree programme at Mona. Nevertheless, the innovative degree remains a respectable offering.

Reconceptualizing Cultural Studies at the University of the West Indies: Theory and Praxis

The ECEM programme can be theorized as a significant break in the focus of cultural studies as it was then practised at the University of the West Indies. Cultural studies had hardly engaged business, except to critique the underlying assumptions of its practice. This approach was understandable, given the discipline's early Marxist influences. However, this history weakened some of the efforts to offer business training to entertainment and cultural enterprise practitioners. Evidence of this could have been seen in the more traditional arts-oriented content of the postgraduate diploma in arts and cultural enterprise management that is offered at the Department of Creative and Festival Arts at the St Augustine campus, developed virtually in parallel with the ECEM programme. I did not know this until months after I had gone through a few drafts of my own. It is undeniable that capitalist praxis needed to be critiqued. However, the exclusive focus on critique can alienate many would-be change makers who find themselves at a disadvantage, holding on to theory-driven knowledge that leaves them without practical skills that are essential for functioning in a world that is decidedly capitalist. Hard business skills, we have come to discover, are no longer a luxury for serious entertainment and cultural enterprise practitioners.

Furthermore, the ECEM programme deliberately avoided any reliance on government and activities of the political directorate, addressing, instead, the very broad scope of the capitalist entertainment enterprise. By the time the programme was being drafted, my ideas of the benefits of wealth creation versus an approach of poverty alleviation had been cemented. Influenced by my reading of Marcus Garvey's philosophies on capitalism and the importance of wealth, self-reliance and entrepreneurship, I recognized that his far-reaching concepts needed to be revitalized as we tested new models of development in our context. Unfortunately, state-led initiatives were failing entire sectors that fell under the entertainment and cultural enterprise umbrella and, increasingly, the call was being made for collective industry action, which was being heralded as a key to achieving the kinds of success we wanted to see in the sector. Entertainment and cultural practitioners were being asked to increase collaboration, form associations and business units, and become shrewd businessmen and women operating modern and efficient enterprises that were to be engaged in global trade. This conception of the industry was entirely consistent with the commitment to collective enterprise that can be found in the writings of Marcus Garvey.

The bold stance of the ECEM degree programme required a clearly articulated vision of the kind of graduate we could expect to produce. The targeted groups for the degree were current industry practitioners as well as entry-level candidates. The ideal graduate would be poised to become a

- dynamic leader and innovator within the entertainment and culture industries;
- highly self-motivated entrepreneur and product manager;
- balanced, dynamic leader and entrepreneur who understands and appreciates both the Caribbean cultural context and the business of culture industries regionally and globally;
- practitioner who is capable of creative application of the knowledge of technicalities within his or her specialization; and
- sensitive presenter of the culture, who eschews demeaning and insensitive commoditizing of the product.

It was very important to me then, and remains so today, that the ECEM programme is seen not as a degree focused on the music business. I was very aware that within Jamaica the words "entertainment" and "music" are used interchangeably. However, entertainment takes on greater meaning globally and it was with this in mind that I included what I labelled the "culture and industry areas of focus", which were as follows:

- computer-based entertainment (gaming, and so on)
- film and television
- music
- fashion
- tourism
- sports (in association with the G.C. Foster College)

- visual and performing arts (in association with the Edna Manley College for the Visual and Performing Arts)

Upon completion of my first draft, the degree programme comprised two options, consistent with the university's degree structure: a "special" (four years) and a "major" (three years). However, because the University of the West Indies was in the process of eliminating the "special", it was the major for which institutional approval was sought.

Beginning the Approval Process

By far, the approval process proved to be the most complicated element of the task. Approximately three months after the birth of the idea, I developed a first draft of the programme for presentation to the appropriate curriculum review committee. It was, in fact, designed as an entrepreneurial business management degree which would have best found a home in the Faculty of Social Sciences at Mona. This was so primarily because many of the existing courses were to be found in the departments of Management Studies at Cave Hill, Mona and St Augustine. The Humanities courses were drawn from the Caribbean Institute of Media and Communication (CARIMAC), the creative arts (CA coded) and two general arts (AR coded) courses. Since there was a need to develop some specific courses for the ECEM degree, any department that took the programme on board and created these new courses would effectively become the owner of the entire programme, at least for the moment. Unfortunately, this was a prospect that did not help us in the early stages. Given the university's structure, programmes cannot be developed without an institutional or departmental home. But no department was willing to develop the programme and run the risk of having it relocated to another department, or faculty even.

My first approach was to present the draft to Joseph Pereira, dean of the Faculty of Humanities and Education and director of the Institute of Caribbean Studies within which the cultural studies programme I was in had been institutionalized. He lauded the effort but, in a frank response, declined to locate the programme in the faculty because of a prior experience with the major in psychology that had been developed by the Faculty of Humanities and Education and appropriated by the Faculty of the Social Sciences. He suggested that I simply present the proposal to the then-dean of the Faculty of Social Sciences, the late Barry Chevannes. With Pereira's assistance, a meeting of all parties was arranged.

Chevannes welcomed the initiative and explained that a department would need to take it on board. He sent us to meet with the then-head of the Department of Management Studies, Alvin Wint, who made a lasting contribution to the name of the programme. He suggested the substitution of the word "enterprise" for "industry", indicating a focus on the units of economic activity rather than their collective output. Up to that point, the initiative had been called the "Programme in Caribbean Entertainment and Culture Industries Development and Management", a rather unwieldy name.

The years 2000 through to 2004 were to come to a close without my being able to garner any further support for the programme. All was not lost, however. The floating drafts foreshadowed some meaningful developments in the Department of Management Studies. From a January 2001 edition of my draft I quote the following: "From the survey done on the Mona campus offerings, one is yet to find a course that speaks directly to entrepreneurial development and innovation. The focus has overwhelmingly been on product management, rather than product 'creation', harnessing and development. One cannot emphasize enough that it is of prime importance that this programme gives focus to issues such as new venture creation, financing new ventures and the science of successful entrepreneurial practice." The analysis was followed up with a note acknowledging the following: "Subsequent to this suggestion the course Entrepreneurship and New Venture Creation was introduced at the Mona campus for summer 2001." It was also satisfying to see that, in 2008, the Department of Management Studies began to offer a minor in entrepreneurship.

Alternative Trajectories

In October 2001, I left the University of the West Indies to accept an appointment at the Ministry of Culture as coordinator of the culture in education programme, a post I held until July 2003. I subsequently joined the staff of the Vocational Training Development Institute as lecturer/coordinator of their Entertainment and Events Management diploma programme, and in October

2004, I became the programme manager for the CARIFORUM Cultural Support Fund until November 2005. Each one of these jobs provided me significant "real world" exposure to Jamaica's entertainment and cultural enterprise operations. The reality was that I had been earning my own stripes within the cut and thrust of the sector through my jobs and had attended a number of meetings and business development initiatives that got their funding from the government, non-profit and international development agencies. Not least of all was my stint at Vocational Training Development Institute in developing courses, coordinating their new diploma and a sustained set of entertainment business professional development courses.

These "real world" experiences repeatedly underscored the fact that there were gaps in the first drafts of the programme that needed to be filled. I, therefore, expanded the scope of the entertainment and cultural enterprise management initiative to include first, the postgraduate diploma mentioned earlier as an offering to be delivered at Mona, through a partnership with the Philip Sherlock Centre for the Creative Arts; second, a series of short courses designed specifically for the music sector; and third, the delivery of consultancy services for the entertainment sectors; as well as the BA programme.

May 2005 would see a new set of meetings at the university and this time the players were different. Tourism interests had come to the table. In April 2006, the Department of Management Studies, Mona, asked for my help in developing a course on entertainment management for their tourism concentration which would be offered to their finalizing students. Work on the course outline began initially with the help of Wayne Wright, who was then the music business consultant at Jamaica Promotions Corporation. The course was approved and, with much behind-the-scenes anxiety, I began delivery in September 2006. It was show time. Fast-forward to November 2007, and I was ecstatic when the second cohort of students in this course mounted the inaugural Entertainment Expo. The successful start of the entertainment management course in September 2006 was a small victory, but it was important in building our cache of courses.

Unlike the Africa and African diaspora studies programme, the ECEM major was one that needed a set of uniquely tailored courses to make it culturally relevant. In the very first draft, while bringing together the many courses existing on other campuses of the University of the West Indies, I had outlined the need for some new courses that were essential for this major. In that draft I proposed the following:

- a specific survey course, possibly titled "Caribbean Entertainment and Culture Industries", which gives the historical development and introduces theories of the specific entertainment and culture industries that are the subject of the programme's focus
- a course examining the legal issues within Caribbean entertainment
- a course to be named "The Business of Producing Culture: Event, Festivals, Music and Film"
- a specific entertainment and culture industries accounting/finance course, and
- the inclusion of an internship

All these have been achieved with the exception of the accounting/finance course. In addition, other relevant courses have made their way to the books, namely "Entertainment and the Digital Convergence"; "Fashion, Culture and Development"; and "Creative Industries Marketing".

With tourism expressing its interest with a clear tourism agenda, Carolyn Cooper and I realized that we needed another game plan for the ECEM degree, as originally conceived. I was very clear about the objective of the programme, and remained committed to cultural relevance. Therefore, I was not willing to allow it to be subsumed under a tourism umbrella, as I felt that the entertainment and culture sector in Jamaica was due to be recognized as a legitimate economic sector on its own. Cooper agreed. Ultimately, we negotiated a minor that would suit the tourism interests, while we began to look elsewhere for institutional support for the major.

So, in August 2006, we approached CARIMAC, located within the Faculty of Humanities and Education, offering them the opportunity to take the programme forward and, in particular, to seek approval for new courses in media. In retrospect, these overtures must be ranked among the most selfless that I have undertaken in my time. In my generosity, I passed on the entire programme and the foundation course I had developed so that CARIMAC could be empowered to deliver the programme as one of their departmental offerings.

As it turned out, CARIMAC dropped the ball. Minimal effort was employed in seeking approval for the new courses. So the Reggae Studies Unit stepped up to the plate, claimed the programme and took full responsibility for getting approval for the ECEM degree. But the somewhat anomalous Reggae Studies

Unit was not a teaching department. Nevertheless, the new dean of the Faculty of Humanities and Education, the late Aggrey Brown, welcomed the initiative and threw the full weight of his office behind it. With the help of Camille Bell-Hutchinson, then deputy dean, the ECEM degree programme was finally institutionalized in July 2007.

Prior to the programme's approval, I ensured that the University of the West Indies reached out to other organizations in order that the programme would have the support of peers. One such initiative was taken in March 2007 when the Reggae Studies Unit and Carolyn Cooper became members of the Music and Entertainment Industry Educators Association, a US-based organization. At the time, it represented music industry and music business programmes from approximately seventy colleges and universities, including programmes from the United States, Australia, Canada and, more recently then, Jamaica. The strides being made were welcome because external recognition and academic validation for the work being done was absolutely critical. The next step then was to ensure that when the students arrived we would help them with the establishment of the student arm, Music and Entertainment Industry Students Association.

The Students Come

The programme began in September with twenty-one students in its first intake. It was an exciting process and I had a hand in the selection of the entrants. There were many who applied but could not be accommodated. Selecting the 2008 intake was even more difficult. My colleagues and I were amazed at the outstanding academic strength of many of the applicants. The Faculty of Humanities and Education had found a new winner. Many students who were prime candidates for the university's prestigious law programme, with excellent grades, were opting to do the ECEM as their first choice. The new degree would certainly enhance the academic profile of the faculty if it lived up to its promise.

As fate would have it, I chose to exit the programme at the end of July 2008, despite Cooper's counsel to stay on. But this was not before I had ensured that even more courses had been written and approved. In my mind, the foundation had been solidly laid and so it was time for me to be on my way to answer another call. As a largely self-taught practitioner, I decided to pursue an MSc in entertainment business at Full Sail University in order to enhance my own competencies in the field.

In 2010, the ECEM major put out its first set of graduates. I did not witness that inaugural graduation ceremony. But, it must have been a moment like few others for those who attended and fully comprehended the arduous journey. Finally, the sacrifices had shown themselves to be well worth it. I am eternally grateful for the opportunity to have made this bit of history. I am proud of the fact that, because of this initiative, these graduates and their successors have been given an opportunity to pursue their dreams.

Contributors

Carolyn Cooper is Professor of Literary and Cultural Studies, University of the West Indies, Mona, Jamaica. She initiated the establishment of the university's International Reggae Studies Centre, and was its director for over a decade. She is the author of *Noises in the Blood, Orality, Gender and the "Vulgar" Body of Jamaican Popular Culture* and *Sound Clash: Jamaican Dancehall Culture at Large*.

Kam-Au Amen invests his time in encouraging the growth of branded entertainment and cultural enterprises. He has served as Deputy Director of Culture in the Ministry of Culture, Jamaica, and has lectured at the University of the West Indies, Mona, Jamaica, where he designed and coordinated the implementation of a Bachelor of Arts programme in entertainment and cultural enterprise management.

Peter Ashbourne teaches at the School of Music, Edna Manley College of the Visual and Performing Arts in Kingston. He is a composer and performer, and his album *Blind Man Swimming* (2001) won the Jamaica Federation of Musicians Union's award for best instrumental album.

Erna Brodber is a distinguished Jamaican writer, sociologist and social activist. Her publications include *The Second Generation of Freemen in Jamaica, 1907–1944*, and *Woodside, Pear Tree Grove P.O.*, and the novels *Myal, Jane and Louisa Will Soon Come Home*, and *The Rainmaker's Mistake*.

Louis Chude-Sokei is Associate Professor of Literature, University of Washington, Seattle. He is the author of *The Last "Darky": Bert Williams, Black-on-Black Minstrelsy, and the African Diaspora* and the forthcoming *The Sound of Culture*.

Brent Clough is the co-founder of Australia's first dancehall sound system, Nasty Tek. He has produced and presented numerous arts and music programmes for the Australian Broadcasting Corporation's Radio National and was producer and presenter of the 2005 BBC World Service series *Pacific Footsteps*.

Cheikh Ahmadou Dieng is Professor of English, Cheikh Anta Diop University, Dakar, Senegal, and a poet.

Samuel Furé Davis teaches in the Department of English, School of Foreign Languages, University of Havana, Cuba. He has written extensively on Rastafari, reggae and racial politics in Cuba.

Teddy Isimat-Mirin is CEO of Strategies Caraibes (LT-SC), an international business development company founded in Guadeloupe in 2003.

Ellen Koehlings is co-editor, with Pete Lilly, of Germany's upscale reggae/dancehall magazine *Riddim*, and co-curator (with Lilly, David Katz and Pier Tosi) of the Reggae University forum at the Rototom Reggae Sunsplash Festival, Benicàssim, Spain.

Pete Lilly is co-editor, with Ellen Koehlings, of Germany's upscale reggae/dancehall magazine *Riddim*, and co-curator (with Koehlings, David Katz and Pier Tosi) of the Reggae University forum at the Rototom Reggae Sunsplash Festival, Benicàssim, Spain.

Amon Saba Saakana lectures at the College of Science, Technology and Applied Arts, Trinidad and Tobago, is the founder of the Karnak House publishing company, and the author of *Jah Music: The Evolution of the Popular Jamaican Song*; *The Colonial Legacy in Caribbean Literature*; and *Colonialism and the Destruction of the Mind: Psychosocial Studies in Race, Class, Religion and Sexuality in the Novels of Roy Heath*.

Roger Steffens is the author or co-author of six books on reggae and Bob Marley and lectures globally on the life of Bob Marley and host of the syndicated radio series *Reggae Beat*. He chaired the Reggae Grammy committee from its inception in 1984 through 2011.

Marvin D. Sterling is Associate Professor of Cultural Anthropology, Indiana University, Bloomington. He is the author of *Babylon East: Performing Dancehall, Roots Reggae and Rastafari in Japan*.

Michael Veal is Professor of Music and African-American Studies, Yale University, New Haven. His publications include *Fela: The Life and Times of an African Musical Icon*; *Dub: Soundscapes and Shattered Songs in Jamaican Reggae;* and the forthcoming *Technotopia 1969: Miles Davis at the Crossroads*.

Leonardo Vidigal is Professor of Cinema, Universidade Federal de Minas Gerais (Escola de Belas Artes [School of Fine Arts]), Belo Horizonte, Brazil.

Klive Walker is a Jamaican-Canadian writer, reggae historian and cultural critic. He is the author of *Dubwise: Reasoning from the Reggae Underground*.

About the Illustrations

The illustrations throughout this volume and the cover art are by Michael Thompson, also known as *FREESTYLEE, artist without borders.* He is the founder (along with Maria Papaefstathiou) of the First International Reggae Poster Contest. Michael studied graphic design at the Jamaica School of Art in Kingston, Jamaica, and is a renowned creative activist and poster artist. He has participated in numerous awareness campaigns for organizations such as National Urban League, African Wildlife Foundation, Living History Forum of Stockholm, Sweden, and Face Africa's clean water efforts in Africa. His works have been exhibited internationally in Berlin, Germany; Benicàssim, Spain; and Dublin, Ireland. His recent exhibitions have been *Freestylee: Artist without Borders*, Drum Arts Centre, Birmingham, United Kingdom, and *Edna Manley's* Bogle: *A Contest of Icons, 2010*, National Gallery of Jamaica, Kingston, Jamaica. His works have also travelled throughout Europe with the *Reggae Movement Exhibition: The Story of the Reggae Sound System's Journey from Jamaica to Europe* (2011).

www.ingramcontent.com/pod-product-compliance
Lightning Source LLC
Chambersburg PA
CBHW022348280326
41935CB00007B/116